Building In-House
Leadership and Management
Development Programs

Building In-House Leadership and Management Development Programs

Their Creation, Management, and Continuous Improvement

William J. Rothwell
and H. C. Kazanas

QUORUM BOOKS
Westport, Connecticut • London

Library of Congress Cataloging-in-Publication Data

Rothwell, William J., 1951–
    Building in-house leadership and management development programs :
    their creation, management, and continuous improvement / William J.
    Rothwell and H.C. Kazanas.
        p. cm.
    Includes bibliographical references and index.
    ISBN 1–56720–258–6 (alk. paper)
    1. Executives—Training of. 2. Supervisors—Training of.
    3. Organizational change—Study and teaching. 4. Leadership.
    I. Kazanas, H. C. II. Title.
    HD30.4.R68 1999
    658.4'07124—dc21   99–14846

British Library Cataloguing in Publication Data is available.

Library of Congress Catalog Card Number: 99–14846
ISBN: 1–56720–258–6

First published in 1999

Quorum Books, 88 Post Road West, Westport, CT 06881
An imprint of Greenwood Publishing Group, Inc.
www.quorumbooks.com

Printed in the United States of America

The paper used in this book complies with the
Permanent Paper Standard issued by the National
Information Standards Organization (Z39.48–1984).

10 9 8 7 6 5 4 3 2 1

To

Marcelina Rothwell and Nuria Kazanas

Contents

Preface

Management plays the key leadership role in planning and deploying organizational assets. Management decisions dramatically affect the lives of other people. Indeed, management employees make strategic decisions about layoffs, mergers, acquisitions, expansions, union negotiations, and bankruptcy filings. They also make tactical decisions about work group structure and individual pay increases, promotions, demotions, dismissals, and transfers. While present trends point toward less arbitrary management decision making in an effort to improve productivity and product or service quality through increased employee involvement, management continues to play a key leadership role whether efforts are focused on authoritatively directing the work of others or participatively guiding it.

At the same time, workers at all levels are increasingly being encouraged—and called upon—to exert leadership. Indeed, leadership is not for management alone. For this reason, then, many forward-thinking decision makers are sponsoring Leadership and Management Development (L & MD) programs in their organizations. The goal of such programs is to encourage, support, and nurture both leadership and management development.

THE PURPOSE OF THIS BOOK

Many people we know have been asked to establish, maintain, renew, or evaluate an L & MD program. Rarely do they know where to turn for help. They invent their own job descriptions and struggle to satisfy the (sometimes conflicting) preferences of executives, managers, and supervisors who see the need for a planned L & MD program but do not know how to establish and operate one successfully.

While many books and articles have been written about L & MD, few books provide practical guidance for those starting up or renewing a planned L & MD program. We wrote this book to serve as a practical, how-to-do-it manual for establishing and administering a planned Management Development (L & MD) program geared to addressing the training, education, and development needs of supervisors, managers, executives, and others who exert leadership in organizational settings. Its purpose is to slake the growing thirst for information about successful L & MD programs.

You may have heard already that many large organizations have enjoyed immense success with planned L & MD programs. Small organizations have also benefited from them, though their triumphs are usually less widely publicized. Many of you may have already worked in—or visited—high-performing organizations in which L & MD programs, while not overtly visible, play important roles in strategic and tactical decisions and actions.

Whatever your interests, this book is intended to give you useful, practical information on how to plan, establish, manage, operate, and evaluate a planned L & MD program in an organizational setting, based on what is known about best practices.

SOURCES OF INFORMATION

As we took up the task of writing this book, we decided that it was important to base it on state-of-the-art practices. To that end, we consulted several major sources of information:

1. *A tailor-made survey.* As an initial step in researching this book, William J. Rothwell surveyed L & MD professionals in 1998 about practices in their organizations. The survey results are published in this book for the first time.
2. *A literature search.* We conducted an exhaustive literature search on L & MD. We provide key references throughout the book so you can delve further into issues of special interest to you.
3. *Firsthand experience.* The first author of this book is an experienced L & MD professional. The fruits of his experience are reflected in this book.

THE SCHEME OF THIS BOOK

Building In-House Leadership and Management Development Programs is written primarily for L & MD specialists, human resource development (HRD) specialists, Workplace Learning and Performance (WLP) practitioners, and human resource managers. But the book also contains valuable information for chief executive officers, chief operating officers, general managers, university faculty members who do consulting on L & MD, and other people who bear responsibilities for developing management talent.

The book is divided into four major parts. Part I consists of one chapter, which serves as the book's prologue. In it we provide background information about L & MD. More specifically, we define a planned L & MD program, distinguish between training, education, and development, explain the purposes of a planned L & MD program, describe the scope of L & MD activities in the United States, distinguish planned from unplanned L & MD efforts, summarize major barriers to a planned L & MD program, and explain ways to overcome those major barriers.

Part II consists of Chapters 2 through 5. It focuses on planning and designing L & MD programs.

Chapter 2 describes how to

1. Set up a committee

2. Determine the purpose of a planned L & MD program

3. Establish program goals and objectives

4. Target groups to be served

5. Prepare a program policy and philosophy

6. Prepare a flexible action plan to guide program startup

7. Establish a regular schedule to review program results

These are initial steps in the startup of most planned L & MD programs.

In Chapter 3 we turn to identifying L & MD needs. This chapter is important because L & MD is carried out to meet individual, group, and organizational learning needs and designed to improve individual, group, and organizational performance. We distinguish between learning and nonlearning needs and explain when corrective actions other than training, education, or development are warranted. The most important part of this chapter focuses on methods for collecting and analyzing information about L & MD learning needs.

In Chapter 4 we describe how to establish a long-term learning plan to meet predictable learning needs. We call such a plan a *curriculum*, and we explain how a comprehensive L & MD curriculum is designed and summarize different ways by which to design an L & MD curriculum.

Chapter 5 poses the following questions:

1. Where should the L & MD function be positioned in the organization's reporting structure?

2. What rewards or incentives should be offered to management to encourage members to accept responsibility for developing themselves and those reporting to them?

3. What kind of leader should direct the planned L & MD program?

4. How should the program leader be recruited, selected, and oriented?

5. How should internal staff members and external vendors be selected, oriented, and trained?

6. How should planned L & MD activities be scheduled?

7. How should budgeting be handled?
8. What records of L & MD activities should be kept?
9. How should L & MD program activities be publicized?

Part III, consisting of Chapters 6 through 9, describes formal, informal, and special L & MD methods. We use the term *method* to mean an organized way by which to meet learning needs and thus bring about individual or group change through learning. *Formal methods* are planned. They are usually focused on meeting group learning needs. *Informal methods* are not planned. They are usually spontaneously focused on meeting individual needs. *Special methods* are on the cutting edge of practice. Sometimes they can be controversial.

Chapter 6 provides two models to help select appropriate L & MD methods to meet identified needs.

Chapter 7 focuses on planning and using formal L & MD methods. These methods include succession planning programs, management career planning programs, internal group training programs, external group training programs, external education programs, job rotation programs, and position assignment programs.

Chapter 8 focuses on planning and using informal L & MD methods, such as on-the-job management training, on-the-job management coaching, management mentoring or sponsorship, management self-development, and management self-study.

Chapter 9 focuses on planning and using special L & MD methods. Among them: adventure learning, New Age Training (NAT), and action learning.

Part IV consists of Chapter 10 only. In this chapter we define evaluation. We also describe different types of evaluation, key obstacles to evaluation, methods to overcome those obstacles, and a step-by-step approach for conducting a program evaluation.

The Epilogue focuses on three special issues affecting L & MD: globalism, downsizing, and team-based management. Our aim in this final chapter is not to address these issues exhaustively; rather, we explain the issues and provide general guidance about reviewing and revamping L & MD programs in light of the recent, pervasive influence of these issues.

Finally, a Bibliography closes the book. It contains not only the notes from all chapters but also additional resources that can lead readers on to other current works and research on Leadership and Management Development.

Part I

Leadership and Management Development: Background Issues

Part I provides background information about Leadership and Management Development (L & MD). We introduce Chapter 1 with a realistic case study. Planned L & MD programs often originate from efforts to handle an isolated crisis like the one dramatized in the case study. In Chapter 1 we also:

- Define a planned L & MD program
- Distinguish between management training, education, and development
- Explain the reasons for a planned L & MD program
- Describe the scope of L & MD activities in the United States
- Distinguish between planned and unplanned L & MD efforts
- Summarize major barriers to a planned L & MD program
- Explain ways to overcome those major barriers

Chapter 1

Defining Leadership and Management Development

INTRODUCTORY CASE STUDY

Josephine Irons is worried. As executive in charge of a large division in a prominent, well-known, and financially stable bank, she has just received word that Leah Smith, one of her most experienced supervisors, will retire in three months. Leah, a 23-year bank veteran, supervises a critically important work unit of 30 employees. Leah has also been an outstanding worker and has been influential in making many positive changes to her work unit.

The announcement of Leah's retirement does not come as a complete surprise to Josephine. The bank recently extended a generous early retirement offer to long-service employees. Josephine has known for six months that Leah would qualify, but Leah did not indicate until recently that she would accept the offer. Amid painful cost-cutting and downsizing efforts, Josephine's division has become so shorthanded that she feels lucky to be getting the work out at all. In some areas her employees have been working 600 hours of overtime annually to hold down staffing needs and employee benefit expenses. Leah is not the only supervisor Josephine will be losing to retirement. But Leah's departure poses the greatest problem because Josephine has not prepared anyone to assume Leah's important, technically oriented, and tough-to-master position.

Josephine can fill the vacancy created by Leah's retirement in several ways. One way is to promote from within, gambling that someone from Leah's work unit can master the job in a reasonable time. In this process she knows she can always ask for Leah's opinion about which employees have the best potential for success in the job. Promotion from within is the bank's time-honored method of filling supervisory openings. In fact, many employees expect a new supervisor to be promoted from within the work unit. Some will be upset if the vacancy is filled in any other way. Unfortunately, Josephine is not convinced that anyone in the work unit is capable of mastering Leah's duties.

Josephine has other ways to fill the vacancy. She can ask other executives in the bank to nominate employees with management potential from their departments. If chosen, such a candidate would be promoted or would receive a lateral transfer to Leah's position. But Josephine knows that moving a worker from another area will touch off moves all over the bank as a replacement is sought for each vacated position, a problem complicated by the early retirement offer. Nor will it be an easy task to convince other managers to give up a trained worker—even for a promotion. During downsizing, some managers hoard workers so they need not justify replacements or take precious time to train newcomers. To make matters worse, the bank has no centralized skill or staffing inventory and has temporarily suspended job posting for supervisory positions. Josephine's efforts to recruit a qualified candidate inside the bank will thus be complicated by lack of information. It could prove to be time-consuming and difficult.

Josephine is also aware that she could hire a supervisor from outside the bank. That option, Josephine worries, is a minefield of potentially explosive problems because ''outsiders'' have established no track record inside the bank. In any case, Josephine would clearly want someone with banking industry experience, preferably someone who has worked at another bank in a position similar to Leah's. Although such people exist, they are rare. Recruiting one will not be easy. Even if a suitable candidate can be located and hired, he or she will lack job-specific and organization-specific knowledge about *this* bank's unique procedures and culture. A new hire, no matter how experienced, also lacks a social support network to ease the transition from outside. Unexpected turnover in Leah's position is an unpleasant prospect for Josephine. But the bank does not have a good record of retaining those hired from outside to fill supervisory positions. Newcomers too often become turnover statistics.

A fourth way to deal with the vacancy, Josephine knows, is to restructure the division to eliminate the need for Leah's position. If that move results in reduced staffing, it will undoubtedly please the CEO, Josephine's boss, because it will reduce the bank's operating expenses. But Leah's duties will have to be shifted somewhere—probably to other supervisors—and Josephine feels that they have already been saddled with too much work. Through their facial expressions and occasional comments, they show evidence that stress and overtime are taking their toll. Josephine is reluctant to push them any harder for fear that several might quit. That would only intensify her staffing problems.

A fifth way to deal with the vacancy is to eliminate the need for any supervisor by making Leah's unit a self-directed work group. If Josephine chose that option, she would redistribute Leah's work to employees of the unit. Josephine would like to experiment with this promising, popular new approach designed to increase employee involvement. But she realizes that employees must first be trained in how to supervise themselves. Three months is not long enough to introduce such a radical change to the work unit's culture, which (like the bank) has long been managed with a top-down approach to decision making. The workers, Josephine knows, are presently ill-prepared to accept such a radical shift of responsibility. (However, Josephine will bear this idea in mind for the future and perhaps introduce it at a later time.)

Despite all these possibilities—and Josephine can think of others as well— she remains unsure of what to do about the pending vacancy in Leah's position. But she knows she is not alone in facing a problem of this kind. The early retirement offer affects too many other people and positions. Perhaps it is time, Josephine reasons, to suggest that the bank introduce a planned Leadership and Management Development (L & MD) program. While starting up such a program now will not help solve the immediate problem created by Leah's early retirement, it may help avoid similar staffing dilemmas in the future. Moreover, Josephine was not all that happy about the "sink or swim" approach she experienced when she entered management. She feels that there must be better ways to train, educate, and develop people. She resolves to find out.

WHAT IS LEADERSHIP?

In the case above, Josephine is looking for someone to exert leadership as well as someone to fill a management vacancy. Many definitions of leadership have been offered over the years. Among other definitions, *leadership* has been described as:

- "Directing the activities of a group toward a shared goal."[1]
- "The process of influencing the activities of an organized group toward goal achievement."[2]
- "The ability to step outside the culture to start evolutionary change processes that are more adaptive."[3]

These definitions share a common thread: *leadership is not linked to position but is linked to the ability to influence others.*

WHAT IS MANAGEMENT?

Management is associated with position. Individuals who are said to be "in management" occupy roles with oversight responsibility for the work of others. In most organizations, management consists of supervisors (who oversee the work of hourly or wage-payroll workers), managers (who oversee the work of supervisors), and executives (who oversee the work of managers).

A point worthy of emphasis is that management is thus a function of position or placement within the organization's chain of command or reporting relationships. But leadership is a function of the ability to influence others. Leadership can be exerted by anyone in an organization.

DEFINING A PLANNED L & MD PROGRAM

As defined in this book, a *planned L & MD program means a systematic effort to train, educate, and develop individuals to influence other people in positive ways. It is conducted on-the-job or off-the-job to meet individual, group, and organizational learning needs and to improve individual, group, and organizational performance.*

A planned L & MD program thus serves many purposes. One purpose is to help individuals perform effectively and efficiently in their present jobs, since good performance in the present job is usually a prerequisite to advancement to other jobs. A second purpose is to meet predictable replacement needs for an organization's management talent, an issue dramatically illustrated by the case study introducing this chapter. A third purpose is to build organizational capacity by identifying, grooming, and encouraging individuals who are able to exert positive influence over others.

In this definition, *planned* means that L & MD should be thought out ahead of time. *Management Development*, in an often-cited but controversial definition, is "an attempt to improve managerial effectiveness through a planned and deliberate learning process."[4] (This definition is controversial because management employees may be developed through unplanned as well as planned methods.)

Systematic means that a planned L & MD program should be:

• Based on a careful review of the organization's leadership and management learning needs

• Designed and delivered to meet those needs

• Evaluated for results

One way to meet learning needs is to train individuals so their knowledge and skills match up to present or future work requirements and organizational needs. In this sense, *training* means "learning, provided by employers to employees, that is related to their present jobs."[5] Management training narrows or closes the gap between what individuals already know or do and what they must know or do to perform competently. Leadership training helps individuals learn methods for exerting influence over others.

A second way to meet learning needs is to educate individuals to prepare them for eventual advancement or increased responsibility. *Education* means "learning focused on a future job."[6] Management education narrows or closes the gap between what individuals already know or do and what they must know or do to qualify for higher-level, or more technical, responsibilities. Leadership education narrows or closes the gap between what individuals already know or do and what they should do to exert more influence over others.

A third way to meet learning needs is to develop people. *Development* means offering "learning experiences, provided by employer to employees, that are not job related"[7] or "changing attitudes or values."[8] In this narrow sense, development refers to opportunities offered to individuals so they can come up with new ideas. Development is just one way to meet learning needs and should not be confused with *Leadership and Management Development* (L & MD), which encompasses management training, education, and development.

Individuals are often the primary targets for change in a planned L & MD program. In one sense, all development is self-development. But, because management employees exert profound influence over others, their individual development greatly influences group or organization performance. For this reason, then, a planned L & MD program is one way by which to effect culture change in an organization, division, department, work group, or team.

By *on-the-job or off-the-job*, we mean that management employees can be developed in more than one setting. Off-the-job L & MD experiences usually afford opportunities to interact with others, while on-the-job L & MD furnishes opportunities to learn while doing.

By *influence other people in positive ways*, we mean that a planned L & MD program can effect change with individuals by giving them increased skills to sway the opinions of others without necessarily requiring authority. Leaders can be made and are not just born. But not all people have the innate talents needed for leadership. They must be shown what skills are needed to influence others and how to apply them.

By *conducted to meet individual, group, or organizational learning needs*, we mean that a planned L & MD program can serve many purposes. It benefits:

- *Individuals* by helping them master job requirements
- *Groups* by helping people learn how to exert effective leadership skills and build teamwork
- *Organizations* by giving workers the skills they need to navigate their organizations through a fiercely competitive business environment

For these reasons, a planned L & MD program is viewed by some supporters as a tool for changing culture, the unspoken roles and norms that guide people's behavior in organizational settings.

By *improve individual, group, and organizational performance*, we mean that one important outcome sought from a planned L & MD program is increased efficiency (*doing things right*) and effectiveness (*doing the right things*).

REASONS FOR A PLANNED L & MD PROGRAM

Why does an organization sponsor a planned L & MD program? What are the chief reasons that they exist?

Exhibit 1-1
Demographic Information about Respondents to Rothwell's 1998 Survey on Leadership and Management Development: Industries

Type of Industry	
Finance	11.3%
Government	7.5%
Health Care	13.2%
Manufacturing	18.9%
Transportation	9.4%
Another Industry	15.1%
Other	24.5%
Size of Organization	
0–99	9.4%
100–249	7.5%
250–499	9.4%
500–1,999	28.3%
2,000–4,999	15.1%
5,000+	30.2%

Source: W. Rothwell, *A Survey about Management and Leadership Development* (unpublished survey results) (University Park, PA: The Pennsylvania State University, 1998).

To answer these questions, we mailed a questionnaire to 300 randomly selected L & MD specialists in June 1998. All survey respondents were members of the American Society for Training and Development (ASTD). Exhibit 1-1 presents demographic information about the respondents' industries and about the size of the respondents' organizations; Exhibit 1-2 presents information about the respondents' jobs within their organizations; and, Exhibit 1-3 lists the chief reasons why an organization sponsors a planned L & MD program. An explanation of each reason is described in the following paragraphs.

Reason 1: Contributing to Implementing Strategic Plans

Our survey respondents indicated that one of the two most important reasons to sponsor a planned L & MD program is to "contribute to implementing the organization's strategic plan." Strategic planning is the means by which organizations prepare for competing in the present and future. Central to strategic success is aligning the right leaders with the right skills in the right places at the right times to achieve desired competitive results.[9] It is this need to match the right leader to the right task that makes a planned L & MD program partic-

Exhibit 1-2
Job Titles of Survey Respondents

Question: *What is your job function?*		
Job Function	**Frequency**	**Percentage**
A Trainer without responsibility for supervising staff	8	15%
B Trainer with responsibility for supervising staff	22	42%
C Other	23	43%

Source: W. Rothwell, *A Survey about Management and Leadership Development* (unpublished survey results) (University Park, PA: The Pennsylvania State University, 1998).

ularly interesting to top managers, who are chiefly responsible for formulating and implementing strategic plans.[10] L & MD can become a means by which to identify and supply the competitive skills necessary for the survival or success of an organization.[11]

Reason 2: Building Skills in People Management

Our survey respondents indicated that the second of the two most important reasons to sponsor a planned L & MD program is "to build skills in people management for individuals who have never received formal instruction on supervision or management." That reason underscores the increasingly critical nature of interpersonal or "people skills" in organizational settings—and the value of human capital.[12]

After all, people are the primary assets in an information society. Financial assets can be acquired through borrowing or through mergers, acquisitions, or takeovers. Technological assets can be purchased. But the skills of people must usually be cultivated over time.

Reason 3: Developing Individuals for More Responsibility

Our survey respondents indicated that the third most important reason to sponsor a planned L & MD program is to "develop individuals for more responsibility."

It is a fundamental fact that the education and experience necessary for individuals to qualify for entry-level jobs are not identical to those necessary for advancement. In many technical specialties—such as engineering, accounting, and data processing—people are hired at entry level for their technical education and experience. But technical success does not necessarily lead to management success, and advancement beyond entry level often requires management

Exhibit 1-3
Reasons for Offering L & MD Programs

Question: There are many reasons why organizations sponsor efforts to improve leadership and management talent. For each reason listed in the left column below, please *circle a response code in the right column* indicating how important you believe that reason to be for your organization. (1 = least important and 5 = most important)				
Reasons for Sponsoring Efforts to Improve Leadership and Management Talent	**Mean**	**Standard Deviation**	**Median**	**N**
1 Contribute to implementing the organization's Strategic Business Plans	4.10	1.25	4	51
2 Build skills in "people management" for individuals who have never received formal instruction on supervision or management	4.10	1.28	4	51
3 Develop individuals for increased responsibility	4.04	1.15	4	51
4 Improve the organization's ability to respond to environmental change	3.78	1.18	4	51
5 Increase the productivity of management employees	3.75	1.28	4	51
6 Improve the organization's ability to respond to technological change	3.67	1.44	4	51
7 Increase the pool of promotable management employees	3.59	1.44	4	51
8 Provide general training to individuals inside the organization	3.37	1.07	3	51
9 Provide increased opportunities for "high-potential" workers	3.39	1.16	3	51
10 Help individuals realize their career plans within the organization	3.35	1.01	3	51
11 Contribute to implementing the organization's succession plans	3.33	1.43	3	51
12 Improve morale of management employees	3.12	1.00	3	51
13 Provide increased opportunities for women	2.71	1.08	3	51

Source: W. Rothwell, *A Survey about Management and Leadership Development* (unpublished survey results) (University Park, PA: The Pennsylvania State University, 1998).

skills.[13] Technical specialists must learn to work with and through others to achieve results,[14] a lesson complicated by their early training to do work tasks by themselves and on their own initiative. Nor can they acquire that ability quickly or easily by taking one or two college courses on management or a few training courses. Courses, whether offered by a college or a training department, serve an important purpose by providing a valuable foundation of theory. But they are seldom sufficiently organization-specific or job-specific enough to give participants opportunities to *observe* a principle in action, *practice* it, or *reflect* on it. More focused, structured, practical, and long-term developmental experiences are often necessary to build leadership and management skills.[15] This purpose can be served by a planned L & MD program.

Reason 4: Responding to Environmental Change

Our survey respondents indicated that the third most important reason to sponsor a planned L & MD program is to "respond to environmental change." Organizations are open systems that depend on the external environment—which includes suppliers, distributing wholesalers, customers, competitors, government regulators, and other such stakeholders. Organizations succeed or fail depending on their ability to satisfy customers and anticipate or react swiftly to dynamic external conditions. A planned L & MD program can be a tool to supply workers at all levels with the knowledge and skills they need to scan the environment for issues affecting their organizations, anticipating or responding as necessary.

Reason 5: Increasing Management Productivity

Our survey respondents cited "increasing the productivity of management employees" as the fifth most important reason to sponsor a planned L & MD program. But management productivity is an elusive concept. In the most simplistic sense, of course, management productivity is defined and measured in precisely the same way as any employee productivity: it is a ratio of inputs to outputs or resources used to results achieved.

The trouble with this definition is that management productivity is often only indirectly measurable. Management employees achieve their results only by working with and through others rather than by their individual efforts. Hence, *management* productivity is measured by *organizational* productivity.

Accountants have long accepted this principle. They apply well-known methods of financial analysis to balance sheet and income statement information and credit or blame the organization's management for the results. They assume management is responsible for an organization's survival, success, or failure. Another reason is that management does not produce unique, tangible work products. Indeed, regardless of industry, management is inherently service-oriented, focusing on customer needs and creating an environment in which employees perform their jobs.

A planned L & MD program contributes to this service orientation by equipping management employees with the knowledge and skills they need to offer these services. Of course, a planned L & MD program can also do more if it is focused more broadly on building leadership talent, which extends the same principle beyond the management ranks to include all employees as potential leaders.

Reason 6: Responding to Technological Change

Our survey respondents indicated that the sixth most important reason to sponsor a planned L & MD program is to "respond to technological change." *Technology*, meaning the application of know-how and machinery to work processes, affects the skills that workers need to perform. Its influence on the knowledge and skills required of management employees is as great as its influence on other employees. Moreover, management employees are often expected to spearhead the introduction of new technology to the work place and thus exert leadership for the applications and acceptance of technology. A planned L & MD program is one way to equip employees with knowledge about technology and its potential applications to work processes.

Reason 7: Increasing the Pool of Promotable Employees

Our survey respondents indicated that the seventh most important reason to sponsor a planned L & MD program is to "increase the pool of promotable employees." A planned L & MD program can help ensure that there is an adequate supply of talent to meet an organization's demands over time. In this sense it is particularly valuable, since nearly three-fourths of all management talent in the United States has historically been promoted from within.[16] That makes it essential to develop sufficient resources at lower levels in an organization to meet management requirements at higher levels over time.

Reason 8: Providing General Training

Our survey respondents indicated that the eighth most important reason to sponsor a planned L & MD program is to "provide general training to individuals inside the organization." Management skills, once necessary only for a handpicked elite, are becoming more closely integrated with the daily work of nonmanagement employees. Increasingly, employees are expected to be self-managing—and self-leading. Employees need to master management and leadership principles if they are to do their jobs more effectively—and with less intrusive, overt, or direct supervision. For this reason, a planned L & MD program can be a means by which to build the management and leadership skills of everyone and thereby diffuse those skills throughout organizations.

Reason 9: Increasing Opportunities for High-Potential Workers

Our survey respondents indicated that the ninth most important reason to sponsor a planned L & MD program is to "provide increased opportunities for 'high-potential' workers." Definitions of *high-potential workers* (HiPos) vary by management philosophy and organizational culture just as definitions of *poor-potential workers* (PoPos) do. In one sense, a HiPo is anyone capable of eventual promotion—a definition which can encompass many employees. In other senses, HiPos may be defined variously as individuals who are:

- Capable of jumping two or more levels in a short time span
- Listed on replacement charts or succession planning forms as likely replacements for incumbents in key jobs or positions
- More highly educated or experienced than others
- Outstanding performers

There are other ways to define HiPos, and most organizations must come to grips with establishing their own definitions.

A planned L & MD program can focus on developing HiPos so that their exceptional abilities are cultivated and harvested in a way that would not happen as quickly or as effectively with unstructured and unplanned methods. A planned L & MD program is a means by which to speed up the development of the best and brightest so they are capable of realizing their potential for their own benefit as well as for their employer's benefit.

Reason 10: Realizing Career Plans

Our survey respondents indicated that the tenth most important reason to sponsor a planned L & MD program is to "help individuals realize their career plans within the organization." In most organizations there are two career ladders. First, there is a *management career ladder* in which status and responsibility are tied to position on a vertical chain of command. The higher the position, the more people a job incumbent supervises and the more responsibility he or she shoulders. Supervisor is the first rung on the management career ladder in most organizations. Then there is a *technical career ladder* in which status and position are tied to position on a horizontal continuum of knowledge, skill, and ability. Position level is tied to level of expertise and experience. Although individuals remain at the same desks and continue performing the same duties, they are promoted as they gain increasing organization-specific, job-specific, and occupation-specific knowledge and experience.

A planned L & MD program can be a tool to promote personal growth and career advancement for both career ladders. For example, it can prepare *nonexempt employees*—those covered by the Federal Fair Labor Standards Act (FLSA)—to enter and advance vertically into the management ranks. Further, L & MD can prepare *exempt employees*—those not covered by the FLSA—to advance from supervisor to manager to executive. After all, individuals must acquire new knowledge and skills if they are to qualify for new responsibilities and positions. A planned L & MD program can be one means by which to provide them with new knowledge and skills through training, education, or development activities.

The same principle applies to a technical career ladder, typical in technical occupations such as data processing. Pay-for-knowledge compensation programs are based on assumptions of technical career ladders. In those cases, individuals become more valuable to an organization as they increase their knowledge and experience in their functional specialties. Promotions provide recognition for their achievements. A planned L & MD program, geared to individuals who supervise others in their functional specialties, can be a tool to help them acquire know-how.

Reason 11: Implementing Succession Plans

Our survey respondents indicated that the eleventh most important reason to sponsor a planned L & MD program is to "contribute to implementing the organization's succession plans." A planned L & MD program is a tool for implementing succession plans to ensure the orderly replacement of management talent.[17] A succession plan addresses such questions as: (1) Who will replace a key executive in the event of sudden death, disability, or other loss? and (2) How can successors be prepared to assume the responsibilities of key positions permanently or temporarily? A planned L & MD program helps answer these questions and address these issues.

Reason 12: Improving Management Morale

Our survey respondents indicated that the twelfth most important reason to sponsor a planned L & MD program is to "improve morale of management employees." Individuals experience all kinds of feelings about their employment situations. They have feelings about their jobs, their immediate organizational superiors, the organization for which they work, their chances for advancement, and other issues. When individual feelings about job satisfaction are viewed collectively in a group, the term *morale* is applied to them.

The relationship between work performance and individual job satisfaction or group morale has long been investigated. But research has not shown a strong correlation between them.[18] However, there *is* a correlation between voluntary turnover and individual job satisfaction and group morale. In other words, people do not have to be happy or pleased with their jobs to perform competently. But if they become dissatisfied and alternative job opportunities become available, they will not long remain tied to a work environment where they feel dissatisfied.

Individual job satisfaction, group morale, and work performance are complex subjects. They are influenced by many factors. In recent years, evidence has surfaced to suggest that management employees—particularly those in middle management—are increasingly dissatisfied, experiencing lower morale than has been traditional at that level. Nor should that trend be too surprising. U.S. corporations, weathering storms of mergers, acquisitions, takeovers, and buyouts in the 1980s, frequently experienced widespread white-collar layoffs and, on more than one occasion, cutbacks at the middle management level. (And middle managers were not protected, as their top management counterparts were, by golden parachutes to soften the blow of involuntary terminations.) In the 1990s, corporations have continued to downsize. That trend seems to be ongoing.[19]

Middle managers have been singled out as a particular target. While management experts point to distinct advantages resulting from cutbacks in the middle management ranks—such as improved communication between top managers and hourly workers—these gains have not been made without significant cost: middle managers feel more insecure about their jobs and careers than ever before. Their insecurity is contagious, affecting the attitudes of others and sending the distressing message to supervisors that promotions for them may be unlikely.

Against this backdrop, a planned L & MD program can help all employees improve and update their knowledge, skills, and abilities. It also raises their self-esteem and promotes the view that top managers care about them. Even better, a planned L & MD program keeps employees attractive in the labor market. It can furnish workers at all levels with the knowledge and skills they need to advance *inside* their organizations—or survive *outside* them in the event of unexpected job loss. As a result, a planned L & MD program can boost management morale at a time when such a boost may be desperately needed.

Reason 13: Increasing Opportunities for Women

Our survey respondents indicated that the thirteenth most important reason to sponsor a planned L & MD program is to ''provide increased opportunities for women.'' If participation in planned L & MD programs is an avenue leading into, through, or up the ranks of management, then it can provide passage into those ranks for women. As females continue to enter the workforce in record numbers, socially responsible organizations are taking steps to open up management opportunities to women. A planned L & MD program, while not a panacea, can nevertheless help achieve this socially desirable goal.[20]

SCOPE OF L & MD PROGRAMS

Executives, managers, and supervisors in the United States comprise roughly 10 percent of the U.S. workforce. Supervisors, managers, and executives oversee productive work activities and mobilize resources to achieve planned results.

L & MD needs, methods, and evaluation techniques differ by worker job category. Nonsupervisory employees receive leadership training to prepare them to play an increasingly self-directed and self-managing role. In the supervisory ranks, where the largest concentration of management employees is located, the tendency is to focus on group-oriented training to meet organizational and individual needs. In the executive ranks, where the fewest people straddle the top of the organizational pyramid, the tendency is to focus on individually oriented developmental experiences.

Nonsupervisory Workers and L & MD

Nonsupervisory workers are individual contributors or team players who do not bear formal responsibility or authority for oversight of other workers. And yet, this group often has the most customer contact and the most direct responsibility for the delivery or manufacture of the organization's services or products. In a bid to hold down supervisory overhead costs and to improve customer service and product quality, many organizations have directed leadership-building efforts to members of the nonsupervisory group. That is particularly true in organizations using teams.

Supervisors and L & MD

Supervisors occupy the first tier of management. They have traditionally been responsible for the work of one unit, function, or assembly line. They devote their time to orienting and training workers, conducting employee performance appraisals, issuing orders, disciplining wayward employees, and dealing with union representatives about daily work in their units. They plan, organize, control, and schedule the workflow of their units. Central to their role is the ability to give direction to other people.[21]

In recent years the supervisor's role has been changing due to improved technology, greater emphasis on product and service quality, and increased expectations about employee participation in decision making. Supervisors are less often expected to *tell* others what to do and more often expected to *coach, counsel*, and *advise* others. Ordering people around, long the stereotypical activity associated with the traditional "straw boss" supervisor, is fading. It is being replaced by a new emphasis on empowering individual workers and facilitating employee teams. In some organizations, the job title *supervisor* has been replaced by *work leader, team leader*, or *work coordinator*. This changing role means that supervisors must become more skilled in handling individual counseling, group dynamics, and structured problem-solving methods. These skills are gradually supplanting the traditional management functions of planning, organizing, scheduling, and controlling.

The precise nature of supervisory duties varies, however, depending on

- *Function*—Differences exist between supervision in marketing, manufacturing (operations), and administration
- *Industry*—Differences sometimes exist between supervision in manufacturing and service organizations
- *Union Status*—Differences exist between supervision in union and nonunion settings
- *Organizational culture*—Differences exist between supervisory skills needed in authoritarian cultures and those needed in participative or empowering cultures

Generally speaking, supervisors in such functions as manufacturing, marketing, and administration devote different percentages of their time to instructing subordinates, managing individuals, representing their staff to higher-level management, planning and allocating resources, coordinating groups, managing groups, and monitoring the outside environment.[22] Supervisors in manufacturing firms deal with the organization's customers less often than those in service organizations do. In unionized settings supervisors must often be prepared to defend their decisions when they are second-guessed by union representatives, an issue not confronting supervisors in nonunionized settings. In authoritarian cultures supervisors shoulder total responsibility for decision making and receive credit or blame for the performance of their work units; in participative cultures supervisors delegate responsibility to those reporting to them. Employees receive credit or blame for their individual or team contributions.

Supervisors occupy a critical juncture point between supervisory and nonsupervisory work. They are the organization's direct representative to their nonexempt employees; they are the nonexempt employees' direct representative to the employer. This dual responsibility can produce considerable stress, since supervisors often feel squeezed between employee and employer concerns. For instance, supervisors recognize keenly when their employees are not enthused about changes in organizational policies, procedures, technology, work methods, or working conditions. Likewise, supervisors are also sensitive to employer concerns, appreciating the need for hard-eyed business decisions such as layoffs or cost-cutting in ways that sometimes escape nonexempt employees who fear for their jobs or fear change itself.

Traditionally, 75 percent of all supervisors in the United States have been promoted from inside their organizations.[23] Most supervisors begin their careers as nonexempt (hourly) employees and are eventually promoted. In rare cases, supervisors enter their positions after gaining experience in other organizations or transferring from other positions or locations.

Despite persisting interest in business and public management careers among college students, only a small percentage of supervisors in U.S. organizations today prepare for their jobs through formal schooling. More often, people enter these jobs from the nonsupervisory ranks. Employers devote less time and money to preparing individuals for supervision than for middle management, even though supervisors often have more direct contact with employees, customers, suppliers, and distributors.

Nonexempt employees prepare themselves to enter supervision in various ways. Apart from maintaining exemplary performance records in their jobs, they may:

- Enroll full-time or part-time in formal degree programs in management, business, or public administration at two-year community colleges or four-year colleges or universities
- Attend nondegree-related seminars offered by colleges, professional associations, private vendors, industry groups, or other sponsors
- View public television programs about supervision
- Listen to audiotape programs
- Take correspondence courses
- Attend conferences
- Read about supervision on their own time
- Talk to experienced supervisors about effective ways to prepare for entering supervision, asking such questions as "What do you know now that you wished you had known before entering supervision?" and "How would you suggest I prepare myself to enter supervision?"

Employers also sponsor training, education, and development to help promising individuals qualify for supervision. For example, employers may:

- Encourage experienced supervisors to identify and prepare promising individuals for promotion through planned or unplanned on-the-job coaching over extended time periods
- Handpick promising individuals to attend carefully selected off-the-job college courses, public seminars, or industry-sponsored educational programs
- Sponsor in-house training to meet the most common needs of people aspiring to enter supervision
- Identify and encourage individuals to attend off-the-job college courses in supervision or management, perhaps using an organization's tuition reimbursement program as a funding source
- Identify job assignments and other activities designed to expose individuals to experiences that will help them learn to deal with special assignments, handle difficult people, mobilize and deploy resources, and master other key skills deemed necessary to succeed in supervision

Of course, these methods may be combined.

Organizations need to do more than sponsor planned L & MD programs tightly focused on preparing people to enter supervision or master new job duties immediately after promotion. Technology, social issues, laws, and other issues change so rapidly that supervisors—like all U.S. workers—need continuous upgrading if their skills are to remain up-to-date. For this reason, some form of *continuing education* is necessary.

To help supervisors stay abreast of new developments, organizations should offer regular briefings, training sessions, and other information-sharing sessions to help supervisors learn about issues affecting their work and their employees' work. To cite a few examples of issues on which supervisors should be regularly briefed:

• Changes in the organization's plans, policies, or work procedures

• New laws, rules, or regulations

• New labor agreements

• New ideas in the practice of supervision

• Brainstorming on common problems

• New techniques that work especially well in other parts of the organization or in other organizations

Managers and L & MD

Middle managers occupy the second tier of management. They number roughly 5 million in the U.S. workforce. They report to senior or top managers, directly oversee the work activities of exempt employees and, through their role as the immediate organizational superiors of supervisors, they indirectly oversee work activities of nonexempt employees. Central to their role is "linking groups."[24]

Managers are traditionally responsible for the work of several related work units or departments. While their specific duties may vary by *functional specialty* (manufacturing/operations, finance, marketing, or human resources), *geographic area* (regions within the United States or abroad), or *product/service line* (type of product or service), their general duties usually involve:

• Establishing intermediate-term goals and objectives to implement strategic plans

• Creating and monitoring budgets and other cost-control methods for their areas of responsibility

• Monitoring the industry and the organization's external environment to identify trends affecting their functions, geographic areas, or product/service lines

• Developing and overseeing annual and sometimes multi-year plans and strategies within their areas to achieve desired results and improved profitability, customer service, and product or service quality

- Staffing key positions within their areas
- Developing people for supervisory and managerial positions
- Structuring their areas of responsibility in ways designed to improve productivity, individual job satisfaction, and group morale
- Establishing policies, procedures, and standards for the work performed in their areas
- Rewarding individuals and groups, within established guidelines of their organizations, for achieving desired results

Job descriptions for managers usually underscore their responsibilities rather than specific tasks they perform to carry them out.

While organizations occasionally hire managers from competitors or other firms in the same industry so as to gain fresh perspectives and avoid "inbreeding," many managers in the United States are promoted from the supervisory ranks. By working in supervision first, managers increase their understanding about

- The organization's purpose (*what is the organization's reason for existence?*)
- Structure (*how is the organization's work divided up, and who does what?*)
- Rewards (*what are the organization's rewards, and how are they gained?*)
- Technology (*how is the organization's work performed?*)
- Leadership (*who are the organization's formal and informal leaders, and what do they value?*)
- Culture (*how are decisions made, and what does the organization really value?*)

As managers plan to implement organizational strategy, their familiarity with these and other issues serves them in good stead.

Since most managers possess a college degree, they usually have an important educational foundation on which to build industry-specific and organization-specific knowledge and skills. While the relationship between a college degree in business and subsequent success in management is difficult to prove, the credential provides the holder with awareness of basic business terminology, credibility with others, a social network of acquaintances who graduated from the same school, and awareness of proven methods by which to approach problem finding and problem solving.

Individuals prepare themselves to enter managerial positions by demonstrating exemplary performance at lower levels of the organizational hierarchy, advertising their interest in advancement to others, building a network of supporters, and acquiring the skills they need to qualify for advancement.

Executives and L & MD

Executives occupy the highest tier of management in most organizations. They number approximately 2.5 million in the U.S. workforce. They report to, and include, the highest level of the organization—such as the senior managers responsible for such functions as finance and human resources. The executive level also includes the chief operating officer (COO), the chief executive officer (CEO), and the board of directors. Executives directly oversee the work activities of middle managers and indirectly oversee the work of supervisors and hourly employees.

Executives are traditionally responsible for the work of several related departments. They chart the course for their organizations, and an organization's survival and success depends on the course they chart. Like managers, their specific duties may vary by *functional specialty* (manufacturing/operations, finance, marketing or human resources), *geographic area* (regions within the United States or abroad), or *product/service line* (type of product or service). Their general duties usually involve:

• Formulating the strategic plan of their organization

• Creating incentives and allocating resources to help realize strategic objectives

• Using their knowledge of the industry to identify and anticipate trends affecting the organization

• Identifying organizational strengths and weaknesses relative to competitors, working to build on strengths or overcome weaknesses

• Staffing key managerial positions within their areas

• Developing managers

• Structuring the organization and their own areas of responsibility so as to conform to the organization's strategic direction

Increasingly, executives find themselves needing to think strategically in a world in which global competition is the norm rather than the exception. At the same time, however, they are often socially insulated from the pressures of daily operations, problems with nonexempt employees, and routine customer concerns. They must thus find ways to gather accurate information about what is happening inside and outside their organizations so they can make informed decisions. That challenge is all the more difficult because, as chief controllers of organizational reward and incentive systems, executives are positioned in such a way that managers, supervisors, and nonexempt employees have vested interests to give them a positive spin on events that are not always positive.

Individuals prepare themselves to enter executive positions in the same ways they prepare themselves to enter middle management. Apart from maintaining exemplary performance records, they advertise their interest in advancement and build a coalition of supporters among their present peers (other managers), their subordinates (supervisors), and their desired peers (executives). For managers to enter the executive ranks, they need luck (positions are available), support (people want them to become executives), and requisite knowledge and skills (they know the industry, function, organization, people, and culture).

Preparing people for executive positions is often a matter of great concern to CEOs, COOs and boards of directors. Methods of preparation are usually highly individualized, tailored to unique strengths and weaknesses of each person. An Individual Development Plan (IDP) may be prepared to plan for the individual's growth. IDPs may call for international assignments, short courses at Ivy League schools, executive MBA programs, domestic and international job rotations, vendor-sponsored education, and other learning activities targeted to meet specific individual needs. Although reviewed annually, an IDP may have a duration exceeding one year—especially if tied to a succession plan and designed to groom replacements for key positions.

Prospective executives are rarely prepared for advancement through classroom training offered by in-house training departments. There are several reasons why:

- Their numbers are small, making it difficult to justify devoting substantial in-house training resources to meet their needs
- Their needs vary widely and are often met best through individualized rather than group learning methods
- Their high-level positions may pose a problem for in-house L & MD specialists, who (in some organizations) are not positioned to command respect or authority in their dealings with executives

Like supervisors and managers, executives must be kept abreast of changes in the external environment if they are to make informed decisions and plan strategically. Organizations are making various attempts to do that, though many efforts to deliver *continuing education* to executives are not labelled by that term. More often than not, executives are kept updated by serving on committees, task forces, or project groups assigned to scan the organization's environment and recommend changes designed to keep the organization competitive. They may also be developed, in part, by employer-sponsored service in community, charitable, or industry-related organizations.

Planned and Unplanned L & MD

Planned L & MD is a deliberate, conscious effort to identify how many people with what skills will be needed by an organization to carry out supervisory, management, and executive duties and to meet those human resource needs through carefully crafted training, education, and development activities. In organizations that have adopted a philosophy of planned L & MD, a continuous effort is made to identify and meet future organizational and individual learning needs.

On the other hand, *unplanned* L & MD is a form of crisis management. No effort is made to identify future management or leadership needs. Vacancies prompt hectic scrambling to find qualified replacements. Sometimes the best applicants are selected, promoted, or transferred; sometimes expediency governs. No preparation is made for filling predictable vacancies stemming from such organizational factors as growth, diversification, or other needs wrought by external conditions and strategic plans; nor is preparation made for filling vacancies caused by death, disability, retirement, transfer, or termination.

Unplanned L & MD is often the first step in a six-step life cycle of L & MD. Subsequent steps include:[25]

- *Isolated tactical L & MD*—Ad hoc efforts are made to address special problems and meet pressing, immediate needs (such as unanticipated vacancies)
- *Integrated and coordinated structural and development tactics*—Steps are taken to anticipate L & MD needs
- *L & MD strategy to implement corporate policy*—L & MD strategy plays a part in implementing corporate strategy
- *L & MD strategy input to corporate policy formation*—Information about the organization's L & MD needs influences the formulation of an organization's strategic plans
- *Strategic development of the management of corporate policy*—L & MD "processes enhance the nature and quality of corporate policy-forming processes, which they also inform and help implement."[26]

Few organizations fit neatly in one step of this six-step life cycle. Indeed, some organizations are positioned at a different stage of the life cycle for different groups, perhaps planning L & MD for supervisors but not for managers or executives. Some sponsor planned L & MD for managers or executives but not for supervisors. Even within organizations, some management employees will do a better job than others in preparing their subordinates for exerting leadership or for entry to management ranks, mastering work responsibilities upon promotion, updating their skills in light of changing conditions, and preparing for subsequent advancement to higher levels.

Few academic research studies have been conducted to compare the value of planned and unplanned L & MD for

- Improving organizational profitability
- Increasing the chances of competitive success
- Ensuring that the right people are at the right places at the right times to meet the organization's needs for management talent
- Holding down turnover in the management ranks
- Encouraging people to enter management

- Reducing the personal anxiety experienced by individuals who move into supervisory, managerial, or executive positions

- Improving an organization's track record to promote women, minorities, and members of other protected labor groups

However, it just seems to make sense that *planned* L & MD efforts will be more effective than *unplanned* efforts in meeting the goals listed above.[27] As the old saying goes, "If you don't know where you're going, you'll have a tough time getting there." The same principle applies to L & MD. If nobody plans to achieve results, then results will be difficult to achieve.

Barriers to L & MD

What barriers stand in the way of successful implementation of a planned L & MD program? Three seem to loom over others: (1) lack of management support; (2) lack of expertise to design or implement L & MD; and (3) lack of resources—such as staff or funds.

Lack of management support means that the organization's senior managers see no good reason to approach L & MD in a planned, systematic way. Citing other important priorities or their own preferences, executives do not believe that L & MD should be planned. Some believe a "sink or swim" approach works best to prepare people to enter management ranks, meet job challenges upon promotion, keep skills current, or prepare people for subsequent advancement. Others are uncomfortable with planned L & MD programs because they worry that such programs may build unrealistic expectations, creating a "crowned prince or princess" syndrome.

Lack of expertise means that the organization does not possess the capability to start up and operate a planned L & MD program successfully. Nor, perhaps, do executives know whom to approach to find and tap such expertise. Obviously, lack of expertise can be a real problem in smaller organizations in which nobody is given full-time responsibility to coordinate L & MD efforts.

Lack of resources means that the organization does not possess the wherewithal to carry out a planned L & MD program, even if support exists or expertise can be found. The willingness of an organization's management to find the resources for a planned L & MD program indicates support, and the inability to find the resources suggests that executives do not attach much significance to planned L & MD efforts. Only organizations in bankruptcy truly lack the resources for a planned L & MD program because much can be done at low cost.

Key problems associated with L & MD programs, identified in Rothwell's 1998 survey and provided in the words of the survey respondents themselves, are listed below. These may also be properly regarded as barriers to the success of such programs.

Key Problems Associated with L & MD Programs

- Competitive pirates.
- No incentives for growth.
- Too many of them, lack of interest, many long-term industry employees, lack of incentives.
- Lack of effort on the part of corporate training.
- Time constraints for training.
- Old culture.
- Lack of qualified candidates for key positions.
- "That's not the way we did it in 1907 when this place opened" mentality.
- "We promote to leadership positions, based on technical expertise."
- No real process in place to distinguish between an individual's *desire* to be a manager and his/her ability to lead. "We're working on that" (succession planning, etc.).
- Poor communication and therefore poor attitudes for learning.
- Lawyers don't want to do leadership things. They want to bill clients.
- Silo mentality "that business unit is trying to steal my best talent."
- (1) Cost prohibitive—budget restrictions; (2) Operations not-buying-in and time constraints—managers get "caught up" in operational situations/emergencies.
- Devoting same amount of time, energy as we do to products, services, finances.
- No program for demonstrating ROI of development.
- (1) Finding the time to pull managers/leaders away from their day-to-day work to attend training; (2) Finding individuals who can coach others in integrating new knowledge.
- Environment in a startup software firm does not allow for management/leadership development at this time.
- Finding time to properly establish curriculum or master plan.
- Lack of commitment/support at senior level.
- Not knowing what/who to train.
- Time to develop.
- Costs at a time when our product cost is decreasing.
- There are few, if any, development opportunities beyond supervisor.
- Sometimes we have people who can't think outside of their reference areas—they forget about being creative—finding or developing people to try new ways of doing things.
- Ongoing commitment of people and resources.
- The organizations responsible for developing plans for management and leadership development have been under constant reorganization themselves, and, it has slowed down the efforts and effectiveness of programs.
- Lack of input from company leaders.
- These folks are often the "busy ones" and want to work us; "being developed."

- None as of this time. We are at the early stage.
- We started our efforts too late—we've been behind in terms of having the necessary number of people ready for promotion and the company doesn't tend to hire outside—likes to promote from within.
- Cultural challenges (various nationalities).
- Lack of accountability to reinforce learning.
- People become more valuable, larger companies lure them away. Time to take training.
- We experienced a rapid growth rate, which led to many inexperienced supervisors being promoted before training, caused fallout in the ranks, was difficult to provide planned training in time.
- Sharing the experience. Poorly designed plans.
- Tends to be a homogeneous group. Tough to "protect" training and development budgets when times are tight.
- Based on relationship with manager. When organization changes, the IDP plans disappear.
- Funding. Empathy.
- Lack of organizational readiness—managers/leaders are so busy "fighting fires" that they don't see the value of and are not willing to commit to developing themselves or their employees.
- Diversity/broad range of skill, experience, and education levels within management group.
- Defining appropriate curriculum at higher levels. Overcoming geographic issues to deliver training.
- Reactive management; adverse employee selection that has led to increased training times, high turnover. Duplicate efforts; no collaboration.
- Coordination across parts of organization. Follow up on development plans.

Overcoming Barriers to L & MD

How do organizations surmount the barriers? The answer to the question depends on how many barriers must be overcome.

To overcome lack of support, key members of the organization's management must become aware of how planned and unplanned L & MD efforts differ and must be convinced that planned L & MD is worth undertaking. Moreover, they must consider the following questions:

- What is in it for them if planned L & MD is undertaken? (*What will they gain from it?*)
- How will planned L & MD contribute to achieving strategic plans, meet needs identified in succession or replacement plans, and help the organization achieve greater competitive success?
- What problems, if any, are stemming from an organization's unplanned approach to L & MD? What is happening now?

• What solutions will planned L & MD offer for those problems, and how will the benefits of planned L & MD match up to its costs?

To convince an organization's leaders to sponsor planned L & MD, some individual or some group must assume a leadership role and become an idea champion or a cheering section favoring it.

It is that person or group who must build management awareness of planned L & MD by circulating articles and books (like this one) favoring planned L & MD, researching what other organizations are doing through benchmarking, gathering complaints about unplanned L & MD practices from the organization's present job incumbents, and identifying possible benefits of a planned L & MD program.

To overcome lack of expertise, some one—or some group—must be given responsibility for coordinating a planned L & MD program. It is important to understand, however, that this individual or committee cannot be given sole authority or delegated the responsibility to "do" L & MD, since many people rightfully have a role to play in "growing" talent. Rather, the individual placed in the role of L & MD leader or the committee assigned the role of overseeing L & MD functions is a focal point for planning activities, carrying them out, and following up to see what works and what does not. Without someone spearheading these efforts, they will usually lack focus. They may not even be launched.

Few academic programs exist to train people to enter and carry out the role of director or coordinator of a planned L & MD program. Organizations lacking the expertise internally will usually need to find qualified individuals externally. Sources of talent include leaders of L & MD programs for other organizations in the same or another industry, leaders of L & MD programs serving industry or professional associations, faculty or continuing education directors in universities or community colleges, and consultants who have worked on L & MD programs in other organizations. Such individuals require special skills.[28]

To overcome lack of resources, the organization's top managers must set the tone by committing their support to a planned L & MD program. Paying lip service to it or playing wait and see will not work. What is needed is a leap of faith at the outset, deciding that such an effort is worth vesting with adequate resources to start up and function.

The key advantages associated with L & MD programs, as they were identified in Rothwell's 1998 survey and as expressed in the respondents' own words, are listed below. They can be regarded as means by which to overcome barriers. The reason: they can be used persuasively to convince skeptics that the benefits of such programs outweigh the problems.

Key Advantages Associated with L & MD Programs
• Flexibility, greater employee effectiveness.
• Strategically oriented executives.
• Broader ability to effectively participate in strategic planning and management.

- Preparation for future; supervisors better able to handle problems.
- Acceptance of new ideas; faster implementation of change efforts.
- Just started this year, too early to tell.
- Industry leadership.
- We have significantly decreased our third-party actions and we are managing our labor dollars better.
- Common skill sets, values, and vision. More effective work relationships and higher results.
- Create understanding of needed organizational competencies.
- Succession planning for managing partner. Creating better practice leaders (department heads).
- Succession management. Culture focus. (Please note: many of our programs are still being developed). Key benefits include better communication skills and awareness of oneself and changing environment and labor force within restaurant industry.
- Increased confidence and competence in handling people.
- Expectation of development as ''earned'' after self-development has been successful equals self-reliant culture.
- The ability to win more engagements.
- Provided the ''tools'' to carry out company's strategic plan—more responsive, reflective leadership—quicker adjustment to leadership roles by new managers.
- The talented stay here for a longer term.
- Decrease in employee turnover; more thorough documentation of direct reports.
- A recognition that well-designed development programs can be very successful.
- A more confident supervisory staff.
- Knowledgeable middle managers—people who have credibility with the employees.
- Reduced turnover—a big issue in our industry.
- Leaders are prepared to take over after significant reduction in DOE funding resulting in downsizing/early retirement.
- Better decisions in a shorter period of time. Quality decisions.
- The individuals are much more effective once they take on their new roles.
- Attention to this group of people. Switching view of training from perk/punishment to benefit.
- Just beginning.
- Less turnover. More timely decision making. More creative problem solving and business development.
- Pool of talent.
- Improved morale; training is seen as a benefit. Improved management ability. Increased awareness of expected behaviors.
- Additional bench strength.
- Aids in recruitment and retention.

- Not very successful in developing in-house, so hire from outside.
- We haven't done enough to realize any benefits.
- Increased performance, and addressing problems among staff. Increased morale in management group. We've been able to fill management jobs internally. We've been able to reduce turnover in management ranks.
- Low turnover. High morale. Successors.

Summary

We introduced this chapter with a case study that dramatizes one problem that can lead to the introduction of a planned L & MD program. We then defined a *planned L & MD program* as *a systematic effort to train, educate, and develop individuals to influence other people in positive ways. It is conducted on-the-job or off-the-job to meet individual, group, and organizational learning needs and to improve individual, group, and organizational performance.* We pointed out that learning needs may be met through training, education, or development. Training is job-oriented; education is individual-oriented; and, development is organization-oriented.

A planned L & MD program is undertaken for many reasons. When the introduction of such a program is contemplated, the benefits should be weighed against the costs. Generally, however, we believe that it is important to plan L & MD rather than leave it unplanned. After all, "if you don't know where you are going, you'll have a tough time getting there!"

Introducing a planned L & MD program is no quick, simple, or easy matter. You will face many barriers. Three barriers generally emerge as most significant: (1) lack of management support; (2) lack of expertise to design or implement L & MD; and (3) lack of resources. Each must be overcome before you proceed to the next steps in starting up the program.

NOTES

1. J. Hemphill and A. Coons, "Development of the Leader Behavior Description Questionnaire," in R. Stogdill and A. Coons, eds., *Leader Behavior: Its Description and Measurement* (Columbus, OH: Bureau of Business Research, The Ohio State University, 1957), p. 7.

2. C. Rauch and O. Behling, "Functionalism: Basis for an Alternate Approach to the Study of Leadership," in J. Hunt, D. Hosking, C. Schriesheim, and R. Stewart, eds., *Leaders and Managers: International Perspectives on Managerial Behavior and Leadership* (Elmsford, NY: Pergamon Press, 1984), p. 46.

3. E. Schein, *Organizational Culture and Leadership* (2nd ed.) (San Francisco: Jossey-Bass, 1992), p. 2.

4. A. Mumford, "Myth and Realities in Developing Directors," *Personnel Management*, Vol. 19, No. 2, p. 29.

5. L. Nadler and Z. Nadler, *Developing Human Resources* (3rd ed.) (San Francisco: Jossey-Bass, 1989), p. 4.

6. Ibid.

7. Ibid., p. 74

8. J. Lawrie, "Differentiate Between Training, Education and Development," *Personnel Journal*, Vol. 69, No. 10, p. 44.

9. D. Hall, "Executive Careers and Learning: Aligning Selection, Strategy, and Development," *Human Resource Planning*, Vol. 18, No. 2, pp. 14–23.

10. M. Cianni, "CEO Beliefs, Management Development, and Corporate Strategy: An Exploratory Study," *Group & Organization Management*, Vol. 19, No. 1, pp. 51–66.

11. S. McClelland, "Gaining Competitive Advantage Through Strategic Management Development (SMD)," *Journal of Management Development*, Vol. 13, No. 5, pp. 4–13.

12. M. Hitt, "Human Capital and Strategic Competitiveness in the 1990s," *Journal of Management Development*, Vol. 13, No. 1.

13. I. Barclay, "A Survey of the Activities, Problems and Training Needs of Technical Managers," *Engineering Management International*, Vol. 3, No. 4, pp. 253–259.

14. W. Ekerson, "Techies Need Training for Management Roles," *Network World*, Vol. 6, No. 14, pp. 27–28.

15. C. McCauley, "Linking Management Selection and Development Through Stretch Assignments," *Human Resource Management*, Vol. 34, No. 1, pp. 93–115.

16. L. Bittel and J. Newstrom, *What Every Supervisor Should Know* (6th ed.) (New York: McGraw-Hill, 1990), p. 7.

17. W. Rothwell, *Effective Succession Planning: Ensuring Leadership Continuity and Building Talent from Within* (New York: AMACOM, 1994).

18. V. Vroom, *Work and Motivation* (New York: John Wiley, 1964).

19. A. Belasen, "Downsizing and the Hyper-Effective Manager: The Shifting Importance of Managerial Roles During Organizational Transformation," *Human Resource Management*, Vol. 35, No. 1, pp. 87–117.

20. B. Betters-Reed, "Shifting the Management Development Paradigm for Women," *Journal of Management Development*, Vol. 14, No. 2, pp. 24–38.

21. A. Kraut, P. Pedigo, D. McKenna, and M. Dunnette, "The Role of the Manager: What's Really Important in Different Management Jobs," *Academy of Management Executive*, Vol. 3, No. 4, p. 287.

22. Ibid, p. 290.

23. Bittel and Newstrom, *What Every Supervisor Should Know*, p. 7.

24. Kraut, Pedigo, McKenna, and Dunnette, "The Role of the Manager," p. 287.

25. J. Burgoyne, "Management Development for the Individual and the Organization," *Personnel Management*, June 1988, p. 41.

26. Ibid.

27. A. Smith, "Management Development Evaluation and Effectiveness," *Journal of Management Development*, Vol. 12, No. 1, pp. 20–32.

28. F. Analoui, "Training and Development: The Role of Trainers," *Journal of Management Development*, Vol. 13, No. 9, pp. 61–72.

Part II

Planning and Designing the Leadership and Management Development Program

Part II introduces key issues to consider when setting up and operating a planned Leadership and Management Development (L & MD) program.

In most organizations, introducing a planned L & MD program requires a change of culture.[1] Leaders must come to grips with what they want from the program, realizing that a planned L & MD program will mean that they will have to think about the competencies necessary for individuals to perform effectively as supervisors, managers, and executives. This process can be more difficult than it sounds, but is absolutely essential if a planned L & MD program is to meet the needs of the organization and the learners it serves.

The four key issues covered in this part are: (1) Establishing program purpose, (2) identifying L & MD needs, (3) establishing an L & MD curriculum, and (4) administering the planned L & MD program.

Chapter 2 describes how to establish program purpose, goals, and objectives and how to identify the program's targeted market. Chapter 3 describes how to assess L & MD needs for individuals and groups. Chapter 4 explains how to establish a curriculum (long-term instructional plan) to guide the planned L & MD program. Chapter 5 describes how to set up the administrative support system for a planned L & MD program.

Chapter 2

Focusing a Leadership and Management Development Program

To introduce a planned L & MD program, you must start out with the support of the organization's leaders. You need their mandate to explore what purpose(s) L & MD should serve, what goals it should seek to accomplish, how it should be initially operated, and whose needs it should meet. Introducing a planned L & MD program requires a culture change. Culture change has figured prominently in books and articles on management in recent years. If published accounts share anything in common it is that making a culture change is a difficult, gut-wrenching, and time-consuming experience. Managers frequently underestimate what it involves. In reality, introducing and consolidating change is like riding a bucking bronco at a rodeo: it is exceedingly difficult at first. However, if people stand to gain personally from a change and are involved in the change process, they will leap on the bronco and their added weight will make taming the beast all the easier.

This chapter is about leaping on the bucking bronco. More specifically, consider this question: *What do you have to do to lay the foundation for a planned L & MD program in your organization?* Assuming leaders of the organization agree that it is worthwhile exploring or undertaking—and, if they do not, then their initial support must be secured before leaping on the bronco!—the first step is to conceptualize the L & MD program, clarifying why it should exist, what results it should initially achieve, and whose needs it should try to meet.

We suggest you begin your planned L & MD program by:

1. Forming a group or committee

2. Determining the program's purpose

3. Establishing program goals and objectives

4. Targeting groups to be served

5. Preparing a program policy and philosophy

6. Preparing a flexible action plan to guide program startup

7. Establishing a regular schedule to review program results

While we plan to address these steps in this chapter, let's add a caveat at the outset: *there is nothing sacred about these steps.* They are suggestions only. However, what works in one organizational setting may not work in others. Therefore, consider these steps in light of previous successful changes introduced in your organization. Modify the steps of introducing a planned L & MD program based on what has worked before when introducing large-scale change in your organization. Examples of previous successful change efforts might include the introduction of new technology, work methods, self-directed work teams, employee benefits programs, or new products or services. Ponder these questions: (1) What steps were taken to introduce those changes successfully? (2) Who was involved in making those changes? (3) What were the most important steps and milestones of that change effort? and (4) What made the change effort successful? Armed with the answers to these questions, you should be able to modify your steps in introducing a planned L & MD program so they follow proven approaches to introducing change and innovation in your organization's unique culture.

OPPORTUNITIES FOR L & MD

The impetus for a planned L & MD program, like other organizational changes, frequently begins when people

- *Complain about the way things are being done.* ("Here we just turn desks around and call people supervisors. That's no way to run a company! We should issue each of them a costume consisting of a red cape, red boots, and a blue suit with a big yellow 'S' emblazoned on the chest. They will need it!")

- *Are hurting due to crisis.* ("Now that Mary is quitting for another job, we have nobody ready to take over for her. Finding and training a replacement is going to be a mess! Why didn't we plan for a backup and prepare someone? Let's *do something* to avoid a similar problem in the future!")

- *Experience pain in making a transition.* ("When I took over this job, nobody trained me. I didn't even know where the restroom was located, and nobody was willing to take time to show me. I don't want anybody to go through that kind of anguish again. I have a stomach full of ulcers from that wrenching experience. Surely that's not how we want to do business!")

- *Discover that major barriers discourage entry to the management ranks.* ("Nobody here wants to be a supervisor, manager, or executive. They can simply earn more as hourly employees eligible for overtime. They end up taking a pay cut just to get a

Exhibit 2-1
The Use of Leadership and/or Management Development Committees

Question: How does your organization encourage the participation and ownership of management in management and/or leadership development efforts? More specifically, which of the following methods does your organization use? For each method listed in the left column below, check a *yes* or *no* response in the right column.				
Response	**Yes**		**No**	
	Frequency	**Percentage**	**Frequency**	**Percentage**
One or more committees composed of representatives from various groups inside your organization?	27	53%	24	47%
One or more committees composed of representatives from various groups outside your organization?	10	19%	42	81%
Learning contracts negotiated between individuals and their immediate supervisor(s)?	17	34%	33	66%

Source: W. Rothwell, *A Survey about Management and Leadership Development* (unpublished survey results) (University Park, PA: The Pennsylvania State University, 1998).

fancy title. That's nonsense! Do we really want to create a disincentive for working in management?'')

- *Demonstrate that high-stakes risk-taking is not rewarded.* (''We don't encourage risk-taking here. The last time someone here had a new idea, she was promptly shipped to Siberia. Let's figure out a way to reward the risk-taking that is essential to leadership for workers at all levels here.'')

Events of these kinds create windows of opportunity when the time is ripe to explore a planned L & MD program.

FORMING A GROUP

Once top managers agree to explore starting up a planned L & MD program, they will want solid information about problems to be solved, action plans, and estimates of costs. To get that information, an administrative structure of some kind is usually required. Such structures include steering committees, task forces, project teams, or similar groups. The results of Rothwell's 1998 survey of L & MD professionals revealed that committees are relatively common (see Exhibit 2-1).

A group can take initial steps, formulating initial parameters for a planned

L & MD program and introducing them to top executives and other stakeholders. The group members also form a nucleus of supporters for introducing and consolidating the change, building a core of support for it in the organization. If the group members include at least one powerful individual—such as the owner of the business, CEO, or division president—the group's existence also creates a political impetus for change, demonstrating that it enjoys top-level sponsorship.

An additional payoff from using a group structure is that the group activity itself provides an opportunity for L & MD. Those participating in the group are directly exposed to setting up a new program, managing significant change, leading (and influencing) a group of people, and other activities that transfer directly to their management jobs. It offers a chance to "learn by doing"—or even "do by learning"—and also builds a stake in success among participants.

Differences in Groups

Of course, different groups can be formed to support a planned L & MD program in the early stages.

- A *steering committee*, as its name implies, is formed to guide and navigate. Members of such a committee should usually include higher-level managers, such as top executives. In small organizations, one committee of 4 to 9 people should be sufficient, and the leader should include—or at least be appointed by—the business owner. In large corporations with many work sites, a committee should be formed at the corporate level, another at the division or Strategic Business Unit (SBU) level, and still others at each work site and/or for each level or function of management served. Leaders at each level should be appointed by the top manager in charge of the facility or plant.

- An *advisory committee* or *coordinating committee* is formed to offer advice or coordinate the L & MD program. It has no power or formal authority to direct others. It exists to make useful recommendations to the chief executive, board of directors, management employees, or the director of MD. It should only be formed with the blessing of the chief executive. (The CEO need not be a member, though his or her membership is desirable.) It establishes initial guidelines for the organization's planned L & MD program, approving the selection (as necessary) of external consultants to provide assistance and/or a full-time L & MD director to administer the L & MD program. The leader of the committee is usually appointed by the owner in a small business or by the CEO or board of directors in a corporate setting. Members are handpicked for their knowledge of management in the organization, their interest in a planned L & MD program, and their credibility with others in management.

- A *task force* is temporary, unlike steering or advisory committees that endure even as individual members rotate on or off them. Once an initial plan for an L & MD program has been developed and implemented, a task force is disbanded. A task force is usually composed of a representative cross-section of employees—such as an executive, a manager, a supervisor, and even several nonexempt employees. The leader is appointed by a top manager or elected by task force members.

- An *annual task force* is a variation of the task force structure. It is formed at the beginning of the year, completes an annual cycle of assigned tasks, and then disbands. Annual task forces are sometimes used to review L & MD needs in light of strategic plans, succession plans, or other plans. (Some top managers favor annual task forces for L & MD since they exist only long enough to complete a specific assignment. They do not contribute to the phenomenon of proliferating committees—a common problem in some corporations.)

- A *project team* is temporary. Composed of four to six individuals and headed by a leader elected by the members, its focus is narrower than a committee or task force. Indeed, project team members may be asked to direct their attention to a handful of issues only. To cite some examples: (1) articulating the purpose of a planned L & MD program for an organization or work site; (2) determining the annual goals or objectives of the program; (3) expressing a policy or philosophy to guide the program; (4) identifying and interpreting L & MD needs for an organization, work site, or targeted market; (5) planning and scheduling specific L & MD practices, such as an internal group training program, an external group training program, or a management job rotation program. When the task is completed, the project team disbands. Project teams are frequently used to design and deliver internal group training on such subjects as production scheduling, statistical process control, or budgeting.

- A *focus group* is a special, temporary group. Originally used in marketing efforts to determine how well a proposed product or service would be received by randomly selected potential customers, they are still widely used in marketing, public relations, and other fields in which public reaction is important. They may also be formed to assess the value of proposed L & MD activities. Participants are chosen to represent different groups—such as executives, managers, supervisors, or aspiring supervisors. They are called together for a short time, such as one to four hours, and are asked to make recommendations about the need for training, education, or development on specific issues. Alternatively, members may be asked to attend a preview of a training course and offer their reactions. If members of the focus group give an effort their stamp of approval, then it proceeds as planned; if they express reservations, their suggestions for change are used to improve the effort.

Forming the Group

The people chosen to serve on a steering committee, advisory or coordinating committee, task force, project team, or focus group will vary—depending on the purpose of the group.

Members of a committee or task force should be chosen based on

- *Their interest.* Does each member favor planned L & MD? If so, they are usually motivated to help make it work.

- *Their knowledge of L & MD practices.* Is each member familiar with L & MD practices in the corporation, industry, or in businesses generally? The greater the knowledge of benchmarks, the faster the group can progress by relating practices in other settings to their own.

- *Their own successful track records in management.* How successful has each member been in entering and progressing through the management ranks? What is each member's potential for future advancement?

- *Their own breadth and depth of management experience.* How broad and deep is each member's management experience as practiced in their own—or other—organizations? Broad experience is gained by many moves; deep experience is gained by long-term exposure to one function or specialty.

- *Their credibility.* How well respected is each group member among the organization's other management employees? Well-respected members will usually give a committee or task force significant influence in the organization.

- *Their willingness to make recommendations and follow through with action.* How willing is each group member to explore new ideas and, more importantly, follow through to see them put into practice?

In contrast, members of project teams should be chosen for their knowledge and skills for the task at hand—whatever that may be. Each member should be thoroughly familiar with the subject matter and possess the skills to follow through on whatever tasks the project requires. On the other hand, members of focus groups should represent a target market or audience. Their collective reactions should provide reliable clues about how a Management Development method—such as an internal group training program or a management job rotation program—will be received.

DETERMINING PROGRAM PURPOSE

A *purpose* is essentially a *mission*, a reason for being. In recent years, purpose has been the subject of much attention. It is, after all, a starting point for formulating—or changing—strategic plans.

An L & MD program should also have a purpose. It can perhaps be best understood as the answer to this question: *Why is the organization undertaking a planned L & MD program?* The answer to the question will provide clarity of direction and suggest goals to be achieved by the program.

Components of Purpose

The purpose of an L & MD program should be stated in writing. Like an organization's written purpose statement prepared during strategic planning, a written purpose statement for an L & MD program should provide clues to answer the following questions:[2]

- What needs should be met by the program?
- What should be the program's major areas of service?
- Whose needs should the program be designed to meet?

- Whose needs should be given priority?
- What should be the responsibilities of participants, sponsors, the organization, and other stakeholders in ensuring program success?

Methods for Determining Purpose

An L & MD program should serve the purposes of the organization and its target market. There are at least three key sources of information about the program's purpose: (1) the organization's leaders; (2) members of management; and (3) employees. Information should be gathered from each source. Appropriate methods for gathering information about program purpose will vary by source.

The organization's leaders are the first key source of information about program purpose. A planned L & MD program has the potential to change the culture of an organization by changing the knowledge, skills, and attitudes of its leadership. Consequently, L & MD is frequently linked to *Organization Development* (OD),[3] otherwise known as a long-term, top-down approach to introducing and consolidating organizational change by energizing and empowering employees.

OD is based on change that is supported by the organization's top managers. With this view in mind, top managers should be polled about *their* opinions on the desirable purpose(s) of a planned L & MD program. Indeed, starting with them is wise so as to build top-level interest, awareness, and support. Better yet, if top managers can help kick off efforts to collect information about the desirable purpose(s) of the program and involve themselves personally in the effort, they will send a strong signal of support. That is one reason many organizations form a steering committee composed of top executives to begin the L & MD effort by clarifying its initial purpose, goals, and objectives. Steering committee meetings are ideal settings for gathering information about the desirable purpose(s) of a planned L & MD program. (See Exhibit 2-2 for a worksheet to draft a purpose statement for an L & MD program.)

Members of management are the second key source of information about program purpose. Few experienced managers in the United States today can dispute that *participation* is a key to building *ownership* and *support*. That principle is no less true for the success of a planned L & MD program than for success in improving product quality or customer service. Consequently, it is important to build support for L & MD by enlisting participation in the process, particularly when formulating the program's purpose.

One way to do that is to release information on program purpose gathered from the organization's leaders and request comment from other members of management. Such information can be presented in "white papers," during informal briefings, or through short electronic mail messages. Experienced managers or supervisors may then be asked for additions, deletions, or modifications.

Exhibit 2-2
Questions about the Purpose(s) of a Planned L & MD Program

Directions: Consider the purpose of a planned L & MD program in your organization. For each question appearing below, provide an answer. When you finish the first five questions, then summarize them by drafting a purpose statement to govern the planned L & MD program in the organization.	
1	What needs should be met by the program?
2	What should be the program's major areas of service?
3	Whose needs should the program be designed to meet?
4	Whose needs should be given priority?
5	What should be the responsibilities of participants, sponsors, the organization, and other stakeholders in ensuring program success?
Draft Purpose Statement:	

Another way is to survey or interview experienced executives, managers, or supervisors individually about the desirable purposes to be served by a planned L & MD program. (The questions posed in Exhibit 2-2 can become the starting point for writing a survey or preparing a list of questions for individual interviews.) The results can then be compiled and fed back to the respondents until the responses begin to converge around common issues. This approach, essentially a Delphi procedure, is advantageous because it (1) Uses a process in which most everyone affected by a planned L & MD program is given a chance to participate in developing its purpose, (2) Keeps everyone informed even as information is gathered and decisions are made, and (3) Builds consensus around a few simple issues, thereby galvanizing support and interest. Workers are a third key source of information about program purpose. They are, after all, affected by a planned L & MD program because their immediate organizational superiors are prospective participants mostly in Management Development (MD)—and they are prospective participants mostly in Leadership Development (LD) of the L & MD program. Moreover, workers have a unique perspective, too seldom valued, for identifying the strengths and weaknesses of their own immediate organizational superiors.

Personal interviewing is probably the best method for gathering information from employees about the desirable purpose(s) of a planned L & MD program. Few employees will want to write down their thoughts—even in organizations where jobs are secure and morale is high. They may fear reprisal from their immediate organizational superiors, so their anonymity should be ensured and protected. The interviewer must be perceived as a trustworthy individual, perhaps someone from outside the organization who is viewed as unbiased. Faculty from local colleges can be employed at reasonable cost to conduct such studies.

First, ask the CEO to notify exempt and nonexempt employees about the

Exhibit 2-3
Questions for Employees about the Purpose(s) of a Planned L & MD Program

Directions: Answer the following questions.
1 In your opinion, what is the best thing about the way workers, supervisors, managers, or executives perform in this organization? (*Cite an example and explain your reasoning, if possible.*)
2 What is your biggest single complaint about the way workers, supervisors, managers, and executives perform in this organization? (*Cite an example and explain your reasoning, if possible.*)
3 What example can you provide in which a worker, supervisor, manager, or executive exerted leadership? (*Cite an example and explain why you believed it was an example of leadership.*)

study in order to give it legitimacy, emphasize its importance, and allay whatever fears may exist about it. Second, select employees randomly from an employee roster or payroll record. Third, contact employees for individual meetings before, during, or after work—or even during lunch hours. Fourth, pose questions like those appearing in Exhibit 2-2. Fifth, feed back the results to managers and employees, starting from the CEO and progressing downward. In light of the results, pose the questions appearing in Exhibit 2-3 to *each layer of management*, recording reactions and feeding them downward to the next layer each time. Sixth and finally, close the feedback loop by conveying the reactions of each layer back to top management. Ask top managers to synthesize the results and finalize the purpose of the L & MD program. By using this approach, all employees participate in establishing the purpose of the planned L & MD program. That will increase its visibility and build commitment at all levels.

ESTABLISHING PROGRAM GOALS AND OBJECTIVES

A *goal* is a result to be achieved. Goals are seldom specific. They grow out of purpose, indicating generally what should be achieved. In some instances, goals may actually be stated as part of a written purpose statement for an organization, division, department, or program.

Examples of goals for a planned L & MD program might include:

- Improving the preparation of individuals for supervisory, management, or executive positions
- Establishing and carrying out programs to ease the transition of individuals hired into, promoted into, or transferred into the jobs of supervisor, manager, or executive
- Helping supervisors, managers, and executives keep their skills current
- Planning and carrying out programs intended to give individuals the skills they need to advance in their management careers

Goals may also be linked directly to the various purposes of planned L & MD programs. For instance, a planned L & MD program may be intended to:

• Contribute to implementing the organization's succession plans

• Contribute to implementing the organization's strategic plans

• Develop individuals for increased responsibility

• Help individuals realize their career plans within an organization

• Improve the morale of management employees

• Improve the organization's ability to respond to environmental change

• Improve the organization's ability to respond to technological change

• Increase the pool of promotable management employees

• Increase the productivity of management employees

• Provide general training to individuals inside the organization

• Build skills in managing people for individuals who have never received formal instruction on supervision or management

• Increase opportunities for women

• Increase opportunities for minorities

• Increase opportunities for "high-potential" workers

It is rarely possible for a planned L & MD program to meet *all* these goals. For this reason, you should limit the goals to the most important ones only. These goals should then be presented for review and approval by higher-level managers and targeted groups. *Objectives* are directly related to, but more specific than, goals. Objectives add elements of time and measurement to goals. Answer the questions appearing in Exhibit 2-4 to convert the general goals of a planned L & MD program to specific objectives.

TARGETING GROUPS TO SERVE

A planned L & MD program can serve the needs of any or all organizational groups. However, during the startup of a new program, you will usually find it necessary to establish priorities and target specific groups for immediate attention. Later, as the program proves its success and is accepted, additional target groups may be added. The effect is the same as a juggler who starts out with a few items but, as a rhythm is achieved, adds more and more items to be juggled.

But how can you conceptualize the various groups to which a planned L & MD program can be targeted? Generally, there are four ways: (1) by job category; (2) by special group; (3) by special program; and (4) by combination. Let's review how each way can be used to establish initial program priorities.

Exhibit 2-4

A Worksheet for Converting L & MD Goals to Objectives

Directions: Use this Worksheet to help you structure your thinking about the goals and objectives of a planned L & MD program for your organization. For each goal listed in column 1 below, rank its importance in column 2. Then convert the goal to an objective by answering the questions appearing in columns 3 and 4. Add paper as necessary. There are no "right" or "wrong" answers for this Worksheet. However, some answers may be more or less useful, depending on the needs of your organization and its workers. When you finish, present your results for discussion to members of a steering committee, advisory/coordinating committee, taskforce, project team or other group assigned to help establish and operate the planned L & MD program in your organization. Repeat this Activity on a regular and periodic basis, such as once a year.

Column 1		Column 2	Column 3	Column 4
Goal		**Rank**	**How can results be measured?**	**What is to be achieved over a specific time period (such as 1 year)?**
1	Contribute to implementing the organization's succession plans			
2	Contribute to implementing the organization's strategic plans			
3	Develop individuals for increased responsibility			
4	Help individuals realize their career plans within an organization			
5	Improve morale of management employees			
6	Improve the organization's ability to respond to environmental change			
7	Improve the organization's ability to respond to technological change			
8	Increase the pool of promotable management employees			
9	Increase the productivity of management employees			
10	Provide general training to individuals inside the organization			
11	Build skills in "people management" for individuals who have never received formal instruction on supervision or management			
12	Provide increased opportunities for women			
13	Provide increased opportunities for minorities			
14	Provide increased opportunities for "high-potential" workers			

By Job Category

Job category is one way to organize a planned L & MD program in an organization. After all, jobs are the nexus or connecting point between individual abilities and organizational responsibilities. By definition, a job is composed of various *duties* or *tasks* (activities with discernible starting and ending points), *desired results* (outcomes to be achieved), or *responsibilities* (continuing results to be achieved). *Job titles* or *job categories* are identifiers for groups of related tasks, desired results or responsibilities across an organization.

Generally speaking, jobs are distinguished by level of responsibility, by proximity to customers or nonexempt workers, or by proximity to the CEO. Nonexempt workers may be categorized as professional, technical, sales, secretarial/clerical, skilled trades, semi-skilled, or unskilled. Additionally, exempt workers may be classified as supervisory, management, or executive. Supervisors are front-line management employees whose work typically involves overseeing the daily activities of nonexempt workers. They must usually have a detailed grasp of how the work is performed. Managers are the next line of management employees, and their work involves overseeing the activities of supervisors *and* nonexempt workers. They require less detailed technical knowledge of how the work is performed but do need more analytical and conceptual skills. Executives are the highest-level management employees. Their work is heavily focused on conceptualizing and planning.

When a planned L & MD program is targeted by job category, L & MD efforts are designed to help individuals (1) Exert leadership over anyone, regardless of level, (2) Prepare to enter management jobs, (3) Orient themselves to the management level to which they have recently been promoted or transferred, (4) Remain current in knowledge, skills, or attitudes appropriate to their job category, or (5) Advance to a new, higher-level job. When targeted by job category, a planned L & MD program must be based on the present and/or future tasks, duties, or desired results of such job categories as supervisor, manager, or executive.

There are several good reasons to focus a planned L & MD program on meeting the needs of learners based on their job categories:

- You should find it relatively easy to distinguish between job categories and explain those distinctions to others.

- Many other organizations focus their L & MD programs based on job category, making it easier to benchmark program initiatives across an industry or geographical area.

- Few skeptics can seriously question the relevance of basing L & MD activities on job-related tasks, duties, and responsibilities.

- Various government regulatory agencies—such as the Equal Employment Opportunity Commission—rely on job categories as a basis for comparing the advancement and training opportunities offered to protected and nonprotected labor groups. Consequently, if you focus your planned L & MD program based on job categories, you should find it relatively easy to report on—and, if necessary, legally defend—affirmative action and Equal Employment Opportunity efforts in your organization.

Of course, there are several drawbacks to using job categories to target groups for planned L & MD programs. One drawback is that management job categories are changing in the United States. It is therefore very important to avoid basing L & MD programs solely on *past* (historical) rather than *present* or *future* responsibilities by job category.[4] At one time a sharp dividing line separated the tasks and duties appropriate at each management level. That line is blurring due to corporate downsizing and advances in information technology. These trends are likely to continue.

A second drawback is that many organizations have more than just three levels of management. For this reason, you must exercise care to classify management job categories in ways that reflect reality in your organizational culture. Indeed, you must start out by identifying the significant management job categories in your organization. One way to do that is to examine an organization chart, identifying how many and what kinds of management positions exist in the organization. Very real differences in duties may also be apparent between *line* (production-oriented) and *staff* (professional, technical, and advisory) supervisory, management, and executive positions. These differences should also be taken into account when you decide what job category or categories are to become the target for an initial planned L & MD program.

By Special Group

Another way to target your market is by special group. In an effort to address the so-called "glass ceiling" that limits advancement opportunities of women and other protected labor groups, some corporations have directed their L & MD programs to improving the opportunities available to these groups. Many large corporations have begun special L & MD programs to increase advancement opportunities for women, minorities, the aged, the disabled, or other groups.

To plan an L & MD program geared to meeting the needs of special groups, you should consider several questions:

1. *Why is such a program needed for the special group?* What is the special purpose of the program? Why is it needed?

2. *Who are they?* Can you identify members of the special groups to be served by a planned L & MD program?

3. *Where are they?* Identify their locations.

4. *What do they need?* Identify their special needs, particularly needs arising from their protected labor status.

5. *Who should plan and operate the program?* Special programs will gain credibility if

they have significant involvement from members of the special groups to which they are targeted.

However, some evidence exists that these special programs in corporations have been turning into *diversity programs* open to all. One reason for this trend is to avoid excluding people from the programs. When people are deliberately excluded, they may begin to harbor suspicion about members of protected labor groups due to the "special treatment" accorded to them. That reaction is, of course, just the reverse of the intended goal. By including nonprotected groups, organizations build their sensitivity to the special needs of protected groups and thereby promote increased understanding and harmonious relations.

By Special Program

Special programs are designed to meet the unique needs of different classes of performers in the management ranks. The underlying assumption is that a corporation may gain special payoffs by concentrating efforts on different groups of performers. For instance, *high-potential* (HiPo) employees participate in programs designed to help them build on their strengths and realize their potential more quickly; *low-potential* (PoPo) employees participate in programs designed to help them overcome their deficiencies. Many corporations operate special *high-potential* programs designed to place selected individuals on the fast track to advancement.

If you choose to target your planned L & MD program by special program, consider these questions:

1. *What desired payoffs are to be achieved by a special program?* Why do you want to direct your initial efforts to performance levels?
2. *How may employees be classified by their performance?* How do you define *high-potential performer, high performer, low-potential performer,* or *low performer?*
3. *What L & MD needs exist for each group of performers?* What should be done for each group?
4. *Which special group or groups should receive primary attention?* How are priorities decided? By whom are they authorized?

Like targeting special groups, however, special programs can also produce significant resentment if not properly handled. If, for example, participants in HiPo programs are viewed as "crowned princes" or "water walkers"—and receive much special attention, high visibility, and choice job assignments—then they may well be disliked intensely by others. Worse yet, some people may deliberately sabotage their work. Great care must be taken to avoid giving the appearance of favoritism and bias in advancement opportunities and job assignments. That raises a special challenge in establishing and operating HiPo programs successfully.

Exhibit 2-5
Targeting Groups for a Planned L & MD Program

Directions: Use this Activity to structure your thinking about whose needs to serve at the outset of a planned L & MD program. Answer the questions appearing below. Compare your responses to the responses provided by other members of management in your organization.	
1	It is not possible to meet the L & MD needs of all members of management at the same time. What group or groups do you feel should receive initial emphasis for an L & MD program? (*By groups we mean job categories such as individuals aspiring to become supervisors, newly promoted supervisors, experienced supervisors, individuals aspiring to become managers, newly promoted managers, experienced managers, individuals aspiring to executive positions, newly promoted executives, or experienced executives. We may also mean special groups, such as women or minorities, or special classes of performers, such as exceptionally high or low performers.*)
2	Why do you feel the way you do? In other words, how do you justify your answer to question 1 above?

By Combination

Of course, it is possible to use a combination of methods by which to select initial target groups for L & MD programs. Indeed, it is possible to target efforts by job category, special group, *and* special need. One example: is a minority-oriented Management Trainee program for HiPos. Exhibit 2-5 gives you the opportunity to structure your thinking about which—or how many—groups you wish to target for your initial efforts.

PREPARING A PROGRAM POLICY AND PHILOSOPHY

In the context of L & MD, a *policy* is a written description intended to coordinate action and fix responsibility, and a *philosophy* is an expression of values. The available research evidence suggests that few organizations have prepared a written *policy and philosophy statement* to govern training, education, or development efforts.[5] For example, one research study revealed that only "22% of the companies reported having a written policy requiring managers to attend formal training and education programs. In 93% of these companies, this policy requires first-level supervisors to participate in formal training/education programs, and in 48% of these companies, this policy also applies to top-level managers. This policy is new within the past five years for 60% of these respondents."[6]

Although few organizations have a written policy and philosophy statement to guide L & MD, there are distinct advantages to having one.

Advantages of a Written Policy and Philosophy Statement

A written L & MD policy and philosophy statement is worth having for several reasons. First, it puts the organization on the record about what the program is intended to achieve. Second, it clarifies the responsibilities of supervisors, managers, and executives in such efforts. Third, it is a starting point for building interest, attention, and ownership in the program. Fourth and finally, it is a tool for communicating about the program to participants, their immediate organizational superiors, and others who are interested.

Without a policy and philosophy statement, an organization may encounter difficulties in its efforts to establish a planned L & MD program. Powerful executives may bend the program to suit their whims. L & MD directors, once hired to lead such programs, will have no clear mandate and may find themselves buffeted about by differing (and possibly conflicting) expectations. The result: the L & MD program will not be as effective as it could have been.

Components of a Policy and Philosophy Statement

What should be included in a written policy and philosophy statement for a planned L & MD program? There is no simple answer to that question because the desirable issues to be addressed may vary across organizations. However, it is possible to list desirable questions to be answered in a policy and philosophy statement:[7]

1. What basic philosophical principles should guide a planned L & MD program?
2. What should be the program's purpose?
3. What should be the program's goals?
4. What should be the relationship between the program and the organization's other human resources practices for management employees?
5. Whose needs should the program be designed to serve?
6. What should be the program's components?
7. How should planned L & MD activities be delivered?
8. How should the program be supported by the organization?
9. What should be the responsibilities of program participants, their immediate organizational superiors, and others?

The first question will prompt decision makers and program architects to articulate a *credo*, a statement of values which the L & MD program is designed to support. The second and third questions will help clarify the program's purpose and goals, showing how the program is designed to support the philosophy. The fourth question will clear up the relationships between a planned L & MD program and such other human resource policies as management performance appraisal practices, compensation, benefits, and selection. The answer to the fifth question identifies the program's targeted groups; the answer to the sixth question identifies program activities; and, the answer to the seventh question clarifies how L & MD activities will be delivered. Questions eight and nine will clarify how much support the program will enjoy and the roles of people who affect program success.

Preparing a Policy and Philosophy Statement

Begin drafting a policy and philosophy statement as soon as top managers signal support for establishing the program. Drafting such a statement should become a central focus of a steering committee or other group early on. The reasons: it surfaces key issues and crystallizes committee thinking.

Use the Worksheet appearing in Exhibit 2-6 to help committee members structure their thinking on key program issues. Pass out the Worksheet before an initial group meeting and ask members to jot down ideas to be shared in that meeting. That should start the group off with a problem-solving focus.

PREPARING A FLEXIBLE PROGRAM ACTION PLAN

A written policy and philosophy statement is only an early step in establishing a planned L & MD program. Another is the development of a flexible *action plan*, a description of steps that must be taken to achieve desired results. You might liken it to a business plan for a small enterprise. An action plan is the product of a focused *vision* about desired results to be achieved, a picture of what a planned L & MD program should eventually look like.

An action plan answers this question: *How will goals, objectives, or desired results be achieved?* It usually specifies what goals or objectives will be achieved, specific steps to take, and the time required. It may also identify who is responsible for doing what.

Why Is an Action Plan Important?

An action plan reduces the likelihood that a desired goal or objective will not be achieved due to uncertainty about who should do what. It also economizes steps, making sure that each step directly contributes to achieving a desired goal or objective. Further, it becomes a basis for judging group and individual performance. On a philosophical level, an action plan is also important because it makes an otherwise vague vision of the future concrete and attainable.

When introducing any change in organizations, try to engineer one or more quick successes to build enthusiasm and support. The same principle applies when introducing a planned L & MD program. One or more action plans should be prepared right away. These plans should be geared to achieving quick, highly visible results. Preferably, the plan should be designed to satisfy a long-standing but relatively simple L & MD problem that has given rise to complaints among supervisors, managers, or executives. While such problems may vary across organizations, one example might be a training course on budgeting for those who are expected to budget but who have never received training on budgeting.

Exhibit 2-6
A Worksheet for Preparing a Written Policy and Philosophy Statement for a Planned L & MD Program

Directions: Use this Worksheet to structure your thinking about key issues to be considered when introducing a planned L & MD program. For each question posed in the left column below and explained in the center column, jot down your answers in the right column. Be prepared to share your thoughts with others. The product of this Worksheet should become the basis for a written policy and philosophy statement to guide the planned L & MD program. Attach more paper if necessary.

	Question	Explanation of the Question	Your Answer?
1	What basic philosophical principles should guide the planned L & MD program?	• What do we believe about the nature of management in this organization? • What do we believe about the value of preparing management employees to do their jobs?	
2	What should be the program's purpose?	• What is the *chief* reason to sponsor this program?	
3	What should be the program's goals?	• What do we hope to achieve from this program?	
4	What should be the relationship between the program and the organization's human resources management practices for management employees?	• What should be the relationship between planned L & MD and • management job descriptions? • management performance appraisals? • management compensation practices? • management recruitment? • Equal Employment Opportunity and Affirmative Action?	
5	Whose needs should the program be designed to serve?	• Should the program be designed primarily to meet the needs of • job categories? • special, protected labor groups? • high, low, or intermediate-range performers in the management ranks? • a combination?	
6	What should be the program's components?	• Should the program rely on such methods as • internal group training? • external group training? • external education? • job rotation? • on-the-job training? • coaching? • mentoring? • other methods?	
7	How should planned L & MD activities be delivered?	• Is there a preference for L & MD activities to be delivered? • on-the-job? • off-the-job • some combination? • What is the reason for this preference?	
8	How should the program be supported by the organization?	• How will it be funded and budgeted for?	
9	What should be the general responsibilities of participants in the program, their immediate organizational superior, and others?	• What are the responsibilities of those who participate in the L & MD program? • What are the responsibilities of the organizational superiors of those participating in the L & MD program? • What should be top managers' responsibilities in the L & MD program? • How will people be informed of their accountabilities? • How will people be held accountable for their L & MD program responsibilities?	

Exhibit 2-7
An Activity for Establishing a Vision for a Planned L & MD Program

Directions: Use this Activity to help you establish a vision and a flexible action plan to introduce a planned L & MD program in your organization. Starting from the left side of the line appearing below, identify different time periods (for example, 5 months, 7 months, 9 months, 12 months, and 5 years). Then, below each vertical line, describe what should be happening in the L & MD program and what results should be achieved. Finally, under the last line at the right side of the continuum, describe the ultimate results to be achieved. In other words, what should be happening, how should the program be functioning, and what results should have been achieved? (*Add paper as necessary.*)

_____ Months	_____ Months	_____ Months	_____ Months	_____ Years

Another example: a training course on employee discipline for those responsible for administering progressive discipline but who are unsure how to apply it.

Why Is "Flexibility" Important?

Don't expect the action plan to cover every problem that will be encountered in starting up the L & MD program. Be flexible. Be willing to modify the action plan as events unfold.

On the other hand, try to anticipate problems. The introduction of any change produces side effects. Some side effects can be predicted; some cannot be. Some are positive; others are not.

The same principles apply to introducing a planned L & MD program in an organization that has always promoted from within or relied heavily on unplanned on-the-job training or informal coaching to prepare individuals for management. Some problems can be anticipated, and strategies for dealing with them should be thought out ahead of time. For instance, upon the introduction of a planned L & MD program, it is common for experienced employees at all levels to worry about how the change will affect them *personally*. Those most worried are likely to be people who would have otherwise expected advancement based on their seniority, popularity, or performance. It is important to allay their fears as much as possible. Do that by communicating about program initiatives and involving others as much as possible.

Use the Activity in Exhibit 2-7 to build flexibility into program planning. Then plan one quick success for the planned L & MD program.

ESTABLISHING A REGULAR PROGRAM REVIEW SCHEDULE

As a final step in introducing a planned L & MD program, establish a schedule to evaluate program success and achievement periodically. The idea is to build in a means to track, and communicate, program successes and achievements. Without such a schedule, it will be easy to forget to do that amid daily work pressures. But if this step is forgotten, L & MD program activities may be scaled back during periods of retrenchment. Unfortunately, many businesses have done that in the past.

We shall have more to say about evaluation in Chapter 10. For now, however, it is sufficient to note that the foundation for program evaluation should be planned from the outset in order to protect the program from budget slashing. A demonstrated track record, widely communicated, goes a long way toward building and maintaining program support. Evaluation is one way to demonstrate that record.

SUMMARY

In this chapter we emphasized the importance of establishing a core group of committed people to work on launching a planned L & MD program. We also explained how to clarify program purpose, goals, and objectives, and how to select a target group to be served by the program. Finally, we described the value of preparing a program policy and philosophy, a flexible action plan for program startup, and a schedule to review program results.

NOTES

1. E. Schein, *Organizational Culture and Leadership* (2nd ed.) (San Francisco: Jossey-Bass, 1992).

2. G. Morrisey, *Management by Objectives and Results in the Public Sector* (Reading, MA: Addison-Wesley, 1976), p. 25.

3. W. Rothwell, R. Sullivan, and G. McLean, eds., *Organization Development: A Guide for Consultants* (San Francisco: Jossey-Bass/Pfeiffer, 1995).

4. W. Rothwell and H. Kazanas, *Human Resource Development: A Strategic Approach*, rev. ed. (Amherst, MA: Human Resource Development Press, 1994).

5. A. Spector, *The Human Resource Development Policy Study: Identification and Analysis of Human Resource Development Policy in Selected U.S. Corporations* (unpublished doctoral dissertation). (Washington, DC: The George Washington University, 1985).

6. L. Saari, T. Johnson, S. McLaughlin, and D. Zimmerle, "A Survey of Management Training and Education Practices in U.S. Companies," *Personnel Psychology*, Vol. 41, pp. 739–740.

7. Morrisey, *Management by Objectives and Results in the Public Sector*, p. 25.

Chapter 3

Identifying Leadership and Management Development Needs

Once you have clarified the purpose of a planned L & MD program, you should begin identifying management learning needs. This step has no definite beginning and ending—assuming that the aim is to continuously improve management performance. To emphasize the importance of this step—the focus of this chapter—we shall start out with a brief but realistic case study.

INTRODUCTORY CASE STUDY

George Smithers was hired to establish a planned L & MD program for a conservative service firm employing 1,500 people. George was hired from outside the firm and the industry, but he started with significant experience in L & MD and college teaching. The company had never planned L & MD before, previously relying on promotion-from-within and on-the-job coaching to help people advance.

On his first day, George was introduced to members of the company's L & MD steering committee, which had been authorized by the company's board of directors and CEO to oversee the start up of a planned L & MD program. The committee members consisted of the company's executive in charge of Management Information Systems, the second-in-command of company Finance, two key middle managers from Operations, and the top Human Resources executive (George's immediate organizational superior).

George was pleasantly surprised to learn that committee members had already clarified the purpose of the L & MD program, established program goals and objectives, and identified prospective and experienced supervisors as initial target groups. Managers, executives, and hourly workers were to be served by the program later, after initial success had been achieved with supervisors. George felt that his next steps were clear. He would coordinate preparation of a program policy and philosophy statement, establish a flexible action plan for program startup, and prepare a schedule of learning experiences. These steps would give direction to the fledgling L & MD program. At the same time, they would provide George with a means to orient himself to the company and build program support.

George also felt that he should conduct a management needs assessment to uncover gaps between what the targeted learners already know or do and what they should know or do. George was aware, after all, that the term *supervisor* does not have a universal meaning. Supervisory duties, tasks, and responsibilities vary dramatically across industries, organizations, and even across people working for different managers in the same organization.

As a first step in needs assessment, George planned to review supervisory job descriptions and recent supervisory performance appraisals. He knew the information they contained would shed light on what supervisors are expected to do in the organization and how well they have been doing it. He should then find it easy to assess individual and group needs against those requirements.

Unfortunately, George soon learned that the organization had no written supervisory job descriptions. Nor, it seemed, did the organization make it a regular practice to require supervisory performance appraisals. Although dismayed by the lack of information, George was undaunted: he decided to conduct a supervisory needs assessment in several steps. First, he would interview a small, randomly selected group of supervisors and their immediate organizational superiors regarding supervisory responsibilities. From the interview results he would draft a supervisory job description and use it as a basis for a written needs assessment survey questionnaire. After having both reviewed by a small group of experienced supervisors and their immediate organizational superiors, he would finalize the questionnaire and send it out to all supervisors and their immediate organizational superiors in the organization. He would use the survey results to identify supervisory learning needs and establish initial priorities for the planned L & MD program. Finally, he decided to feed back the results of his efforts to members of the steering committee and survey respondents. Feedback would communicate the necessity of the L & MD program and validate a direction for it.

In time, George also wanted to pinpoint the competencies of successful performers at all levels, create a full-circle multi-rater assessment survey questionnaire based on the competencies of exemplary performers, clarify the values of the organization so that corporate culture could be purveyed by experiences in the program, and establish a management curriculum in the organization to ensure consistent preparation of individuals to meet predictable learning needs resulting from promotion to supervision. Comprised of planned learning experiences, it would be flexible, lending itself to individualized planned learning experiences in various media as necessary.

DEFINING NEEDS

As the introductory case study implies, a *need* is traditionally viewed as a performance gap separating *what is* from *what should be*. In this context, *performance* means *desired results*. Performance should not be confused with the observable or unobservable behavior or activities of job incumbents.

Learning versus Nonlearning Needs

There are three categories of needs:[1]

- *Learning needs*: A performance gap is caused by lack of necessary knowledge or skill.
- *Nonlearning needs*: A performance gap is caused by an obstacle in the work environment. Nonlearning needs are sometimes called *management needs*, because the work environment is controlled by management.
- *Learning and nonlearning needs*: A performance gap is caused in part by lack of necessary knowledge or skill and in part by an obstacle in the work environment.

A simple example should help clarify the differences described above: newly promoted supervisors experience learning needs when they *do not know how* to fill out reports, conduct employee performance appraisals, or prepare work schedules. But they experience nonlearning needs when they already know how to perform these supervisory tasks but fail to do so for other reasons—such as lack of proper tools (they are not given necessary equipment to write out reports), sufficient time (they have conflicting work assignments), or proper attitude and motivation (they do not consider the work tasks important enough to warrant attention).

For the most part, a planned L & MD program focuses on meeting individual or group learning needs. Its typical purpose is to build individual competencies so that individuals can perform effectively. However, those responsible for coordinating L & MD programs should pay close attention to nonlearning needs stemming from problematic recruitment, selection, reward, and other practices. Questions that can help distinguish learning from nonlearning needs appear in Exhibit 3-1.

Sources of Learning Needs

Where do learning needs come from? Most authorities agree with the view, first proposed in 1961,[2] that needs stem from at least three primary sources: (1) *The organization*: What performance is required of an individual or group by the organization's strategic plan, culture, and activities? (2) *The job*: What do people have to know or do to be able to perform their jobs competently? (3) *The individual*: What does the individual or group already know or do? How does that compare to what the individual must know or do to perform compe-

Exhibit 3-1
Questions for Distinguishing Learning from Nonlearning Needs

When confronted with problem performance or a problem situation, pose the following questions to find out more about the problem and its causes:	
Major Questions	**Related Questions**
What is happening?	• What is happening now? • Who first reported the problem? • When was the problem first noticed? • How was the problem first noticed?
What should be happening?	• What is the desirable or ideal state? • What performance or behavior is expected? • What performance standards or objectives provide benchmarks against which to measure what should be happening? • What organizational policies, common business practices, or governmental laws, rules, or regulations apply to this situation or problem?
How wide is the performance gap between what is happening and what should be happening?	• What is the difference between *what is happening* and *what should be happening*?
How important is the performance gap between what is happening and what should be happening?	• What are the consequences of this performance gap? • How important is the performance gap to • Customers, suppliers, or other external stakeholders? • The organization? • Divisions, departments, work groups, or work teams? • Individual management employees? • Other individuals or groups? *(If the problem is not important, ignore it. Otherwise, continue to the next step.)*
What is the cause of the performance gap?	• Is the problem caused *chiefly* by a lack of knowledge or skill? (Do people know what to do in situations like this one?) • Is the problem caused *chiefly* by an obstacle to performance? (Do people have the resources they need to perform? Do they want to perform? Are they capable of performing?) • Is the problem caused *chiefly* by a combination of a lack of knowledge or skill *and* an obstacle to performance?
What solution(s) will address the cause(s) of the performance gap most effectively?	• If the performance problem is caused chiefly by lack of knowledge or skill, can it be most effectively addressed by designing and delivering training? Designing and offering job aids to help people comply with a policy or follow procedure at the time they need to perform? Giving people an opportunity to practice a skill or master knowledge on their own—either on-the-job or off-the-job? Modifying selection practices to choose people who have more knowledge or skills at the time of a job change—such as at time of hire, promotion, or transfer? Modifying job duties so that only those already possessing appropriate knowledge or skills handle problems? Establishing expert systems so as to minimize the need for human decisions and/or actions? Choosing another strategy to address the deficiency of knowledge or skill? • If the performance problem is caused chiefly by an obstacle to performance, can it be cost-effectively addressed by: Clarifying work standards? Improving feedback about individual or group performance? Providing more appropriate tools, materials, procedures, policies, or other resources to do the work? Holding individuals or groups more accountable

Exhibit 3-1 (continued)

When confronted with problem performance or a problem situation, pose the following questions to find out more about the problem and its causes:	
Major Questions	**Related Questions**
	for their performance by applying disciplinary methods when appropriate? Changing/improving the match between performance and rewards or incentives? Choosing another strategy designed to overcome obstacles to performance outside the direct control of individuals? • If the performance problem iscaused by a combination of lack of knowledge or skill and a barrier to performance, can the problem be broken down into components based on their causes and can appropriate, cost-effective solutions be selected for each component? If yes, continue to the next step. If no, devote time to analyzing the problem so it can be broken down into components suitable for corrective action.
What negative or unintended side effects may result from the solution(s) selected, how can they be anticipated, and how can their effects on performance be minimized?	• What problems are likely to result from the corrective action that is planned? • What can be done before or during corrective action to minimize the problems, negative or unintended side effects?

tently? Since 1961, authorities have added a fourth source of learning needs: *the external environment*. It consists of the world outside the organization, and it affects learning needs through requirements posed by customers, stockholders, competitors, regulators, and other stakeholder groups. Identifying stakeholders' expectations for an organization and/or its products or services can be a vital first step in formulating organizational strategic plans, establishing a Total Quality Management (TQM) effort, re-engineering work processes, and identifying the learning needs of exempt and nonexempt employees.

Organizational, job, individual, and external environmental requirements should be clarified and then compared to existing conditions to determine the gap between what is and what should be.

DEFINING LEARNING NEEDS ASSESSMENT

Learning needs assessment is the process of identifying performance gaps, caused by lack of knowledge or skill, that separate *what is* and *what should be*. It answers such questions as: (1) How large is the performance gap? (2) How important is the performance gap at present and in the future? *Leadership and Management Development learning needs assessment* (L & MDNA) is the process of identifying the learning needs of management employees or individuals who can or should exert leadership. It is a crucial starting point for planning learning experiences.[3] Without L & MDNA, it will not be possible to determine what learning needs exist—or which needs deserve priority attention.

Unfortunately, relatively few organizations make it policy to conduct systematic L & MDNA routinely. One survey study revealed that only 27 percent of the survey respondents' organizations conduct needs assessment for management employees.[4] Needs assessment is most often conducted for supervisors and least often conducted for top managers. Large organizations are more likely than small ones to use needs assessment to identify the learning needs of management employees.

Identifying Whose Needs to Assess

Begin L & MDNA by identifying the learning needs of the first group targeted for attention in your planned L & MD program. For instance, you may choose to start with L & MDNA for aspiring supervisors, high-potential employees (HiPos), or protected labor classes. Start with the group whose needs are perceived to be greatest.

In addition—or, as an alternative—conduct a *benchmarking* study.[5] Identify well-known competitors or organizations renowned for their L & MD programs. Prepare questions to determine (among other issues) which groups in those organizations are receiving priority attention for leadership or management development efforts. Contact representatives of those organizations. Visit them, if at all possible, to see firsthand what is being done. Take along representatives of key stakeholder groups in the organization—such as members of the L & MD steering committee, top managers, targeted learners, and others—to build an impetus for change and for program success. Presently, a small but growing number of organizations are benchmarking their L & MD programs.

Differences Between Macro and Micro Learning Needs

L & MDNA may be conducted for long-term or short-term learning needs. Long-term needs are relatively enduring or may affect many people. They are called *macro needs*.[6] On the other hand, short-term needs may change rapidly. They are created by topical problems facing an organization, individual, or job category. They may also result from individual deficiencies. They are called *micro needs*.[7]

Examples of *macro* and *micro* needs are easy to point out. Suppose supervisors, the initial targets of a planned L & MD program, interview job applicants. When supervisors are hired, promoted, or transferred into their positions, few know how to conduct legally defensible employment interviews. Hence, employment interviewing presents a *macro learning need* because it affects all supervisors in the organization. It will endure as long as supervisors are expected to conduct employment interviews.

Suppose that new laws are enacted, court rulings are handed down, or company policies are instituted that affect employment interviewing practices—as occurred with the enactment of the Americans with Disabilities Act or the Family Medical Leave Act.[8] Such a change affects everyone, including those experienced in employment interviewing. Changes of this kind also create *macro learning needs* affecting many people.

On the other hand, individuals vary in the knowledge and skills they bring to their jobs. Some newly promoted supervisors may know already how to conduct employment interviews in conformance with company policy and legal requirements. Forcing them into learning the basics will be a waste of time. Others may not be conducting interviews properly, even though they have been doing them for some time without receiving training first. They experience *micro needs*, which are unique needs stemming from their individual strengths and weaknesses.

THREE APPROACHES TO L & MDNA

There are three general ways by which to conduct L & MDNA: the *top-down approach*, the *bottom-up approach*, and the *combination approach*.

The *top-down approach* focuses primarily on macro needs. A plan is prepared to guide the preparation, orientation, and training of all members of an identified group. All group members participate in the learning experiences identified as appropriate for them. In short, it is a one-size-fits-all approach. Critics of L & MD complain that this approach is used far too often and is usually ineffective.[9]

The *bottom-up approach* focuses on micro needs. Individual needs are assessed. That information is fed upward to higher-level management levels and/or to a centralized L & MD function. When aggregated, individual needs become the basis for a collective learning plan. It is a way of identifying common needs shared by individuals so that appropriate action can be taken to address them. Individual needs falling outside the envelope of common needs for the group can be met by sending individuals outside the organization to attend public seminars sponsored by local colleges, universities, or training vendors.

The *combination approach* strikes a balance between the top-down and bottom-up approaches. First a plan is prepared to guide the preparation and orientation of a group. Then individual needs are compared to group needs. Individuals participate only in learning experiences appropriately geared to *their* needs. Planned learning experiences are selected from a smorgasbord of available options.

CONDUCTING L & MDNA

L & MDNA is conducted by systematically collecting, analyzing, and using information about learning needs. Various techniques may be used to compare what workers already know or do and what they should know or do to perform efficiently and effectively. The most common approaches to collecting information about management learning needs are listed and summarized in Exhibit 3-2. Each has distinct advantages and disadvantages, as the exhibit shows. Some are used more often than others, as Rothwell's 1998 survey of ASTD members revealed, and some are perceived as more effective than others by the respondents to Rothwell's survey. (See the survey results summary appearing in Exhibits 3-3 and 3-4.)

HOW OFTEN SHOULD L & MDNA BE CONDUCTED?

Ideally, L & MDNA should be conducted at least annually. Both macro and micro needs should be examined at that time. It is also important to integrate the planned L & MD program with the organization's needs, as they are expressed in strategic plans and succession plans. Consequently, L & MDNA should be conducted on a schedule linked to those other organizational activities.

Individual (micro) needs should be assessed at least once each year, at the end of projects, or upon the discovery of individual deficiencies. Some organizations tie individual needs assessment to performance appraisals; others keep them separate, preferring instead to tie individual needs assessment to career planning or succession planning activities. Individual Development Plans (IDPs), prepared annually, are often a guiding force for L & MDNA.

WHO SHOULD PARTICIPATE IN L & MDNA?

Participants in L & MDNA, like those participating in assessing learning needs for other occupational groups in organizations,[10] may include

- Targeted participants
- Immediate organizational superiors of targeted participants
- Peers
- Organizational subordinates
- Professional or industry associates
- Customers, suppliers, or other stakeholders
- Spouses or family members of targeted participants
- Predecessors
- Mentors or sponsors of targeted participants

When all these groups participate in L & MDNA, it is called *full-circle multi-rater assessment* because the providers form a circle around the targeted learners.[11]

Targeted participants are an important source of information about their needs. Their perceptions should not be minimized, and their participation and involvement in L & MDNA can build their ownership and support. Immediate organ-

Exhibit 3-2
Techniques for Conducting L & MDNA

Assessment Center. A process rather than a place, an assessment center usually consists of a series of activities based on the requirements of a job in an organizational setting. Assessment centers are often associated with the process of selecting those deemed suitable for promotion into the management ranks, but they can also be used to identify individual learning needs.

Steps in Conducting L & MDNA Using the Technique	Advantages and Disadvantages
1 Conduct a detailed job analysis for the job category (such as supervisor, manager, or executive).	**Advantages:** • The results are usually easily accepted by management. • The approach is based on job requirements, and assessment centers can be more effective than selection interviews and other methods for selecting management employees and/or identifying their training needs.
2 Design management activities—such as in in-basket exercises, simulations, or role plays—to assess an individual's abilities to meet the requirements of each job.	**Disadvantages:** • Expensive to design and to set up. • Tend to perpetuate existing management methods and organizational culture.
3 Train assessors who are usually experienced job incumbents from the client organization.	
4 Test out the activities.	
5 Implement the assessment center	
6 Evaluate results of the assessment center over time.	
7 Use the assessment center to: • Select individuals for management positions. • Identify individual training needs.	

Competency Model. A description of desirable knowledge, skills, and abilities of job incumbents in an entire job category—such as supervisor, manager, or executive. A competency model, once agreed upon, can be immensely useful in selecting management employees, training them, and preparing them for advancement from one management level to another.

Steps in Conducting L & MDNA Using the Technique	Advantages and Disadvantages
1 Review literature on previous competency models of management.	**Advantages:** • Results have high face validity and are accepted by management easily. • The approach lends itself to future requirements (implied by strategic plans) as well as past requirements.
2 Identify exemplary performers in the organization to participate in the study.	**Disadvantages:** • A vendor or outside assistance may be required to establish a valid competency model. • The results of the competency model may be too general to be helpful.

Exhibit 3-2 (continued)

	Steps in Conducting L & MDNA Using the Technique	Advantages and Disadvantages
3	Draft a survey for use with exemplary performers to capture their views about essential roles, competencies, work outputs, and quality requirements for each management job category.	Disadvantages:
4	Test the survey for clarity.	
5	Conduct the survey.	
6	Compile the results.	
7	Compare individual profiles to the ideal profiles in the competency model.	
8	Use the competency model to: • Select individuals for management positions. • Identify individual training needs.	

DACUM method. An acronym formed from the first letters of the phrase Developing A CurriculUM. DACUM has been widely used in establishing vocational and paraprofessional curricula in community colleges. This approach can also be used to help a group of experienced job incumbents focus on changes they need to make in preparation for adopting a new role for management—such as the new role for management implicit in a "team" environment.

	Steps in Conducting L & MDNA Using the Technique	Advantages and Disadvantages
1	Assemble a panel of experienced job incumbents, preferably the best performers.	Advantages: • The results are usually easily accepted by management. • The approach is fast and relatively inexpensive. • A body of knowledge exists about using the approach.
2	Set up an agenda for a one- or two-day meeting for each job category to be analyzed.	Disadvantages: • The approach is limited to the experience and knowledge of the participants. • The approach tends to be based on present or past duties, rather than future ones (although DACUM can be modified to focus on future work requirements).
3	Begin the meeting by explaining that its purpose is to focus on what incumbents do on their jobs.	
4	Go around the panel of participants, and ask for activities or tasks performed (one from each participant initially).	
5	Record tasks on large index cards or sheets of paper, and affix them to the wall.	

Exhibit 3-2 (continued)

	Steps in Conducting L & MDNA Using the Technique	Advantages and Disadvantages
6	Adjourn the group briefly and establish several general descriptive categories in which to classify two or more activities/tasks each.	**Disadvantages:**
7	Change the wall chart to reflect the categories established.	
8	Convene the group and ask group members to verify that the descriptive categories are appropriate to use, making changes as needed.	
9	Go through each activity or task again, asking panel members to verify, revise, or delete them.	
10	Adjourn the meeting and reduce the wall chart to a one-page handout (called a DACUM chart).	
11	Create a written questionnaire based on the DACUM chart for use in assessing individual knowledge, skills and abilities.	
12	Ask each job incumbent and each organizational superior of a job incumbent to use the questionnaire for assessing skill levels.	
13	Use the survey results to: • Identify selection criteria. • Identify individual training needs. • Establish an internal group training curriculum.	

Focus Groups. A focus group is a small group formed to "focus" on an issue of concern to group members. This approach has proved its value in marketing research. A focus group typically consists of a randomly selected group of customers called together to assess reactions to a new product or service. A focus group may also be established to examine management learning needs. Such a group may consist of external stakeholders (customers, suppliers, or distributors) or internal stakeholders (exempt or nonexempt employees).

	Steps in Conducting L & MDNA Using the Technique	Advantages and Disadvantages
1	Select a small group of people at random from: • External stakeholders (customers, suppliers, distributors), and/or • Internal stakeholders (nonexempt or exempt employees).	**Advantages:** • Fast. • Relatively inexpensive. • Offers a unique perspective that is difficult to obtain from other methods.

Exhibit 3-2 (continued)

	Steps in Conducting L & MDNA Using the Technique	Advantages and Disadvantages
2	Call the group together in a central location.	**Disadvantages:** • It can be difficult for members of a focus group to separate management learning needs/performance from organizational needs/performance. • Employees in a focus group may not "open up" to identify problems/concerns.
3	Ask group members to list: • Problems they have encountered in doing business with the organization and/or in performing in the organization. • Management learning needs they can infer from those problems (this assumes management is responsible for all such problems).	
4	Compile results from the focus group, using them as a basis for: • Establishing learning plans for management. • Feeding back results to management employees as they plan their own learning activities.	

Individual Development Plans (IDPs). An IDP, synonymous with an individual learning plan, is designed to orient one person to a new job, upgrade skills in preparation for a new job, or rectify a deficiency of knowledge and skill for an experienced performer. Learning needs are individually assessed on some periodic basis, such as once a year.

	Steps in Conducting L & MDNA Using the Technique	Advantages and Disadvantages
1	Prepare a form and procedures to encourage periodic discussions between management employees and their immediate organizational superiors, focusing on: • Individual needs (stemming from job requirements, personal strengths and weaknesses, and organizational requirements/issues). • Learning objectives to meet the needs. • Learning methods (how to meet the needs). • Evaluation methods.	**Advantages:** • Highly individualized. • Easily administered. • Easily focused on needs stemming from the job, the individual, and/or the organization. • Capable of aggregation so that macro needs, shared by more than one person, can be identified and met.
2	Encourage management employees and their immediate organizational superiors to meet to discuss learning needs on some regular basis.	**Disadvantages:** • Requires time commitment by each management employee and his/her immediate organizational superior. • Depends heavily on the interaction of superior/subordinate and their ability to identify learning needs.

Exhibit 3-2 (continued)

	Steps in Conducting L & MDNA Using the Technique	Advantages and Disadvantages
3	Offer advice and support in meeting the learning needs, ensuring some kind of follow-up.	**Disadvantages:**

Interviews. An interview is a planned or unplanned conversation. When used in needs assessment, an interview may be conducted with randomly selected members of a targeted learner group—such as supervisors or managers—and/or with their immediate organizational superiors for the purpose of identifying the common learning needs of that group.

	Steps in Conducting L & MDNA Using the Technique	Advantages and Disadvantages
1	Randomly selected for interviews group members from any/all of these groups: • Targeted learners (such as supervisors, managers, or executives). • Immediate organizational superiors of the targeted learners. • Peers of the targeted learners. • Subordinates of the targeted learners.	**Advantages:** • Easy. • Simple. • Fast. • Dialogue with others serves to build interest and expectations for change.
2	Meet with them, asking what they perceive to be the greatest learning needs/performance deficiencies/improvement possibilities of the targeted learners.	**Disadvantages:** • Tends to be heavily influenced by past or present problems rather than future organizational requirements. • May build unrealistic expectations for improvement/change.
3	Identify common themes identified across interviews, considering them to be learning needs typical of the job category in the organization.	

Management Diagnostic Questionnaires. In recent years much interest has been expressed in numerous management diagnostic questionnaires that purport to identify individual styles of interacting with others. Perhaps the best known is the Myers-Briggs Type Indicator, though others are also frequently used.

	Steps in Conducting L & MDNA Using the Technique	Advantages and Disadvantages
1	Purchase questionnaires from an external vendor.	**Advantages:** • May increase individual motivation to learn. • May heighten individual appreciation of learning styles. • May lead to experimentation in interpersonal interaction.
2	Target individuals to take the questionnaires, explaining beforehand: • What the results do and do not mean. • How the results will be used—and by whom.	**Disadvantages:** • Unethical or unschooled users may misuse the results and/or breach pledges of confidentiality.

Exhibit 3-2 (continued)

	Steps in Conducting L & MDNA Using the Technique	Advantages and Disadvantages
3	Administer the questionnaires.	Disadvantages:
4	Score results and/or allow individuals to self-score.	
5	Facilitate discussion about: • What the results mean. • How the results may be used appropriately. • Issues of ethics and confidentiality.	
6	Plan learning activities, if learners desire, to meet identified group/individual learning needs.	

Management Tests. Written—or performance—tests of: (1) Management theories or (2) Individual approaches to common (or unusual) problems encountered in the practice of management. Individual learning needs are identified by comparing an individual's test score to some absolute score (such as a national or international benchmark), the average score of other management employees in the organization, or the score of the "best" management employees in the organization.

	Steps in Conducting L & MDNA Using the Technique	Advantages and Disadvantages
1	Purchase examinations from an external vendor or prepare examinations in-house.	Advantages: • May heighten individual motivation to learn. • Job-related testing is more "objective" than relying on the perceptions of others.
2	Target individuals to take the tests, explaining beforehand: • What the results do and do not mean. • How the results will be used, and by whom.	Disadvantages: • Test scores may be misused by unschooled or unethical people. • May create disparate impact (that is, produce discriminatory results).
3	Administer the test.	
4	Score results and/or allow individuals to self-score.	
5	Facilitate discussion about: • What the results mean. • How the results may be used appropriately. • Issues of ethics and confidentiality.	
6	Plan learning activities, if desired, to meet identified group/individual learning needs.	

Exhibit 3-2 (continued)

<table>
<tr><td colspan="2">

Written Needs Assessment Surveys. A very popular method of collecting information about learning needs for L & MD, as well as for employee training generally, a written needs assessment survey typically consists of a series of questions about the needs for different training courses (or other planned learning experiences). Such a survey is usually sent to targeted learners, their immediate superiors, and/or other stakeholders in L & MD. Written surveys may be regarded as "interviews reduced to written form."

</td></tr>
<tr><td colspan="2">**Steps in Conducting L & MDNA Using the Technique**</td><td>**Advantages and Disadvantages**</td></tr>
</table>

	Steps in Conducting L & MDNA Using the Technique	Advantages and Disadvantages
1	Draft a written survey to assess management learning needs in one or more management job categories in an organization by: • Purchasing (or locating) a survey questionnaire from a publisher or other source and modifying it in a way that is in compliance with copyright restrictions, or • Using results of interview questions to draft a tailor-made survey.	**Advantages:** • Allows much information to be collected and analyzed quickly. • Heightens expectations for change by involving many people in the needs assessment process. • Relatively inexpensive (compared to the cost of conducting on-site interviews or even focus groups).
2	Pretest the survey by calling together a group of stakeholders (prospective learners, their immediate organizational superiors, or their immediate subordinates) and, going through the survey item by item, working to improve the clarity of the questions posed before the survey is sent out.	**Disadvantages:** • May build unrealistic expectations for change. • Not everyone sends in a completed survey, leading to incomplete results.
3	Select a sample to receive the survey.	
4	Select analytical methods.	
5	Test the survey, if appropriate, by selecting a small group of stakeholders at random and sending the survey to them. Use the test results to assess response rates and to identify questions needing possible revision.	
6	Revise the survey, as appropriate.	
7	Administer the survey.	
8	Analyze the survey results.	
9	Feed back the survey results to stakeholders.	
10	Plan learning activities based on identified learning needs.	

Exhibit 3-2 (continued)

Critical Incident Technique. A very effective approach to collecting information about L & MD needs, the critical incident technique was first used to train military pilots and spies. The aim of this method is to collect information about needs that are of life-and-death importance (hence the use of the term *critical*) on the basis of specific and relatively common situations encountered in the past (hence the term *incident*). In its purest form the method is quite simple: Ask experienced management employees about the worst situations they have encountered in the past, and use their answers to ensure that the newly hired, newly promoted, or newly transferred are trained how to handle those situations.

	Steps in Conducting L & MDNA Using the Technique	Advantages and Disadvantages
1	Select a group or panel (6–15 people) of experienced job incumbents, such as supervisors, managers, or executives.	**Advantages:** • Fast. • Very appealing to no-nonsense/skeptical management employees. • Focused on the most difficult, hard-to-handle issues/situations.
2	Call a meeting of the panel.	**Disadvantages:** • Tends to be oriented to past or current problems rather than those that may arise in the uncertain future. • Lacks a logical flow from one incident to others (that flow must be imposed).
3	Answer these questions: • What is the critical incident technique? • How can the results be used? • What will be done in the meeting?	
4	Ask panel members to write down: • A description of the most difficult situations each of them has encountered in his or her career. • A description of how the situations were handled. • A description of how the situations should be handled if they should happen in the future.	
5	Share the situations with the group.	
6	Prioritize the training on the situations (on the basis of group members' input).	
7	Include coverage of critical incidents in: • Classroom training. • On-the-job training. • Other methods.	

Exhibit 3-2 (continued)

	Steps in Conducting L & MDNA Using the Technique	Advantages and Disadvantages
	The Delphi Procedure. This method of collecting information about learning needs takes its name from the ancient Greek oracle of Delphi. The method is not solely associated with L & MD; rather, it has been widely applied to futures research. When using the Delphi procedure, choose a panel of experts in the job category and conduct numerous rounds of surveys until results converge around common themes.	
1	Select a group or panel (6–15 people) of stakeholders in L & MD—such as experienced job incumbents, their immediate organizational superiors, their organizational subordinates, customers, and/or others.	**Advantages:** • Has a long and venerable history. • Lends itself to examinations of the future as well as of the past or present. • Requires minimal time commitment from busy management employees.
2	Ask the group members to participate in a Delphi study of management learning needs by job category—that is, for such groups as supervisors, managers, or executives.	**Disadvantages:** • Takes some time to reach a conclusion. • May require several rounds of surveys to obtain good results for all management job categories. • Results may become outdated quickly as new challenges face the organization.
3	Draft a written survey about issues of importance to the organization, individuals, and job categories and/or about perceived L & MD needs for each job category.	
4	Ask a small group (2–3 people) to review the survey's clarity and contents before it is shared with the Delphi panel.	
5	Revise the survey.	
6	Send out the survey to the Delphi panel.	
7	Compile results and develop a second survey based on key issues and/or needs identified in the first survey.	
8	Ask a small group (2–3 people) to review the clarity and contents of the second survey before it is shared with the full Delphi panel.	
9	Revise the second survey.	
10	Send out the results of the first survey and the second survey to the Delphi panel.	
11	Repeat steps 7 through 10 until the responses of the Delphi panel converge around common issues of importance and/or learning needs by job category.	
12	Use results of the Delphi panel to identify issues/needs affecting each job category and to assess individuals' learning needs against those results.	

Exhibit 3-2 (continued)

Nominal Group Technique (NGT). NGT, like the Delphi procedure, has been widely used in assessing the learning needs of employee groups other than management. The basic idea is to call together a group of experienced employees and/or their immediate organizational superiors and to give them a series of questions to which they respond in writing. Then the responses are shared.

	Steps in Conducting L & MDNA Using the Technique	Advantages and Disadvantages
1	Select a group or panel (6–15) of people who are knowledgeable about a management job category in the organization.	**Advantages:** • Same as for the Delphi procedure.
2	Ask the group members to participate in a Nominal Group to identify: • Key issues affecting management employees. • Learning needs for each job category of management employees in an organization.	**Disadvantages:** • Same as for the Delphi procedure.
3	Call a meeting of the group or panel.	
4	Hand each panel member a 3" x 5" index card and ask him or her to identify key issues affecting a management job category in the organization.	
5	Ask panel members to: • Place one issue on each card. • Work in silence. • Hand in their cards as they finish them.	
6	Place the ideas on a flipchart, blackboard, or overhead transparency.	
7	Ask group members to vote on the relative importance of each issue (the highest vote "wins" top priority).	
8	Ask group members to vote on issues they believe should be the focus of planned learning experiences (L & MD activities) for one job category—such as supervisor, manager, or executive (the highest vote "wins" top priority).	
9	Compile the results after the meeting, and distribute them to participants and other stakeholders.	
10	Use the results as a starting point for setting L & MD priorities and for assessing individual, group, and organizational learning needs by job category.	
11	Repeat the approach for other job categories.	

Exhibit 3-3
How Often Are Different Techniques of L & MDNA Used?

Question: There are various ways by which to assess training and development needs for management-level or for leaders of an organization. For each method listed in the left column below, circle an appropriate response in the right column below to indicate how often your organization makes use of the method. Use the following scale: **1 = Not at all; 2 = Seldom; 3 = Sometimes; 4 = Frequently; 5 = Always.** In the right column, circle an appropriate response to indicate how effective you perceive that method to be in identifying the development needs of management-level workers and/or for leaders. Use the following scale: **1 = Not at all effective; 2 = Seldom effective; 3 = Somewhat effective; 4 = Effective; 5 = Very effective.**

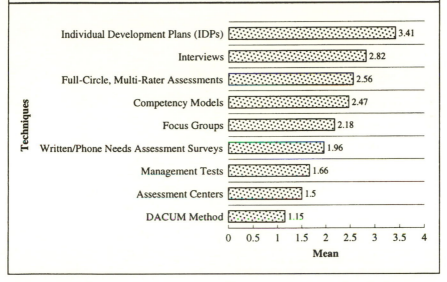

Source: W. Rothwell, *A Survey about Management and Leadership Development* (unpublished survey results) (University Park, PA: The Pennsylvania State University, 1998).

izational superiors are uniquely positioned to detect individual needs, provide coaching, and identify individual strengths and weaknesses. They can also assess the individual's potential for advancement. Peers, organizational subordinates, professional associates, industry associates, customers, spouses, family members, predecessors, and mentors or sponsors are uniquely positioned to observe management employees in other ways. Generally, the more opinions collected and the more perspectives taken into account, the more powerful and rounded will be the needs assessment of individuals—or groups.

SUMMARY

In this chapter we defined needs as performance gaps separating what management employees already know or do and what they should know or do. Needs

Exhibit 3-4
How Effective Are Different Techniques of L & MDNA?

Question: There are various ways by which to assess training and development needs for management-level or for leaders of an organization. For each method listed in the left column below, circle an appropriate response in the right column below to indicate how often your organization makes use of the method. Use the following scale: **1 = Not at all; 2 = Seldom; 3 = Sometimes; 4 = Frequently; 5 = Always.** In the right column, circle an appropriate response to indicate how effective you perceive that method to be in identifying the development needs of management-level workers and/or for leaders. Use the following scale: **1 = Not at all effective; 2 = Seldom effective; 3 = Somewhat effective; 4 = Effective; 5 = Very effective.**

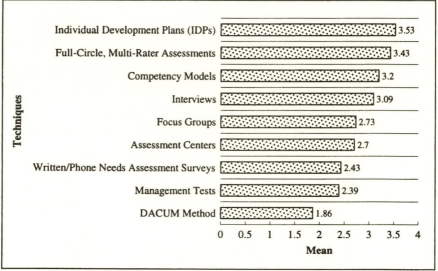

Source: W. Rothwell, *A Survey about Management and Leadership Development* (unpublished survey results) (University Park, PA: The Pennsylvania State University, 1998).

are identified through an assessment process designed to uncover and prioritize those performance gaps. Many different methods may be used to collect and analyze information about learning needs.

NOTES

1. W. Rothwell and H. Kazanas, *Mastering the Instructional Design Process: A Systematic Approach* (2nd ed.) (San Francisco: Jossey-Bass, 1998).

2. W. McGehee and P. Thayer, *Training in Business and Industry* (New York: John Wiley, 1961).

3. M. Kubr and J. Prokopenko, *Diagnosing Management Training and Development Needs: Concepts and Techniques* (Geneva: International Labour Office, 1989).

4. L. Saari, T. Johnson, S. McLaughlin, and D. Zimmerle, "A Survey of Manage-

ment Training and Education Practices in U.S. Companies," *Personnel Psychology*, Vol. 41, p. 734.

5. R. Camp, *Benchmarking: The Search for Industry Best Practices That Lead to Superior Performance* (Milwaukee, WI: Quality Press; White Plains, NY: Quality Resources, 1989).

6. D. Laird, *Approaches to Training and Development* (2nd ed.) (Reading, MA: Addison-Wesley, 1985), pp. 49–50.

7. Ibid.

8. W. Rothwell, "HRD and The Americans With Disabilities Act," in W. Rothwell, ed., *The Emerging Issues in HRD Sourcebook* (Amherst, MA: Human Resource Development Press, 1995).

9. T. Quick, *Training Managers So They Can Really Manage: Confessions of a Frustrated Trainer* (San Francisco: Jossey-Bass, 1991).

10. W. Rothwell and H. Sredl, *The ASTD Reference Guide to Professional HRD Roles and Competencies* (2nd ed.), 2 vols. (Amherst, MA: Human Resource Development Press, 1992).

11. T. Davis, "Whose Job Is Management Development? Comparing the Choices," *Journal of Management Development*, Vol. 9, No. 1, pp. 58–70.

Chapter 4

Establishing a Leadership and Management Development Curriculum

As we explained in Chapter 3, L & MD learning needs are performance gaps indicating differences between what employees with leadership potential already know or do and what they should know or do to perform competently. Non-learning needs should be met by removing obstacles to individual or group performance; learning needs should be met through planned learning experiences such as training, education, or development. This chapter focuses on establishing a long-term learning or instructional plan, otherwise known as a *curriculum*, to guide a planned L & MD program and meet predictable learning needs.

IDENTIFYING AND MEETING LEARNING NEEDS

When you set out to meet learning needs, you will soon discover that it makes sense to approach the task in an organized way. By structuring and planning what you do, you will make the process of meeting learning needs more efficient for you and more understandable to learners. In contrast, a disorganized approach leaves you unsure what needs to meet or when precisely you have met them. Worse, it subjects learners to anxiety about when they know enough to perform competently on their own.

Example

Perhaps a simple example will dramatize the importance of identifying and meeting learning needs in an organized way.

Suppose you are a manager setting out to train two recently promoted supervisors. One way you can approach their training is to cover problems as they come up. You simply tell them what to do and how to do it as need arises. If you use this approach, you do not have to invest any time planning their training. But you will have to keep your fingers crossed and hope that they eventually learn their jobs well enough to function on their own through gradual and unstructured exposure to everyday work experience. Only after an extended time will the learners develop to the point that you will trust them to handle typical daily problems on their own. In the meantime, they will be tortured by self-doubts and may grow dissatisfied. You may have trouble remembering what training they have received, and that will complicate your ability to hold them accountable for what they have learned. After all, you will be unsure just what problems they have experienced through exposure to daily crises. Too much—or too little—of your valuable time will be devoted to their individualized coaching. On occasion you might not be available when they need help, and they will be forced to muddle through emergencies they have not been trained to deal with or are not mentally prepared to handle.

Another way to approach their training is to cover work duties and responsibilities logically, scheduling activities so that individual progress will be clear. You begin by preparing a detailed job description and deciding how you will judge supervisory performance on each responsibility or desired result. In this process you clarify your own expectations. By examining the job description carefully, you see that some supervisory responsibilities are shared by all supervisors in the organization; some are shared only by supervisors in one division or department; and, some are unique to one work unit or function. You also see that it will be relatively easy to train newcomers on some issues but not so easy to train them on others. Some responsibilities listed on the job description are logically related and can be effectively treated at the same time. Others will not be logically related, and training will require special instructions and more time.

From this information you can begin to prepare an individualized training plan to guide the orientation of each new supervisor. That plan should sequence learning activities logically and should be based on a detailed job description, individual strengths and weaknesses, organizational needs or plans, and external environmental trends or demands. It should clearly establish a basis for accountability by listing what training your new supervisors will receive, when the training will be offered, how it will be handled, and how results will be evaluated. You should share the entire learning plan with each new supervisor at the outset of training, thereby reinforcing the plan's importance and establishing learner accountability. Armed with this plan, you should be able to proceed through new supervisory training in an organized fashion. Even better, you can sidestep the necessity of wasting time on spoon-feeding or hand-holding.

If you follow the approach just outlined, you will have taken the first steps toward devising a *management and/or leadership training curriculum*. The same approach can be usefully applied to the training of newly hired, newly transferred, or newly promoted managers and executives. Alternatively, it can be designed to meet the learning needs of a special group or contribute to the implementation of a special program. On a broad conceptual level, then, a *leadership and management development curriculum* goes beyond a training curriculum to integrate leadership and/or management training, education, and development.

The Role of a Centralized Leadership and Management Development Function in Meeting Learning Needs

Macro learning needs can be more economically, efficiently, and consistently met by a centralized L & MD function or department than by numerous managers who separately sponsor their own learning experiences for their employees. A centralized L & MD function usually focuses on meeting shared learning needs across a job category, special group, or special program. That frees individual managers so they can devote more attention to meeting learning needs unique to their work functions and individuals reporting to them.

DEFINING CURRICULUM

Curriculum is derived from the Latin word for *foot race*.[1] The term eventually became associated with a course of study rather than the course of a foot race. Today it is widely applied to educational course requirements that students must meet before they are eligible to graduate from an elementary school, a secondary school, a trade school, or a college. Taken more generally, a curriculum simply means *a learning plan or an instructional plan*. It need not refer solely to programs sponsored by degree-granting educational institutions. A curriculum may refer to *any* planned learning—whether delivered to learners on-the-job, off-the-job, or in some combination of on-the-job and off-the-job learning experiences. These learning experiences may range in length from one minute to many years.

Curriculum development implies an evolutionary process of discovering appropriate learning experiences; *curriculum design* implies a systematic approach to the planning of learning experiences.

Distinctions Between Training, Educational, and Developmental Curricula

Recall from Chapter 1 that training is job-oriented, education is individually oriented, and development is organizationally oriented. In practice, that means training focuses on helping people meet their job responsibilities; education focuses on preparing individuals for advancement; and development focuses on evoking new insights about the organization, industry, community, society, or culture of which the learners are members.

A curriculum can be designed to meet any or all these needs. It is thus a broad-scope plan for orienting people to new jobs, correcting problems with present performance, upgrading skills, preparing people for advancement, and evoking new ideas.

Reasons for Establishing an L & MD Curriculum

As individuals enter—or prepare to enter—new positions, they must change and adapt to meet new job and organizational requirements. Most people adapt to change best when they are gradually prepared to assume new responsibilities and challenges. Few are capable of making a quantum leap from performing one job to performing a very different job without any help.

The same principles apply to L & MD. By using an L & MD curriculum to prepare, orient, and upgrade the skills of workers, organizations ensure that high-potential people are properly equipped to meet new responsibilities. As Julia Galosy observed, "curriculum design requires that we view the whole fabric of management learning in its totality; learning experiences are created from this holistic perspective. The challenge of curriculum design is to build a coherent, sequential plan which will provide structure and unity to the full gamut of planned learning experiences."[2] The idea is thus to create a unified view of learning experiences that can help exempt employees meet their learning needs.

APPROACHES TO CURRICULUM DESIGN FOR L & MD

There is no "one best way" to design an L & MD curriculum. In fact, there are four basic approaches to developing a curriculum:[3] (1) The subject-centered approach, (2) the objectives-centered approach, (3) the experience-centered approach, and (4) the opportunity-centered approach. Their labels imply the chief distinctions between the approaches. A subject-centered approach bases learning plans on topics or subjects; an objectives-centered approach bases activities on the knowledge or skills the learners are expected to possess after participating in planned learning experiences; the experience-centered approach makes the planning of learning an experience of its own; and the opportunity-centered approach provides individuals with choices about what they learn, leaving it up to them and their immediate organizational superiors to discover opportunities.

The Subject-Centered Approach

The subject-centered approach to curriculum design is perhaps the best known—even among people who know little about how to plan learning experiences. It is widely used in American education. Consequently, most people have at least a rudimentary grasp of how it works.

Put simply, the subject-centered approach bases instruction on subjects or course titles. Students in educational institutions take courses geared to grade level. Needs assessment is carried out centrally, the province of state boards of education (at the elementary or secondary level) and accrediting bodies (at the college level). Planning course details within a curriculum is left to teachers, and instructional delivery methods rarely vary. Despite advancing technology, educators still rely heavily on classroom delivery rather than video-based, audio-based, or computer-based alternatives. Nor is hands-on field experience common. Instructional evaluation is often minimal and indirect: students take tests and receive individual grades. Little is done to evaluate the daily performance of individual students or teachers to provide prompt, specific feedback of use in improving their performance.

As a simple example of a subject-centered curriculum, consider the courses required to earn a Master's of Business Administration Degree (MBA). Many public and private schools allow entry into MBA programs through two routes: one route for those who completed an undergraduate major in Business Administration; another route for those who completed an undergraduate major in another discipline. The core subjects in a typical MBA curriculum include Production/Operations Management, Marketing, Finance, Organizational Behavior, and Business Policy/Strategic Planning. Students with undergraduate business majors take these courses and electives; students without undergraduate business majors also complete prerequisite courses in Economics, Statistics, Accounting, and other business-related subjects.

The subject-centered approach to curriculum design can also be applied to developing curricula for job categories, special groups, or special programs in a planned L & MD program. Needs assessment is carried out centrally—and sometimes informally—by an L & MD director, an L & MD coordinator, a steering committee, a coordinating committee, or a project team. Planned learning experiences are identified to correspond to the major job responsibilities of the targeted learners. Methods of planning each learning experience are left up to trainers or vendors. Instructional delivery methods may vary. Evaluation is carried out chiefly by participants.

To design a subject-centered L & MD curriculum, take the following steps:[4]

1. Update job descriptions for the targeted job category, making sure to obtain a list of key responsibilities

2. Formulate a course title to correspond to the knowledge or skills needed to meet each key responsibility identified on the job description

3. Group together, as appropriate, related knowledge or skills based on job responsibilities to reduce the course titles to a manageable number

4. Sequence the course titles in the order of their importance—based on the needs of individuals who are

   A. Preparing to enter the job category (what "subjects" should the participants learn about first, second, and so on?)

   B. Orienting themselves to the job category

   C. Upgrading their skills, having already gained experience

   D. Preparing for movement to other job categories or other life changes

5. Design each planned learning experience in the subject-centered curriculum in greater detail, focusing on the individual or collective group needs of the participants

See Exhibit 4-1 for a Worksheet to use in devising a subject-centered leadership and management curriculum for supervisors. (The same approach would be used to design a leadership curriculum for other workers at the exempt or nonexempt levels.)

The subject-centered approach has unique advantages and disadvantages. The chief advantages: it is quick, dirty, and cheap. You can prepare a curriculum in short order for aspiring supervisors, experienced supervisors, aspiring managers, experienced managers, aspiring executives, and experienced executives. People who want to see quick results are generally happy with how quickly a subject-centered approach can produce a unified L & MD curriculum.

There are disadvantages, however. Because the curriculum design process is handled quickly and rarely permits much participation, only a few people feel any ownership in the results. Others may complain that the subjects have little or nothing to do with daily work activities—and that is a significant problem. The subjects identified may not be treated consistently, varying across instructors or vendors, and that will lead to inconsistencies in preparation and subsequent work performance across program participants. If internal group training is the primary vehicle for delivering the instruction, then scheduling can become problematic in today's lean organizations in which the workers' ranks have been cut so dramatically that it becomes difficult for people to steal time away from daily work pressures to attend planned learning experiences away from their work sites. Every hour spent in the classroom is an hour away from the job. If training is offered on nonworking time, some people will not show up—and it will be difficult to force them to do so. Course evaluations based on participant reactions will carry little weight with results-oriented managers who want to know how much money was saved or what performance problems were solved as a result of investments in planned learning experiences.

The Objectives-Centered Approach

The objectives-centered approach to curriculum design is widely associated with technical training. However, it can also be applied to planned L & MD. It takes its name from its emphasis on *performance objectives*. Objectives are the explicit results to be achieved from planned learning activities. They are articulated in writing. Performance objectives are matched directly to meeting learning needs: each objective represents a desired *solution* to an identified need, problem, or deficiency of individual knowledge, skill, or attitude. The objectives-centered approach is usually based on existing work requirements, though it is possible to identify possible *future* work requirements and base the curriculum on those. Needs assessment focuses on identifying performance gaps between actual and desired work performance and organizational requirements.

Exhibit 4-1
Creating a Subject-Centered L & MD Curriculum

Directions: Use this Worksheet to practice creating a subject-centered L & MD curriculum based on a supervisory job description. For each responsibility listed in the left column of Part I below, write a course title in the right column. Then, in Part II, group together all related or similar responsibilities under a reduced number of course titles. Finally, in Part III, establish a tentative supervisory training curriculum by sequencing the course titles as you feel they should be delivered to aspiring, newly-promoted and experienced supervisors.

Part I	
Supervisory Responsibilities Listed on a Job Description (Supervisors will . . .)	**Course Titles**
Take daily attendance of employees	
Schedule workflow, exceptions to normal workflow, and work on backlogs	
Manage time of self and workers	
Monitor productivity of workers assigned	
Train employees on procedures and products	
Coordinate unit activities with other units and departments	
Document changes in work procedures	
Performs cost/benefit analysis of projects	
Conduct employee performance appraisals	
Coach and positively reinforce employees	
Correspond with suppliers, wholesalers, retailers, and customers	
Set goals and objectives with employees	
Interview prospective employees	
Discipline and, on occasion, terminate employees in compliance with organizational policy and applicable laws, rules, and regulations	
Prepare budget for the work unit in consultation with manager	
Identify need for backup workers and oversee worker cross-training	
Order supplies and raw materials	
Conduct staff meetings with employees	
Prepare payroll for the work unit	

Exhibit 4-1 (continued)

Supervisory Responsibilities Listed on a Job Description (Supervisors will . . .)	Course Titles
Schedule vacations	
Authorize overtime	
Perform overtime calculations for employees	
Ensure employee compliance with general safety and accident procedures for assigned employees	

Part II	
Group together all related or similar responsibilities under a reduced number of course titles, based on your response to Part I.	

Related Responsibilities	Course Titles

Part III	
Basing your work on the results of Part II, sequence the course titles as you feel they should be delivered.	

Job Categories/Targeted Groups	List Course Titles in the Sequence You Feel They Should Be taken by Members of the Targeted Group
Aspiring Supervisors Preparing for Promotion	
Newly Hired, Promoted, or Transferred Supervisors	
Experienced Supervisors who require updating, retraining, or preparation for advancement	

As needs are identified, they become the basis for performance objectives, and objectives are grouped together and logically sequenced to form courses and other planned learning experiences. Learning experiences are based on the objectives and leave little room for the subjective opinions of L & MD specialists, participants, top managers, or others.

To design an objectives-centered L & MD curriculum, take the following steps:[5]

1. Assess

    A. Management or leadership work requirements

    B. Organizational requirements

    C. Individual strengths and weaknesses

2. Analyze

    A. The group targeted for participation

    B. The work environment

3. Conduct L & MD needs assessment

4. Develop performance objectives based on needs

5. Prepare written or performance-based tests to assess learner achievement based on performance objectives

6. Identify strategies to meet the performance objectives

7. Prepare, locate, or locate and modify materials to meet the objectives and thereby meet the learning needs

8. Deliver or facilitate planned learning experiences

9. Evaluate L & MD methods and/or the L & MD program

These steps are systematic because the results (*outputs*) of each step become the starting point (*inputs*) for subsequent steps.

The objectives-centered approach has its own advantages and disadvantages. A chief advantage is its focus on job-related performance and learner accountability. After all, performance objectives signify the results to be achieved from planned learning, and they are directly linked to needs, instructional content, and tests. This approach is very detailed, and skeptical managers who want to see effective results are generally pleased with this approach. That is a major selling point for it.

However, there is one big disadvantage to the objectives-centered approach: The process of designing planned learning experiences can be very time-consuming and costly. Effectiveness is achieved at the cost of speed. Targeted participants and their immediate organizational superiors may complain that it takes too long to prepare and deliver planned learning experiences designed in this way, though few will question their value once they have been designed.

The Experience-Centered Approach

The experience-centered approach is often linked to Organization Development (OD), a long-term approach to planned organizational change relying heavily on behavioral science techniques. Like OD, the experience-centered approach

• Bases planned L & MD experiences on the highly participative *action research model* that consists of such phases as data collection, feedback, problem solving, implementation, and evaluation. Needs are identified by learners and other stakeholders; strategies for meeting needs are identified by the same group. The steps of this process are continuous, making them ideal to integrate with increasingly popular Total Quality Management (TQM) efforts, employee involvement (EI) programs, and work-team-directed efforts.

• Is geared to achieving long-term cultural and organizational change. L & MD becomes a tool for changing organizations by involving the leadership in a highly participative and long-term planned learning experience.

To design an experience-centered L & MD curriculum, take the following steps:[6]

1. Identify performance problems separating

   A. What employees with leadership potential or responsibilities should know and do from

   B. What they already know or can do

2. Feed the results of step 1 back to each level of management and/or the organization

3. Facilitate efforts by each level of worker to

   A. Diagnose the cause(s) of these gaps

   B. Plan L & MD experiences designed to solve the problems and thereby meet needs

4. Involve members of management in each step of implementing planned L & MD experiences. These steps include:

   A. Assessing learning needs

   B. Selecting methods to meet the needs

   C. Delivering planned learning experiences

   D. Evaluating results

5. Feed the results of steps 1–4 back to all members of management to ensure that the process is highly participative and oriented toward continuous improvement

The experience-centered approach is advantageous for one major reason. Since developing an experience-centered curriculum is highly participative, the process builds strong ownership among those it serves. In time, aspiring and experienced leaders at all levels will come to accept an L & MD curriculum that they and their predecessors have established and have continued to refine.

But there are two major disadvantages to using this approach: it tends to be very time-consuming and focuses on solving past performance problems. A participative approach simply takes more time than other approaches to design and deliver. And, because a participative approach involves workers with leadership potential in identifying needs, there is a tendency to base learning experiences on performance problems experienced in the past—particularly worst-case situations that are more easily remembered than routine ones.

The Opportunity-Centered Approach

Identifying and meeting *individual* L & MD needs is the chief focus of the opportunity-centered approach, which is customarily designed from the bottom up. The curriculum is thus planned to meet individual, rather than group, needs.

The centerpiece of the opportunity-centered approach is an *individualized learning plan* (IDP) or *learning contract* prepared for each employee with leadership potential each year. (The terms *individualized learning plan* and *learning contract* are synonymous.)

To design an opportunity-centered L & MD curriculum, take the following steps:[7]

1. Establish a program in which workers with management and/or leadership potential meet with their immediate organizational superiors at some regular interval, usually once each year, in order to discuss

   A. Individual performance gaps (needs stemming from past and present performance)

   B. Individual career goals (needs stemming from future aspirations)

   C. The organization's future goals (needs stemming from plans)

2. Establish an individualized plan to meet the needs through planned L & MD experiences. This plan should be reached by mutual agreement between individuals and their immediate organizational superiors.

3. Establish a means by which to hold both individuals and their immediate organizational superiors accountable for achieving results

4. Feed the results of IDPs at all levels to

   A. Top managers

   B. The L & MD director, L & MD coordinator, or an L & MD committee

5. Aggregate the IDPs to identify common needs shared by many people

6. Prepare an instructional plan to meet common needs through internal group training, external group training, or other L & MD methods

7. Establish a means by which to offer consulting advice to meet uniquely individual needs, as needed

8. Track and monitor activities and results against IDPs so as to provide information for future planning

One big advantage of the opportunity-centered approach is that it is directed toward *individualizing* learning plans. Supervisors, managers, and executives—as leaders in each of their functions—often face unique challenges. As leaders, their influence over others makes their individual strengths and weaknesses critical to organizational success. Indeed, as people advance to higher-level responsibilities, how they *personalize* their jobs becomes more important. One value of the opportunity-centered approach is that it is tailor-made to deal with uniquely individual needs, dovetailing nicely with strategic and succession plans.

Another big advantage of the opportunity-centered approach is that it is highly participative, giving management employees a chance to meet with their immediate organizational superiors to identify needs and plan for the short-term and long-term training, education, and development to meet those needs. The results of IDPs are, in turn, fed back to (1) Higher-level managers so they are familiar with individual and group L & MD needs and issues, and (2) A centralized L & MD function that can track individual and group needs, monitor achievement, and provide support and technical assistance to meet the needs.

Finally, an opportunity-centered approach does not preclude the use of other approaches. For instance, the organization can establish a subject-centered L & MD curriculum for training courses. When an IDP indicates that an individual experiences a learning need that can be met by a regularly scheduled internal group training session, the individual merely signs up to participate. There is one major disadvantage of the opportunity-centered approach: it places heavy emphasis on the relationship between individuals and their immediate organizational superiors. While few can dispute that the employee–boss relationship exerts profound influence over individual development, not all organizational superiors are equally adept at or motivated to develop those reporting to them. In addition, management employees—like all employees—are subject to a pigeonholing or stereotyping effect in which their immediate organizational superiors' impressions of their present performance and future potential can be difficult to change. If those impressions are unfair or inaccurate, they pose a very real stumbling block to individual development.

The Leadership and Management Development Curriculum: What Are Other Organizations Doing?

Research reveals that organizations are not adequately planning their L & MD efforts,[8] even though more money per employee is spent on developing supervisors, managers, and executives than is spent on developing individuals in other occupational groups.

Rothwell's 1998 survey revealed that recently promoted and experienced supervisors are the two groups for which most organizations have established curricula (see Exhibit 4-2). That indicates an L & MD curriculum exists more often at lower rather than higher management levels.

SUMMARY

In this chapter we explained that curriculum design means planning learning experiences, a process intended to satisfy needs. There are four basic approaches to curriculum design for L & MD. Each approach implies different steps. They are not mutually exclusive; rather, they may be used in combination. A curriculum is implemented through specific L & MD activities, including on-the-job or off-the-job training, education, and developmental experiences.

NOTES

1. K. Egan, "What Is Curriculum?" *Curriculum Inquiry*, Vol. 8, No. 1, pp. 65–72.

2. J. Galosy, "Curriculum Design for Management Training," *Training and Development Journal*, Vol. 37, No. 1, p. 48.

Exhibit 4-2
What Management Groups Tend to Be the Focus of a Planned Curriculum?

A *curriculum* is a long-term, standing series of planned learning experiences—such as training courses—for individuals, work units or job categories. Indicate below for which groups your organization has a curriculum.

Does your organization have a Leadership/Management Development curriculum for ...

Job Category	Yes		No	
	Frequency	Percentages	Frequency	Percentages
People who aspire to become supervisors (where *supervisor* is defined as "one who oversees the work of hourly workers")	17	33%	34	67%
Recently promoted supervisors	29	57%	22	43%
Experienced supervisors	26	51%	25	49%
People who aspire to become middle managers (where *middle manager* is defined as "one who oversees the work of supervisors")	15	29%	36	71%
Recently promoted middle managers	19	38%	31	62%
People who aspire to top management/executive positions (where *top manager/executive* is defined as "one who oversees middle managers")	10	20%	41	80%
Recently promoted top managers/executives	16	31%	35	69%
Experienced top managers/executives	15	29%	36	71%
Nonmanagement employees who show leadership potential	12	24%	39	76%

Source: W. Rothwell, *A Survey about Management and Leadership Development* (unpublished survey results) (University Park, PA: The Pennsylvania State University, 1998).

3. W. Rothwell, "Strategic Curriculum Design for Management Training," *Journal of Management Development*, Vol. 3. No. 3, pp. 39–52.

4. Ibid.

5. Ibid.

6. Ibid.

7. Ibid.

8. W. Rothwell and H. Kazanas, "Curriculum Planning for Training: The State of the Art," *Performance Improvement Quarterly*, Vol. 1, No. 3, pp. 2–16.

Chapter 5

Administering a Leadership and Management Development Program

This chapter describes how to set up an *administrative support system* consisting of the policies, procedures, and activities necessary to ensure that a planned L & MD program is carried out. With an administrative support system, an organization's action on L & MD will be an outgrowth of coordinated, consistent, and effective action.

WHAT TO CONSIDER

As you establish a planned L & MD program, consider the following questions:

1. Where should the L & MD function be positioned in the organization's reporting structure?

2. What rewards or incentives should be offered to encourage people to accept responsibility for developing themselves and others?

3. What kind of leader should direct the planned L & MD program?

4. How should the program leader be recruited, selected, and oriented?

5. How should internal staff members and external vendors be selected, oriented, and trained?

6. How should planned L & MD activities be scheduled?

7. How should budgeting be handled?

8. What records of L & MD activities should be kept?

9. How should L & MD program activities be publicized?

Exhibit 5-1
A Worksheet on Administrative Issues Regarding a Planned L & MD Program

Directions: Use this Worksheet to structure your thinking about important administrative issues to consider when establishing and operating a planned L & MD program. For each question appearing in the left column below, jot down your answer(s) in the right column. Add paper as necessary. There are no "right" or "wrong" answers in any absolute sense, though some questions may be more or less appropriate—depending on the organization's culture, top managers' attitudes about L & MD, and the organization's expressed policy and philosophy for L & MD.

Questions		Your Answers
1	Where should the L & MD function be positioned in the organization's reporting structure?	
2	What rewards or incentives should be offered to members of management so they are encouraged to accept responsibility for developing themselves and their management subordinates?	
3	What kind of leader should direct the planned L & MD program?	
4	How should the program leader be recruited, selected, and oriented?	
5	How should internal staff members and external vendors be selected, oriented and trained?	
6	How should planned L & MD activities be scheduled?	
7	How should budgeting be handled?	
8	What records of L & MD activities should be kept?	
9	How should L & MD program activities be publicized?	

In this chapter we shall address these questions. Before reading the chapter, however, pause a moment to formulate your own answers to these questions by completing the Worksheet appearing in Exhibit 5-1. As you complete the Worksheet, think about the written program policy and philosophy governing the planned L & MD program. Does it provide clues to answer the questions? If not, you may wish to modify it so that it does. Pose the questions on the Worksheet to members of a committee, task force, or project group involved in the L & MD program.

POSITIONING LEADERSHIP AND MANAGEMENT DEVELOPMENT

Where should the L & MD function be positioned in the organization's reporting structure? That is an important first question to answer about the administrative support structure. The best answer may depend on the size of the organization, the issue of responsibility, and the options available.

Differences by Organizational Size

Large organizations of 1,000 or more employees will often have a unit or department charged with responsibility for coordinating L & MD; smaller organizations, rarely having an L & MD unit or department, are more likely to make its operations a committee or task force responsibility. In both cases, however, somebody *must* be charged with program responsibility. Otherwise, grand ideas will founder on crude procedures. Indeed, L & MD will soon be forgotten amid the daily pressures to get the work out.

One result of such neglect is that, in smaller organizations, no successors will be prepared to carry on after the founder's death, retirement, or disability. In larger organizations, the inability to place the right leaders in the right places at the right times will sound the death knell for strategic plans. In addition, because managers tend to hire and promote individuals like themselves, and most organizations are dominated by white males, the lack of planned L & MD may limit the advancement opportunities available to women, minorities, the disabled, and people over age 40.

Who Bears Responsibility?

It only seems logical to position L & MD where greatest responsibility for it rests. However, in an important sense worth emphasizing, L & MD is pervasive: all supervisors, managers, and executives bear an important responsibility to develop themselves and the people reporting to them. Like strategic planning, an organization's responsibility for L & MD rests with the highest official: in large organizations that is usually the CEO; in small organizations it is the owner, founder, or proprietor.

Options for Positioning

Even though L & MD is a pervasive responsibility, someone must be charged with the responsibility for coordinating and carrying out L & MD activities, ensuring they are scheduled and managed. Most often, L & MD can be positioned within the following departments or units:

1. Training and development

2. Human resource management

3. Planning or development

4. The office of the chief executive

5. A line department

6. A department reporting to the CEO

7. The corporate board of directors

Each placement has advantages and disadvantages.

When placed in the Training and Development (T & D) or Human Resource Development (HRD) Department, L & MD is linked to the key function to which it is commonly associated—planned learning activities carried out for performance improvement. That is a major advantage. It can lead to a desirable cross-fertilization of ideas about an organization's employee training, education, and development activities. Moreover, it can produce a powerful integration of all HRD efforts—including technical development, sales development, leadership and management development, and professional development. But this placement can be disadvantageous in the diminishing number of organizations in which T & D or HRD is placed two or more levels below the CEO on the organization's chain of command. That placement complicates access to top managers. One result: a predictable focus on the needs of target groups at or below the placement of the person carrying out L & MD–related activities.

Another disadvantage can stem from placing L & MD with T & D or HRD. Some T & D or HRD specialists view their function as *solely* a "corporate schoolhouse" intended to offer classroom courses.[1] Off-the-job, rather than on-the-job, learning experiences are emphasized. When linked to that philosophy, the L & MD function may emphasize management *training* at the expense of *management education, management development, leadership training, leadership education*, or *leadership development*. Yet most L & MD, like most employee learning generally, occurs outside classrooms and on the job.

When placed in the Human Resource Management (HRM) or Personnel Department, L & MD is linked to an important function that contributes to planning and meeting the organization's leadership needs. That placement can produce a results-focused orientation in which the planned L & MD program is linked directly to Human Resource (HR) plans. Moreover, placement in HRM connects L & MD with other important activities that influence it. Among them: job/work analysis, performance appraisal, compensation, benefits, recruitment, selection, and OD.

There are two primary disadvantages to this placement. First, L & MD is removed from the CEO by at least one level, as is also true when L & MD is placed with T & D. Making matters worse, some HR managers are hesitant to allow the director of L & MD to work directly with other managers in the organization, serving as a resource person and internal consultant. They prefer communication be handled formally through the chain of command so that all messages from higher-level managers pass through the HR manager first. That practice can compromise the value of L & MD as a means by which to offer consulting services and advice to others. Second, placing L & MD with HRM encourages managers to view L & MD as a staff or advisory function. That turns out to be a spot with low credibility in many organizations. Conflict between "line" and "staff" managerial officers has been the subject of problems—and discussion[2]—for many years.

At first glance it would seem natural to place L & MD with an organization's planning or development function. L & MD should be viewed from a long-term perspective, a view that should be common among planners and developers. When the organization's planning or development function coordinates strategic planning and L & MD efforts are linked to it, important long-term benefits can be realized.

Unfortunately, planners and developers often focus their attention on financial forecasting or budgeting issues and exclude or downplay HR issues. Some do not know *how* to plan for HR. (Indeed, one chief of planning in a very large corporation once told the authors that "we tried HR planning and systematic L & MD activities, and we couldn't make them work.") If there is no willingness to attempt L & MD in a systematic way that is tied to the organization's needs and strategies, then placing L & MD with corporate planning or development will not usually work out.

Placing L & MD in the office of the CEO can achieve goodness of fit only when the CEO is a champion and supporter of planned L & MD. This placement gives the director of L & MD access to the individual who, by virtue of position, should be most interested in L & MD. It also provides a platform for the director of L & MD to work comfortably with top-level and middle-level managers.

But this placement also has its drawbacks. Chief among them is that, when the CEO is not a supporter of L & MD, the director of L & MD will not feel secure in the position—and probably will not last there for long. Another drawback is that placement with the CEO may create reluctance among managers to discuss their subordinates and themselves realistically. They will be hesitant to be frank. Some will be tempted to paint an overly optimistic picture for the CEO's benefit, thereby creating a positive impression about L & MD in various divisions in which conditions are not positive.

L & MD can be placed directly in a line management department—such as Marketing, Finance, Operations, or Production. That places it near to the largest group of potential customers. After all, line management departments traditionally have more employees at all levels than staff departments do.

But this placement is not ideal. Whatever line department L & MD is placed in will tend to become the prime—and sometimes the only—"customer." Managers in other departments will be reluctant to ask for help from an L & MD director whom they may view as tied to one organizational function, since they may reason that he or she devotes efforts to that function exclusively. Even when that is not true, it can lead to an unfortunate reticence among others to ask for support.

L & MD can be a department in its own right but yet not be part of the CEO's office. In that case, the director of L & MD reports directly to the CEO and appears on the organization chart as a peer of other first-tier managers.

There can be real benefits to this placement. The director of L & MD has access to the CEO and to other first-tier managers but is not viewed as a member of the CEO's staff. Managers in other parts of the organization are likely to view L & MD as a source of help, and assurances of confidentiality will be easier for them to believe.

Finally, the L & MD function can be placed directly under the board of directors—perhaps as a board-authorized committee. This placement enshrouds the function with the aura of the board's power and gives L & MD an independence from other activities that is hard to find anywhere else. Unfortunately, too few boards of directors take a firsthand interest in L & MD as they do in financial matters. That makes this placement most unusual. Nevertheless, it is worthy of exploration.

ENCOURAGING L & MD THROUGH REWARDS AND INCENTIVES

While theories of motivation differ dramatically, two conclusions about motivation seem inescapable: people will do what they are rewarded for doing and will not do what they are punished for doing. The same principle applies to L & MD: executives, managers, and supervisors will take a dedicated interest in the training, education, and development of themselves and employees reporting to them only when they rewarded for doing so. If they are overtly or inadvertently punished for it, they will avoid action. It is important to understand that the success or failure of any planned L & MD program rests heavily in the hands of the participants and their immediate organizational superiors. Moreover, it should *not* be viewed as the sole responsibility of a L & MD director or L & MD coordinator. The responsibility for L & MD cannot—and should not—be delegated down an organization's chain of command or shoved onto a staff administrator; rather, that responsibility must be shouldered by *every* executive, manager, and supervisor.

But how does an organization encourage employees to take an interest in self-development and the development of those reporting to them? There are at least four basic approaches: (1) Responsibility for L & MD can be made explicit, and employees at all levels can be routinely held accountable for it; (2) The organization can offer incentive bonuses for L & MD; (3) The organization can offer nonpecuniary rewards for L & MD results; (4) The three approaches can be combined.

One way to encourage employees to take a personal interest in self-development and the development of co-workers or management employees reporting to them is to make that responsibility explicit and subject to periodic review. For instance, the responsibility for L & MD can be listed on job descriptions. That makes it clear that the responsibility is an important one. If this approach is chosen, it is important to make clear that workers are responsible for their own development as well as for those reporting to them.

You can also determine how well the responsibility is being carried out by making L & MD an item for discussion during performance appraisals, salary reviews, and career counseling sessions. Employees will be influenced by whatever they believe affects their salary raises and their chances for advancement. By listing L & MD as an issue for consideration in employment decisions, the organization demonstrates powerful support for it.

Another approach: put in place an organizational policy that management employees can only be promoted or transferred when they have groomed their own replacements. While extremely powerful, this policy must be monitored carefully. It may not produce dependable or consistently reliable results because some management employees will not be sure how to interpret this vague policy. Specific directions must be given about how to groom a replacement and how satisfactory results will be measured.

One alternative to imposing explicit requirements for L & MD is to create incentives for it. An incentive is perhaps best understood as an inducement or a means of encouragement. An incentive system, as the term is commonly used in compensation practice, is based on the assumptions that people (1) Are able to perform what is desired, (2) Believe they can perform what is desired, (3) Believe that what they do will result in more money—or other rewards—for them, (4) Value the rewards they will receive, and (5) Will not be forced into pursuing conflicting priorities by the incentives. Finally, incentives must be based on measurable results that vary across people.

At least two kinds of incentive programs, both using managerial bonuses, can be established to encourage L & MD: (1) A program geared to the immediate organizational superiors of one or more targeted individuals, groups or job categories; and (2) A program geared to the targeted individuals, groups, or job categories directly. In both cases, bonus funds are established from the organization's profits—or, in the case of government agencies or not-for-profit enterprises, from appropriations or revenues—to pay for the bonuses. They usually range from 20 percent to 80 percent of base pay, depending on the job category receiving them.[3]

In both cases, measurable objectives for L & MD are established at the beginning of a year. They should be based on measurable criteria. Among them:

• *Number of hours*. How much time is spent by each employee each year participating in internal group training, external group training, external education, or other learning experiences?

- *Planned objectives versus achieved results.* What planned learning objectives were negotiated between employees and their immediate organizational superiors? What results were achieved? How well do results match objectives?

- *Fulfillment of certification requirements.* A certification program is a curriculum of planned learning experiences. Completion should indicate (certify) that the individual has completed a program that relates to individual, job, or organizational requirements or plans. Employees should progress at their own speeds but must make minimal progress to be eligible for a pay raise. If they progress faster than expected and their job performance is at least satisfactory, then they are eligible for a higher-than-average pay raise. This approach is comparable to a pay-for-knowledge program.[4]

- *Number of people promoted to other responsible positions in the organization.* Some organizations recognize, and encourage, employees who prepare their people for advancement to other positions in the organization or who coach and mentor others. Such people acquire a reputation as "people developers," and those who work for them are sometimes sought out by others in the organization.

There are good reasons to establish incentive programs for both employees and their immediate organizational superiors. In this way, employees are encouraged to develop themselves, and their immediate organizational superiors are also induced to encourage that development.

When most people think of rewards, money is usually the first thought that crosses their minds. But money has long been viewed as a questionable motivator. Its effects are short-lived. Once people receive raises they want others almost immediately. Using money as a reward is also difficult in today's cost-conscious organizational environments, where it is becoming increasingly difficult to fund the swelling expenses of employee health care benefits *and* salary increases sufficiently exceeding annual inflation rates to be viewed by employees as real rewards for exemplary performance. In many organizations, pay raises for exemplary performers seldom exceed 5 percent at a time when annual inflation averages between 3 and 5 percent in the United States. It is small wonder that many employees confuse merit raises with cost-of-living adjustments. For this reason and others, some organizations adopt *nonpecuniary rewards* as a means of recognizing and encouraging those who develop themselves or their employees. There are two types:[5] *intrinsic* (stemming from the work itself) and *extrinsic* (stemming from the job environment). Intrinsic rewards include increased job autonomy, task control, power, influence, visibility, or achievement. Extrinsic rewards include organizational or supervisory recognition and social interaction.

Various intrinsic and extrinsic rewards may be offered to employees who develop themselves or encourage the development of those reporting to them. Note that some rewards are inexpensive, but they do acknowledge that participation in L & MD is important and worthwhile.

These include:

Examples of Activities That May Be Rewarded

- Encouraging employees to plan their careers
- Providing management employees with job-related and career-related coaching
- Serving as mentor or sponsor for management employees who are or are not reporting directly to a supervisor, manager, or officer
- Attending or delivering training in organizationally sponsored training courses
- Serving on steering committees, advisory committees, project teams, or other L & MD groups in
  - Organizational settings
  - Community college or university settings
- Participating in, or providing support for, planned job rotation programs
- Participating in, or delivering presentations at, management conferences
- Serving on industry-related educational committees
- Publishing books or articles

Examples of Nonpecuniary Rewards

- Seeing that memos/letters are sent from the CEO or others
- Awarding desired job assignments
- Awarding high-visibility assignments
- Allowing desired geographical transfers
- Setting up executive mentoring for the employee
- Providing the opportunity to serve in loaned executive programs
- Awarding certificates
- Reporting about the person in the organization's in-house publications
- Honoring people at banquets or giving other special recognition

Finally, if sufficient support exists to offer encouragement for L & MD, the approaches may be combined. While that can be an expensive strategy, it can pay off by creating conditions in which people really *want* to develop themselves and help others develop.

IDENTIFYING THE RIGHT KIND OF LEADER FOR THE L & MD PROGRAM

Finding the right leader at the right time is often cited by CEOs as crucially important for the strategic success of new ventures, startups, or turnarounds. This principle applies as much to the leadership of a planned L & MD program as for other ventures. If a program lacks the right leader—someone possessing the right mix of skills and positive attitudes—then it is doomed to failure from the outset. In fact, if you wish to destroy a program, a fast way to do that is to place someone in charge of it who lacks the right skills, lacks a positive attitude, or lacks credibility.

L & MD Director or Coordinator?

Many large organizations employ at least one person to oversee and coordinate L & MD efforts. In the largest corporations, there may even be separate full-time positions devoted to supervisory development, manager development, and executive development. However, for the sake of simplicity, we shall use the term *L & MD director* to refer to a full-time professional assigned to L & MD. Of course, other job titles are also possible: Leadership Development Director, Director of Executive Education and Development, Assistant Vice President of Leadership and Management Development, Vice President of Executive Development, or Senior Vice President of Corporate Executive Development.

L & MD directors are full-time professionals assigned to spearhead planned L & MD programs. They work directly with executives, managers, and supervisors, and they have usually received previous education or training on L & MD. They conduct L & MDNA, design and/or deliver training geared to the workers, and locate sources to meet identified L & MD needs.

On the other hand, small organizations rarely employ sufficiently large numbers of management employees to justify full-time positions to oversee and coordinate their planned L & MD programs. In those cases, a committee oversees L & MD activities. For want of a better term, we shall use the term *L & MD coordinator* to refer to the elected or appointed chairperson of such a committee. He or she carries out committee recommendations, ensuring they are implemented. He or she also communicates about committee initiatives with others.

L & MD coordinators devote only part time to the planned L & MD program. They work full-time in other capacities. They have rarely participated in previous education, training, or work experience focused on administering a planned L & MD program, though they are usually enthusiastic advocates of L & MD.

What to Look for

Before selecting an L & MD director or appointing an L & MD coordinator, key decision makers of the organization and/or members of an in-house L & MD committee should first decide what they want from the planned L & MD program. It is at this point that a written program policy and philosophy statement and a tentative first-year action plan become invaluable. Armed with this information, committee members can draft a *job description* for an L & MD director or a *role description* for an L & MD coordinator and then circulate it among decision makers for additions or other modifications.

A *job description* is a list of responsibilities. Since an L & MD director is a management employee, his or her responsibilities should be summarized in such a description. But L & MD coordinators are only part-time employees who chair internal committees composed of people who are interested in L & MD. Coordinators already have job descriptions for their full-time jobs in the organization, but they do need guidelines for enacting their roles as L & MD committee leaders. These are called *role descriptions*.

The purpose and philosophy driving the planned L & MD program greatly affects the appropriate knowledge, skills, and attitudes of the ideal candidate chosen to spearhead the program. For instance, if the program's purpose centers around offering internal group training, then it only makes sense to recruit someone for L & MD director who has previously designed and delivered training of that kind. If the program's purpose centers around executive development, then someone should be chosen for the job who feels comfortable working with executives. If the program's purpose centers around starting and operating a management or leadership job rotation program or a high-potential program, then the best candidate will be someone who has already done that. If the L & MD program is to be *comprehensive*—meaning that it is intended to meet the needs of many targeted learners through a combination of training, education, and developmental methods—then the ideal candidate should possess education and experience commensurate with such a challenging undertaking.

By way of a starting point, review the sample job description appearing in Exhibit 5-2. Modify it as necessary to meet the demands of the planned L & MD program in your organization. You may also narrow it to create a role description for an L & MD coordinator.

RECRUITING, SELECTING, AND ORIENTING A PROGRAM LEADER

Take the following steps when recruiting, selecting, and orienting a program leader:

- Decide first whether to recruit a full-time L & MD director or a part-time L & MD coordinator

- Based on the L & MD program's purpose, goals, policy, philosophy, and first-year tentative action plan, prepare a job or role description for the L & MD director or L & MD coordinator

- Ask others in the organization to review and finalize the job or role description so as to build ownership in the selection process

- Receive approval to fund the job, setting the salary at a competitive level (for salary information about L & MD specialists, consult the annual survey results in a November issue of *Training Magazine*)

- Position the job within the organization's chain of command, involving the immediate organizational superior of the L & MD director

Exhibit 5-2
A Job Description for an L & MD Director

Summary	Administers L & MD activities for the organization; oversees internal training and external education for all levels to encourage leadership development; coordinates participation in industry-related, association-related, and university-related management and leadership programs.	
Responsibilities	1	Analyzes management and leadership performance problems, distinguishing learning from nonlearning needs.
	2	Assesses job-specific learning needs for workers, supervisors, managers, and executives, using needs assessment results to establish and maintain a planned L & MD program.
	3	Establishes performance objectives for training programs.
	4	Offers consulting assistance to determine whether the leadership and management development learning needs of workers, supervisors, managers, or executives will be met best through internal or external group training or other programs.
	5	Designs and delivers internal leadership, supervisory, management, and executive training programs to meet identified needs.
	6	Sources external training, education, or development programs as necessary to meet unique, individual needs.
	7	Prepares and negotiates contracts with external vendors or consultants, as appropriate, to meet supervisory, management, and executive learning needs.
	8	Manages and oversees assigned external vendors and consultants, ensuring they meet contractual requirements.
	9	Selects media for planned learning activities, choosing classroom-based, video-based, audio-based, computer-based, individualized instruction or other delivery methods when appropriate.
	10	Selects and purchases audiovisual equipment, as necessary, to support internal training for leaders, supervisors, managers, and executives.
	11	Establishes and maintains close working relationships with key executives, managers, supervisors, and other workers as appropriate to build ownership in— and support for—the planned L & MD program.
	12	Sets up and coordinates various management and project committees to support the L & MD program.
	13	Prepares instructional materials for internal training, including trainer guides, participant workbooks, checklists, videotape scripts, audiotape scripts, participant activities, and on-the-job checklists.
	14	Prepares training schedules.
	15	Provides individualized assistance to line managers to address the specialized L & MD needs of their management employees.
	16	Prepares and distributes invitations to internal training and briefing sessions for executives, managers, supervisors, aspiring supervisors, and other leaders.
	17	Oversees a specialized Leadership Development program for high-potential talent, recruiting and overseeing selection of such employees.
	18	Oversees internship and summer programs for individuals with leadership potential.

Exhibit 5-2 (continued)

Responsibilities	19	Provides special advice and assistance on recruiting, selecting, hiring, and orienting leadership talent for the organization.
	20	Arranges meeting facilities, as appropriate, to support classroom sessions, self-study, management briefings, and other activities.
	21	Budgets for the L & MD program.
	22	Delivers training programs and briefings to leaders at all levels, aspiring supervisors, experienced supervisors, managers, and executives—including (but not limited to) such topics as orientation to supervision, conducting performance appraisals, communicating effectively, motivating employees, on-the-job training and coaching, career planning, selection and interviewing methods, and discipline methods.
	23	Conducts rehearsals of training programs to elicit reviews and suggestions for improvement by supervisors, managers, and executives.
	24	Evaluates training, education, and development programs.
	25	Ensures transfer of learning from training, education, or developmental settings to on-the-job work settings.
	26	Establishes and maintains a management and leadership skill inventory for use in succession planning, HR planning, and the organization's strategic planning.
	27	Offers career counseling to aspiring and experienced supervisors, managers, executives, and other leaders.
	28	Provides outplacement and recruitment services, when necessary, for employees.
	29	Promotes and coordinates external educational activities linked to such efforts as executive MBA programs, night school MBA programs, and other educational activities linked to L & MD.
	30	Identifies and coordinates policy for external management and leadership seminars and conferences.
	31	Coordinates efforts to develop company leadership talent via work experience through planned job rotations and other methods.
	32	Educates leaders at all levels about their responsibility to train, educate, and develop their peers and/or subordinates.
	33	Provides advice and suggestions about job descriptions, performance appraisals, and compensation.
Qualifications		Requires the knowledge, skill, and mental development equivalent to the completion of a master's degree with specialized courses in employee training, human resources management, adult learning, and instructional design.
		Requires general knowledge of the history, structure, and operations of the organization and the industry of which it is part.
		Requires experience in leading training, education, and/or development activities.
		Requires ability to establish and maintain effective interpersonal relations with employees at all levels of the organization, with external vendors, with college faculty, and other groups.
		Requires strong written and oral communication skills.
		Requires familiarity with such instructional media as video-based, computer-based, and self-study instruction.
Date Prepared:		

After taking these actions, prepare to recruit, select, and orient the L & MD director or L & MD coordinator.

Recruitment Strategy

There are two primary sources for recruiting an L & MD director or L & MD coordinator—outside or inside the organization. Decide at the outset where to look for the best applicant. Typically, a full-time L & MD director will be hired from *outside*, assuming the organization employs no one with the requisite expertise to meet the program's unique requirements. On the other hand, a part-time L & MD coordinator will be selected from *inside*, often by appointment from the CEO or by election of members of a steering or advisory committee.

If the decision is made to undertake an *outside* search for an L & MD director, start by looking at recent employment applications already on file. List the position with the local job service; advertise in local newspapers and in newsletters of local chapters of the American Society for Training and Development. If necessary, extend the search nationally through search firms specializing in T & D that advertise regularly in *Training and Development, Training, Personnel Journal, HRMagazine*, and *HR Executive*. List the position with the referral service of the International Society for Performance Improvement. Place notices on appropriate web sites.

On the other hand, if the decision is made to restrict the search to *inside* the organization only, begin by posting a job description on electronic or physical bulletin boards or listing it in the organization's internal publications. Do not be shy about using other sources—such as word-of-mouth recruitment. It is also advisable to list the opening with the organization's Equal Employment Opportunity or Affirmative Action Office.

No matter where the advertisements are placed, they should indicate *minimum* job qualifications. If special restrictions apply, those should be listed; so, too, should *essential job functions* as defined in the Americans with Disabilities Act. The salary range should also be listed so as to prompt inquiries and applications from serious candidates only.

Selection Strategy

Clarify selection strategy and criteria before applications or resumes are received. Decide how to weigh applicant education and experience, screen resumes or applications, conduct job interviews with applicants, and make the hiring decision. If more than one person will participate in making the selection decision—an advisable move—be sure it is clear who is to do what in the selection process.

Start developing selection strategy with the job or role description. Involve members of L & MD steering or advisory committees in the screening, interviewing, and hiring process. Formulate interview questions based on responsibilities listed on the job description, adding questions about each applicant's background to a core of questions that will be posed to all of them. If possible, ask applicants to provide relevant work samples—such as management courses they have designed and delivered. You may even wish to request videotapes of group presentations from applicants—assuming the job requires platform skill. Have several people interview each applicant and write down their observations immediately and independently after each interview. Then compare the observations later. Make an offer only to the one applicant who is most positively received.

Orientation Strategy

Orientation is designed to increase the speed of the socialization process, reducing the unproductive breaking-in period during which a newcomer learns the job, role, department, and organization. A well-planned orientation can also reduce the chance of avoidable turnover. Of all training and development activities, orientation is the one activity that is the most commonly sponsored by organizations. Several practical guides to employee orientation have been published and are readily available.

The most important question to ask, before formulating orientation strategy, is this: *was the leader for the L & MD program hired from inside or outside the organization?* Generally, someone hired from outside will require a more thorough orientation than someone transferred or promoted from inside. Plan the orientation to ensure success. Never assume it will happen on its own.

To orient an L & MD director hired from outside the organization, begin by sending him or her to the organization's in-house orientation. (Many organizations offer such in-house programs, sponsored by the HRD, to summarize key employee benefits and the organization's work rules.) Give the newcomer

- The organization's HR manual
- Recent annual reports
- The organization's written L & MD policy and philosophy
- Tentative action plans for L & MD
- Minutes of an in-house L & MD committee

Then give the newcomer an orientation to the area of the organization in which the job is positioned. If possible, convene a special meeting of an L & MD steering or advisory committee to offer initial suggestions about the newcomer's orientation.

It can also be very helpful to arrange one-on-one informational interviews between the newcomer and key people. Such interviews serve several purposes. First, they help socialize the newcomer quickly so he or she knows—and is known to—key people. Second, they provide an opportunity for the newcomer to hear many views about L & MD in a short time. Third, they can help the newcomer learn about the organization's culture, history, structure, and strategic plan.

Orienting an L & MD director or L & MD coordinator hired from inside the organization should be easier. He or she should already be familiar with the organization's rules, benefits, culture, history, structure, and strategic plan. But it will still be necessary to provide detailed background information about the L & MD program. That, too, may not be necessary if the person has been serving as a member of an L & MD steering or advisory committee.

SELECTING, ORIENTING, AND TRAINING STAFF AND VENDORS

Internal staff members consist of full-time or part-time people hired to support the planned L & MD program; *external vendors* are consultants or other service suppliers whose special skills are needed for the L & MD program. Both internal staff members and external vendors support the program and report to the L & MD director or coordinator. They carry out varied activities—such as conducting needs assessment, writing performance objectives, preparing performance tests or written tests based on objectives, locating or writing instructional materials for on-the-job or off-the-job use, identifying sources of planned learning experiences to meet *macro* or *micro* needs, delivering instruction, or evaluating instruction.

When Are They Needed?

Full-time internal staff members should be hired for L & MD only when the number of targeted learners is sufficiently large to warrant it. Otherwise, external vendors or part-time staff members can be used to meet short-term, one-time, or specialized needs. (Use the flowchart appearing in Exhibit 5-3 to help decide whether to hire internal staff members, rely on external vendors, or use a combination of internal staff and external vendors.)

Selecting, Orienting, and Training Staff or Vendors

The process of selecting, orienting, and training internal staff members and external vendors does not differ markedly from the process of selecting and orienting an L & MD director or coordinator. Typically, they are recruited and selected by the L & MD director or coordinator, often after consultation with other people who have a stake in these decisions.

First: the L & MD director or coordinator should decide just what the staff members or vendors are expected to do. Many L & MD staff members and vendors assist in developing instructional materials *or* delivering classroom pres-

Exhibit 5-3
A Flowchart for Deciding whether to Hire Internal Staff, Find External Vendors, or Rely on a Combination of the Two to Meet the Needs of the L & MD Program

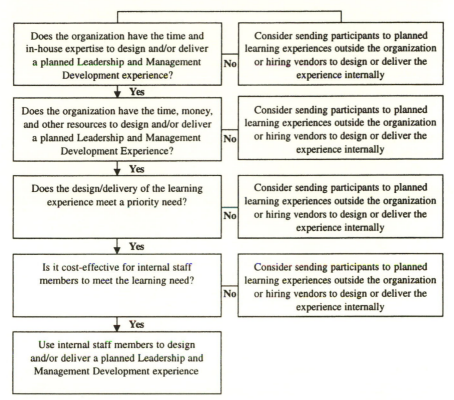

Does the organization have the time and in-house expertise to design and/or deliver a planned Leadership and Management Development experience?	**No** → Consider sending participants to planned learning experiences outside the organization or hiring vendors to design or deliver the experience internally
↓ Yes	
Does the organization have the time, money, and other resources to design and/or deliver a planned Leadership and Management Development Experience?	**No** → Consider sending participants to planned learning experiences outside the organization or hiring vendors to design or deliver the experience internally
↓ Yes	
Does the design/delivery of the learning experience meet a priority need?	**No** → Consider sending participants to planned learning experiences outside the organization or hiring vendors to design or deliver the experience internally
↓ Yes	
Is it cost-effective for internal staff members to meet the learning need?	**No** → Consider sending participants to planned learning experiences outside the organization or hiring vendors to design or deliver the experience internally
↓ Yes	
Use internal staff members to design and/or deliver a planned Leadership and Management Development experience	

entations. The demand for L & MD specialists is expected to increase for the foreseeable future.

Second: the L & MD director or coordinator should draft a job description (for staff members) or a work plan (for external vendors). Circulate it to interested people for their suggestions and modifications before it is finalized. This process builds ownership through participation. A job description or work plan should list the primary responsibilities to be shouldered by the prospective staff member or vendor.

Third: the L & MD director or coordinator should obtain approval to hire the staff member or contract with the vendor. Approval to hire usually requires the completion and approval of a job requisition. Approval to contract usually begins with a "Request for a Proposal" that lays out project requirements for a vendor.

Fourth: the L & MD director or coordinator should plot out and implement recruitment strategy. As in recruiting an L & MD director or L & MD coordinator, sources of talent may be found inside or outside the organization. Internal recruitment may be carried out through job posting, word-of-mouth recruiting, and searches of skill inventories. External recruitment may be carried out through newspaper advertising, newsletter announcements, personal contacts, or specialized search firms. Vendors may be identified through published sources, professional contacts of the L & MD director/coordinator, or professional advertising.

Fifth: the L & MD director or coordinator should use a job description or work plan as the basis for preparing selection criteria and interview questions. Applicants for internal staff positions should be screened and interviewed. Prospective vendors should be similarly screened, based on their proposals, and then interviewed.

Sixth: the L & MD director or coordinator should select the staff member or vendor. The choice should be made as objectively as possible, preferably based on the results of interviews with several people. Once vendors are chosen, they should be required to sign a contract that clearly indicates project expectations, objectives, time frames, and maximum amounts to be spent on each activity.

Seventh: the L & MD director or coordinator should orient the staff members or vendors. If staff members are chosen from within—or if vendors have previously worked with the organization—then a lengthy orientation should not be necessary. Otherwise, a thorough orientation should be planned.

SCHEDULING L & MD PROGRAMS

The scheduling of planned L & MD activities is more important than it may seem at first glance. Four issues are particularly important when scheduling: (1) Organizational needs, (2) Work cycles, (3) Individual needs, and (4) L & MD activities.

Organizational Needs

When a planned L & MD activity is specifically designed to support an organizational need, then scheduling becomes critically important. Indeed, the organization's chances of meeting its needs may depend on L & MD activities. When that is true, then scheduling L & MD assumes a commanding position.

Consider driving issues identified in strategic plans. They make organizational needs explicit. For instance, assume an organization's leaders have decided to make customer service training a high priority. It will make sense, then, to identify what managers and employees need to know or do relative to that need. L & MD activities may be required, and they must be scheduled to help meet the need.

Work Cycles

Organizational work cycles vary, depending on the business. For instance, retailers are particularly busy during the holiday season. Manufacturers are busy when they receive larger-than-normal orders. Some financial service firms are busiest at year end—from October through December.

When possible, L & MD activities should not be scheduled during peak work cycles. If they are, targeted participants may face conflicting priorities with their work and may not be able to participate in off-the-job learning experiences or devote time to on-the-job experiences.

The point to bear in mind is that L & MD activities should be scheduled at times when they do not conflict with peak work cycles. If you are unsure when the peaks of the work cycle occur, ask others these questions: (1) When is the organization's work cycle at its peak? (2) When does the organization's work activity drop off? (3) What is the best time of year for people to participate in planned L & MD activities?

Individual Needs

Individuals are eager to participate in L & MD activities when they feel the need to learn. This feeling, what adult educators call a *teachable moment*, is most intense just before and immediately after a change affects an individual. To ensure that the timing of L & MD activities matches up to predictable needs, scan the organization to determine if there will be any special time in the future when a larger-than-normal group is to be promoted or transferred. (Such phenomena can occur immediately after a large group leaves an organization due to an early retirement offer or a layoff.) Do this scanning at the beginning of each year—or immediately after announcements are made that have sweeping implications for the organization. Adjust planned L & MD activities accordingly.

The same principle applies when individuals are promoted, demoted, transferred, hired, or outplaced. Any change prompts individuals to learn more because learning is a mechanism for coping with change. People are often highly motivated to learn at such times, so these times are especially opportune to approach them about developing learning plans.

L & MD Methods

Not all L & MD methods require the same amount of time, and these differences affect scheduling. For instance, internal group training is finite: each experience has a definite beginning and ending for participants. Job rotation programs often last longer than internal group training efforts, so they require advance timing and scheduling commitments. External group training may—or may not—require on-the-job time commitments for study or learner follow-up.

On the other hand, self-study efforts, on-the-job coaching, and other individualized learning activities are quite flexible, allowing participation as time permits.

When scheduling L & MD activities, pay attention to group activities demanding the most time from the largest groups. Schedule them so they do not interfere with the organization's peak work cycles or in the wake of upheavals created by buyouts, mergers, acquisitions, or layoffs.

PROGRAM BUDGETING

Budgeting a planned L & MD program should stem from an action plan, usually established on an annual basis. However, few organizations budget separately for L & MD, choosing instead to fund L & MD by dividing costs among several participating departments so that digging the pertinent figures out of individual budgets can be a difficult task.[6] When L & MD programs are budgeted on a corporate or SBU level, they are often treated from a zero-based perspective because L & MD activities are not necessarily the same from year to year; rather, L & MD programs are driven by organizational, individual, and job needs that may vary somewhat over time.

Start the budgeting process by tentatively planning each project in each program area. In organizations that target L & MD participants by job categories, program areas mean *annual learning plans for each job category*. Projects mean *specific planned learning experiences*. In organizations that target participants by special group or program, the group or the program becomes the basis for budgeting. Projects will also mean specific activities for each group or program.

List the projects planned for each program area during the future year. If possible, develop a simple list of activities for each project. Then prepare a simple *project budget* based on the staff, equipment, and other necessary resources. Base estimates on information supplied by vendors or historical experience. When you finish, tally up the resources that will be required in each project in each program area and then budget for equipment, instructors' salaries, instructors' benefits, facilities, and travel. Be sure to follow organizational policies, practices, and accounting methods when preparing the final budget.

KEEPING PROGRAM RECORDS

Recordkeeping is essential to meet management and legal obligations. Records are useful from a management perspective because they indicate *who* participated in *what* L & MD activities. Without records, management will not find it possible to access information about individual participation in L & MD activities to aid decision making about who should (1) Qualify for a promotion, (2) Receive a higher-than-average pay raise, (3) Receive a desirable transfer to another part of the organization to cultivate needed skills, (4) Be assigned to what jobs or short-term assignments. Without records, L & MD specialists will also lose an important source of information about L & MD needs.

From a legal perspective, organizations are required to avoid discrimination in all employment matters. As Equal Employment Opportunity and Affirmative Action requirements dictate, people must be given equal access to all avenues associated with hiring, promotion, and training. Without records of who participated in planned L & MD, your organization may not be able to defend itself against a charge of unfair employment discrimination if one is ever filed.

Some state governments even require professionals to complete a specific statutory number of continuing education hours each year as a condition for maintaining their state licenses. When your organization functions in an industry in which continuing education is important, then recordkeeping for L & MD can be critical.

Two sets of records should be kept: one about participants and one about programs.

Participant records may or may not be linked to an organization's Human Resource Information System (HRIS) containing employment, payroll, and benefits information or to confidential recordkeeping for succession plans. It is desirable if they can be linked, though L & MD records may become so detailed as to become unwieldy. For each individual participating in a planned L & MD program, you may want to keep at least the following information:

- Complete name (and any changes resulting from marriage or divorce)
- Names and locations of schools attended
- College majors
- Degrees earned
- Degrees in progress
- Dates of graduation
- Fluency in foreign language(s)
- Professional designations earned or licenses held
- Professional designations in progress
- Training programs attended, including sponsor's name, dates of attendance, and location
- College courses attended (or in progress)
- Published articles and books
- Major presentations made to professional, industry, or organizational groups
- Jobs held in previous organizations, including job titles and dates of employment
- Jobs held in the present organization, including titles, dates of movement in and out of them, and location
- Other issues of particular interest and value for L & MD purposes—including performance appraisal results and identified individual learning needs

Program records should contain information about each L & MD program, organized as it is in your organization by job category, special group, or special program. Each project record should at least contain information about:

- What it was (descriptive title)
- Who participated (list of participants)
- When it was held (dates)
- Where it was held (location)
- How it was held (delivery method)
- Why it was held (how did it satisfy a business or individual need?)
- What happened (what evaluation results are available? how were they gathered?)

Information about internal group training is easiest to record, while information about on-the-job training may be the most difficult. Information may also have to be added to program records if continuing education requirements must be satisfied. For instance, employees who are also accountants may need special information about each planned learning activity in which they participated, so as to comply with statutory requirements.

In small organizations with fewer than 100 employees, paper records about individuals and L & MD programs will probably satisfy most requirements. But in large organizations employing more than 100 employees, automated record-keeping is essential. Numerous vendors sell computerized recordkeeping software, typically designed for use on a personal computer.

A software package can be purchased and installed quickly. However, not every software package for recordkeeping permits easy modification to meet specific organizational needs, so be sure to check it out carefully before making a purchase. (Most vendors will be willing to supply you with a *demo disk* so you can check it out.) Review several software packages before choosing one.

PUBLICIZING L & MD ACTIVITIES

It is not enough for an organization merely to sponsor a planned L & MD program. Information about program activities and results should also be publicized so targeted learners and their immediate organizational superiors will be inclined to participate in it and support it. Publicity is thus a vital tool to build program support and visibility by trumpeting successes.

Publicity and L & MD Philosophy

Not all organizations have cultures that are equally open; not all organizations have top managers or middle managers who are equally supportive of a planned L & MD program. Top managers or middle managers in some organizations may be unwilling to publicize information about planned L & MD programs for fear they will be swamped by promotion seekers, only some of whom are worthy of promotion. In such organizations, managers may prefer to make information about L & MD activities available only to those they are willing to nominate and sponsor for participation. For this reason, be sure to clarify the organization's philosophy about publicizing the L & MD program before doing it through in-house periodicals or community newspapers.

Some managers may also consider L & MD activities proprietary and may prefer to keep information about them confidential. Since the L & MD program should be closely linked to corporate strategy and succession plans, information about it is treated as top secret. Prospective participants and their immediate organizational superiors are only clued in to program activities on a need-to-know basis.

That can also be a reflection of an organization's general employment philosophy. Organizations that take this stance with L & MD will usually shroud other employment matters in secrecy as well. For instance, they may be unwilling to share information about pay ranges, job classifications, or job descriptions. They may also be unwilling to clarify the criteria used in making promotion or pay decisions.

However, recent work place trends favoring participative management generally discourage secretive approaches to L & MD. Managers are learning that employees today want to know the reasons underlying employment decisions. When left in the dark, cynical and skeptical employees often assume that employment decisions are not being made fairly or legally. That perception can lead to costly litigation. For this reason, then, it is advisable for most organizations to be open about L & MD activities so long as proprietary organizational rights and individual rights to privacy are not violated.

How Should a Planned L & MD Program Be Publicized?

There are three methods by which to publicize a planned L & MD program: (1) Mass media, (2) Group approaches, and (3) Personal selling. It is usually not a matter of choosing one method in preference to others; rather, most organizations seek an effective combination of methods.

Mass media are geared to reaching many people, usually with a simple message. The aim is to build awareness. In organizational settings, you can use the following mass media approaches to publicize L & MD efforts:

- Place articles in community newspapers or in-house publications
- Place announcements on bulletin boards
- Provide information about L & MD efforts by electronic mail bulletin boards
- Sponsor career/education ''fairs'' in the organization
- Provide large group presentations to 100 or more employees

• Send direct-mail brochures and memos to everyone qualified to participate in L & MD experiences

Direct-mail methods are often most effective, although there is (admittedly) no assurance that people will read what is mailed to them.

Group approaches are focused on building awareness and interest for L & MD in a specific niche market. In organizational settings, group approaches might include presentations to all employees working in the same function or department or reporting to the same person. These presentations may be made before, during, or after succession planning or individual career planning activities so as to reinforce the value of L & MD as a tool for realizing organizational and individual goals.

But our favorite approach is personal selling, though it is by far the most time-consuming. It involves one-on-one contact with prospective participants and/or their immediate organizational superiors. The aim is to target the message to the specific needs of a handful of individuals.

To do personal selling, arrange a meeting with managers in charge of various departments or work units. Then explain what the planned L & MD program can *do* for them and their employees. Finally, ask for their support, cooperation, and participation. End the meeting, like any good salesperson, by asking for enrollments, participation, or other evidence of a "sale."

SUMMARY

In this chapter we described the administrative support system necessary to operate a planned L & MD program. As we explained, early issues to consider when starting up a planned L & MD program include any or all of the following:

1. Where should the L & MD function be positioned in the organization's reporting structure?

2. What rewards or incentives should be offered to induce people to accept responsibility for developing themselves and their workers?

3. What kind of leader should direct the planned L & MD program?

4. How should the program leader be recruited, selected, and oriented?

5. How should internal staff members and external vendors be selected, oriented, and trained?

6. How should planned L & MD activities be scheduled?

7. How should budgeting be handled?

8. What records of L & MD activities should be kept?

9. How should L & MD program activities be publicized?

NOTES

1. R. Zemke, "In Search of a Training Philosophy," *Training*, Vol. 22, No. 10, pp. 93–94, 96, 98.

2. M. Dalton, "Conflicts Between Staff and Line Managerial Officers," *American Sociological Review*, Vol. 15, pp. 342–351.

3. F. Hills, *Compensation Decision Making* (Chicago: The Dryden Press, 1987).

4. D. Feuer, "Paying for Knowledge," *Training*, Vol. 24, No. 5, pp. 57–58, 60, 61–66.

5. Hills, *Compensation Decision Making*.

6. R. Fulmer, "Corporate Management Development and Education: The State of the Art," *Journal of Management Development*, Vol. 7, No. 2, p. 65.

Part III

Selecting, Planning, and Using Formal, Informal, and Special Methods

Part III focuses on methods for changing individuals or groups, providing them with the knowledge, skills, or attitudes they need to perform competently, prepare themselves for advancement, or gain new insights about the problems they face on their jobs.

Change rarely comes about on its own. That principle holds true in L & MD as well as in other organizational change efforts, of which L & MD may be part. For this reason, many organizations use three methods to bring about these changes: formal methods occur off-the-job and lend themselves to group planning; informal methods occur on-the-job and require planning between one employee with leadership potential and his or her immediate organizational superior; special methods are unique, cutting-edge, or controversial.

This part of the book, then, focuses on these methods. Chapter 6 provides two models for selecting appropriate L & MD methods. Chapter 7 describes how to select, plan, and use formal L & MD methods; Chapter 8 describes how to select, plan, and use informal L & MD methods; and Chapter 9 describes how to select, plan, and use special L & MD methods.

Chapter 6

How Should Recruitment and Selection Be Used as Part of a Leadership and Management Development Program?

Earlier chapters indicate that the startup of a planned L & MD program requires many issues to be addressed:

- What is the purpose of the planned L & MD program?
- What goals and objectives should the L & MD program strive to realize initially? eventually?
- What policy and philosophy should guide the L & MD program?
- What targeted job category, special group, or special program should be initially served by the L & MD program?
- What action plan should guide program startup?
- What needs are evident for the targeted groups?
- What instructional plan (curriculum) should guide the organization's planned L & MD program?
- What administrative support will be necessary for the program?

Once these questions are answered, you are ready to pose these questions: *By what methods should learning needs be met? How should the L & MD curriculum be implemented?* (By *methods* we mean *modes of delivering planned L & MD activities.*)

When working in L & MD, you may be tempted to skip the preliminary questions and jump to the questions about methods immediately. By doing that, you will endear yourself to zealots who want to take immediate action. Unfortunately, the action taken may be ill-conceived because it is hastily contrived. It may fail to meet the L & MD needs of targeted groups in the organization.

Exhibit 6-1
How Often Are L & MD Methods Used?

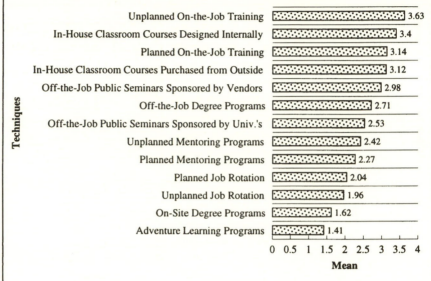

Question: What methods are used to develop management and/or leadership talent in your organization? For each method listed in the left column below, circle a response in the center column that indicates how often your organization uses that method. Use the following scale: **1 = Not at all; 2 = Seldom; 3 = Sometimes; 4 = Frequently; 5 = Always.**

Techniques	Mean
Unplanned On-the-Job Training	3.63
In-House Classroom Courses Designed Internally	3.4
Planned On-the-Job Training	3.14
In-House Classroom Courses Purchased from Outside	3.12
Off-the-Job Public Seminars Sponsored by Vendors	2.98
Off-the-Job Degree Programs	2.71
Off-the-Job Public Seminars Sponsored by Univ.'s	2.53
Unplanned Mentoring Programs	2.42
Planned Mentoring Programs	2.27
Planned Job Rotation	2.04
Unplanned Job Rotation	1.96
On-Site Degree Programs	1.62
Adventure Learning Programs	1.41

Source: W. Rothwell, *A Survey about Management and Leadership Development* (unpublished survey results) (University Park, PA: The Pennsylvania State University, 1998).

Hasty action will only frustrate those you serve and damage the long-term credibility of the L & MD program in a way that will not be easy to repair.

We suggest you take a more deliberate course of action. Resist impatient zealots. Be thoughtful about what you do. While not falling into the paralysis of analysis, avoid the temptation to follow those who cry "fire, aim, ready." Instead, pick one important issue early on—and address it so extraordinarily well that you establish a reputation for quality.

With that thought in mind, we'll turn our attention in this chapter to the process of choosing methods designed to meet the learning needs of targeted groups. At this point our aim is simply to explain when to use methods common to L & MD. In Chapters 7, 8, and 9 we'll describe these methods in detail.

METHODS USED IN L & MD PROGRAMS

Rothwell's 1998 survey of ASTD members focused on the most frequently used and the most effective L & MD methods. (See Exhibits 6-1 and 6-2.)

Exhibit 6-2
How Effective Are L & MD Methods?

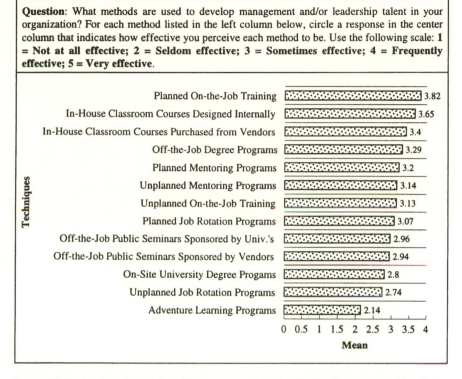

Question: What methods are used to develop management and/or leadership talent in your organization? For each method listed in the left column below, circle a response in the center column that indicates how effective you perceive each method to be. Use the following scale: **1 = Not at all effective; 2 = Seldom effective; 3 = Sometimes effective; 4 = Frequently effective; 5 = Very effective.**

Techniques:

Technique	Mean
Planned On-the-Job Training	3.82
In-House Classroom Courses Designed Internally	3.65
In-House Classroom Courses Purchased from Vendors	3.4
Off-the-Job Degree Programs	3.29
Planned Mentoring Programs	3.2
Unplanned Mentoring Programs	3.14
Unplanned On-the-Job Training	3.13
Planned Job Rotation Programs	3.07
Off-the-Job Public Seminars Sponsored by Univ.'s	2.96
Off-the-Job Public Seminars Sponsored by Vendors	2.94
On-Site University Degree Progams	2.8
Unplanned Job Rotation Programs	2.74
Adventure Learning Programs	2.14

Source: W. Rothwell, *A Survey about Management and Leadership Development* (unpublished survey results) (University Park, PA: The Pennsylvania State University, 1998).

According to the results of that survey, the mean response indicates that the *most frequently used* methods include unplanned on-the-job training, in-house classroom training, and planned on-the-job training. However, planned on-the-job training was cited by Rothwell's survey respondents as the *single most effective* method.

GUIDELINES FOR SELECTING L & MD METHODS

The models appearing in Exhibits 6-3 and 6-4 should be helpful in sorting out key issues for consideration when selecting L & MD methods to meet learning needs and implement an L & MD curriculum. Review them. Then read the following discussions about them. While not foolproof, these models do provide worthwhile guidance for selecting appropriate L & MD methods to meet organizational, individual, or job-related needs.

Exhibit 6-3
A Model for Selecting L & MD Methods Based on Group versus Individual Needs

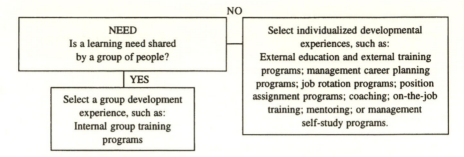

Model 1: Methods Based on Group or Individual Needs

Sometimes a temptation exists to treat L & MD as an exercise in ''sheep dipping.'' Everyone is to be given exposure to the same planned learning experiences. However, such an approach is usually costly and unwise. Indeed, the trend is away from a one-size-fits-all mentality and toward learning experiences geared to addressing *individual* rather than *group* L & MD needs.[1]

However, there are still numerous occasions when group experiences are highly appropriate. As the model in Exhibit 6-3 indicates, the key question to ask is this: *is the learning need shared by a group of people?* Examples of such group needs may include any of the following situations:[2]

- New laws, rules, or regulations are enacted affecting the organization, and management employees are not familiar with what those legal requirements mean to them.

- New organizational policies, procedures, or strategic plans are adopted. They have far-reaching scope that will be difficult to implement successfully unless everyone is familiar with them.

- New, far-reaching technology is introduced to the organization, and employees at all levels are expected to spearhead its introduction.

- Employees experience changes in their job duties or role expectations due to promotions, downsizing, transfers, or other widespread changes. The changes share enough in common that group training is more economical than individualized training.

On the other hand, individualized methods are more appropriate to use when learning needs are not widely shared across many people. A typical example: a newly promoted supervisor, manager, or executive from a technical background such as accounting, engineering, or data processing may have difficulty exercising appropriate interpersonal skills upon promotion to management. Group training is too expensive to offer because everyone promoted does not experience this need. Hence, individualized methods are more appropriate. (In this example, some organizations opt to send employees to external educational seminars on Human Relations.)

Model 2: Methods Based on Types of Needs

Experts on adult development have long contended that learning needs are not all the same; rather, they differ by type.[3] Five types are commonly identified: (1) Cognitive or informational needs, (2) Psychomotor or skill needs, (3) Affective, feeling, or attitudinal needs, (4) Advancement or educational needs, (5) Developmental needs. Different instructional methods should be used to meet these needs.[4] These needs are the basis for selecting L & MD methods in Exhibit 6-4.

Cognitive or *informational* needs have to do with knowledge. Examples of such needs include definitions and concepts. Cognitive or informational training is perhaps the most common planned learning experience sponsored by organizations for employees demonstrating leadership potential, and most external seminars, like off-the-job college courses, are focused on meeting cognitive or informational needs as well. They are especially appropriate for those who have never had any courses in management or leadership.

Cognitive or informational training addresses *what* questions and *what* needs. Examples: "what is motivation?" and "what methods may be used to delegate work to employees?" It is also used as a means of kicking off a new program, since employees will naturally have to know "what is a self-directed work-team?" before they can help establish one or "what is Total Quality Management?" before they can introduce such a program.

As the model indicates, if you are trying to meet cognitive needs, you should consider knowledge-based internal group training programs, on-the-job coaching, or on-the-job training. These methods are particularly well suited to addressing cognitive needs, since they can answer *what* questions particularly well. Knowledge-based training is usually focused on introducing content rather than describing procedures.

Psychomotor or *skill* needs are frequently associated more with technical personnel than employees showing leadership potential. Learning experiences designed to meet these needs address *how-to* questions—such as "how do you fix this machine?" or "how do you prepare a production report?" Note that these questions are directed to technical issues. But it is still possible to design and deliver planned learning experiences to employees who show leadership potential based on skill issues. Indeed, a common complaint among employees is that they do not receive enough of this training.

As the model in Exhibit 6-3 indicates, psychomotor or skill needs may be met through skill-based internal group training programs or on-the-job coaching/training. Skill-based training is well suited to address *how-to* questions.

Affective, feeling, or *attitudinal* needs have to do with establishing new values, lifestyles, or philosophies about life, work, management, and people. Short-term

Exhibit 6-4
A Model for Selecting L & MD Methods Based on the Types of Needs

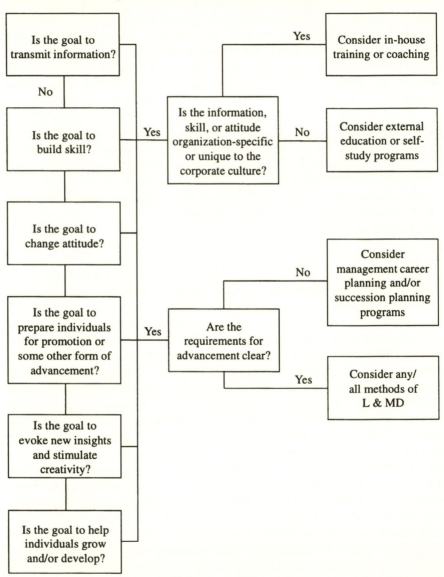

planned learning experiences alone will rarely produce such sweeping changes in internal beliefs; long-term experiences are usually necessary to do that. Learning experiences of this kind usually focus primarily on *why* questions—such as "why should employee participation be valued?" and "why is Total Quality Management worth pursuing?"

The attitudes of employees showing leadership potential have long been important, because their opinions exert a strong influence on the job satisfaction of individuals and the morale of employee groups. To employees, their immediate organizational superiors exemplify and embody management, so the opinions of their organizational superiors are (they reason) no doubt shared by others in authority. Many of the challenges facing U.S. organizations today center around attitudinal issues. To mention a few, organizations have needs to:

• Offer exemplary customer service

• Improve product or service quality

• Build employee involvement in decision making

• Address the pervasive cynicism of U.S. workers in the wake of numerous scandals that have sullied the reputations of otherwise sterling corporations

• Deal with a changing work ethic

• Cope with waning employee loyalty

Often, however, efforts to meet affective learning needs require broad-based action extending beyond such short-term planned learning experiences as one-shot internal group training courses. In fact, it often requires paying attention to all factors influencing performance—including compensation, benefits, recruitment practices, and selection practices as well as job design and work group structure. Training, geared to changing individuals, is inadequate by itself to change organizational culture. The reasons: on-the-job reinforcement is often insufficient following training and too few people are trained at one time to create a critical mass favoring change. For these reasons, then, learning needs linked to attitudes or feelings may require increased attention to on-the-job coaching, on-the-job training, individual career planning, and mentoring or sponsorship programs. By paying more attention to coaching, training, individual career planning, and mentoring or sponsorship programs, managers and other organizational leaders can provide individuals with prompt, concrete, and specific feedback about performance or behaviors.

Advancement needs are linked to vertical (promotional) or horizontal (technical) job advancement opportunities. They are closely associated with employee education, intended to prepare people for the next job rather than the present job. Management and leadership education focused on meeting these needs addresses *future what, how-to,* and *why* questions. For example, to a supervisor aspiring to a manager position, consider these issues: "What should a manager do?'' ''How should the responsibilities of a manager be met?'' and ''Why are certain attitudes so important for managers?''

As the model in Exhibit 6-4 indicates, advancement needs can only be met effectively when the organization has clarified and communicated the responsibilities linked to advancement. To that end, management and leadership career planning programs and succession planning programs—both methods of clarifying what is needed from the individual and organization—are essential for clearing up *what* needs to be learned and *how well*.

Once learning needs are clear, many L & MD methods may be brought to bear on a performance gap separating what individuals already know and what they should know to meet future requirements. Short-term methods may be used, such as internal group training, coaching, or on-the-job training programs; long-term methods may also be used, including external education, job rotation (to other functions), position assignment, or management/leadership self-study programs.

Developmental needs are linked to organizational growth through individual creativity. They stem from the deep human need to realize one's potential. Development focuses on evoking new ideas for the benefit of individuals and their organizations. Creativity is a human need, and development is associated with it.

L & MD focused on meeting developmental needs addresses *what's new* questions. For example, to a manager aspiring to an executive position, consider these issues: ''How do departments other than your own function?'' and ''What new methods can be used to address organizational problems in your department or in others?'' As the model in Exhibit 6-4 indicates, developmental needs are worth meeting only when some recognizable payoff will be realized. However, the nature of that payoff varies, and the results of developmental experiences are often difficult to quantify. If it is not possible to see any value resulting from the experience—such as sending an employee off to an Executive Development program, basket weaving, aerobics, a community leadership program, or an adventure learning encounter—then perhaps time, attention, and resources should be devoted to other methods in which the payoffs are more easily identified.

Any L & MD method may be used to meet developmental needs, thereby broadening individual horizons and stimulating new ideas in an organization. As in management or leadership education, developmental experiences may be short term or long term. Of course, new ideas may come from inside or outside the organization; new ideas may come from such planned learning experiences as internal group training or external educational programs. They may also be elicited through coaching, on-the-job training, job rotation, position assignments, or management/leadership self-study programs.

SUMMARY

As we explained in this chapter, *methods* refer to *modes of delivering planned L & MD activities*. While it is tempting to select L & MD methods immediately, we advise you to first address questions about the L & MD program's purpose, goals, objectives, policy, philosophy, targeted group(s), action plan, needs to be served, curriculum, and administrative support. Only then should you pose the questions: *By what methods should learning needs be met? How can the L & MD curriculum be implemented?*

NOTES

1. T. Quick, *Training Managers So They Can Really Manage: Confessions of a Frustrated Trainer* (San Francisco: Jossey-Bass, 1991).

2. D. Laird, *Approaches to Training and Development* (2nd ed.) (Reading, MA: Addison-Wesley, 1985), pp. 49–50.

3. R. Gagné and L. Briggs, *Principles of Instructional Design* (2nd ed.) (New York: Holt, Rinehart and Winston, 1979).

4. H. Ellington, *Producing Teaching Materials: A Handbook for Teachers and Trainers* (London: Kogan Page, 1985).

Chapter 7

Planning and Using Formal Methods

In this chapter we turn to planning and using *formal L & MD methods*. These approaches to L & MD are carefully planned and deliberately executed to meet learning needs and to improve the performance of management workers and others who demonstrate leadership potential. They include:

- Succession planning programs
- Management or leadership career planning programs
- Internal group training programs
- External group training programs
- External education programs
- Job rotation programs, and
- Position assignment programs

These L & MD methods, while seemingly unrelated, lend themselves to planning and to centralized administration and oversight. Formal L & MD methods may thus be coordinated by an L & MD director or L & MD coordinator for an organization.

SUCCESSION PLANNING PROGRAMS

Succession planning is an apt starting point for introducing formal L & MD methods because it is helpful in identifying gaps between existing and desired management or leadership talent. *Succession planning is a systematic approach for identifying, assessing, and developing successors for positions in organizational settings.*[1] Successors are typically, but not always, identified from within

organizations by their immediate organizational superiors for higher-level positions. They are assessed over time spans ranging from short to long and developed to assume those higher-level or more technically sophisticated positions.
While most succession plans focus on replacing the incumbents of key positions,
succession plans can also be extended throughout the organization.

The Importance of Succession Planning

Many corporations use some form of succession planning. It is important for

- Creating a surplus of skills beyond those minimally necessary to ensure organizational
  survival.
- Identifying individuals capable of assuming more responsibility (*vertical advancement*)
  or achieving greater technical expertise (*horizontal advancement*).
- Ensuring continuity of operations in the event of the sudden death, disability, retirement, resignation, or other loss of key management employees or individuals demonstrating leadership potential.
- Identifying individuals as possible replacements for key incumbents of critically important positions.
- Pinpointing positions in which no successors have been identified so that contingency
  plans may be established.
- Creating a talent pool of likely candidates for succession from inside—and sometimes
  even from outside—the organization.

When Should Succession Planning Be a Programmatic Focus of L & MD?

Succession planning is a process, a form of long-term internal recruitment in
which decision makers identify possible replacements for incumbents occupying
important positions in the organization. The process is *long term* because few
succession plans assume that incumbents must be immediately replaced. The
process focuses on *possible* replacements because few succession plans assume
that identified successors will always become permanent successors. Indeed, an
actual placement ratio of 60–70 percent is indicative of a successful program.
Higher ratios make it appear that key replacement decisions are ''fixed'' or
''rigged'' to restrict opportunities for members of protected labor groups.

Succession planning should be one guiding force for the organization's
planned L & MD program. Succession planning can pinpoint the need for replacements or successors in key management positions and for leadership talent
throughout the organization. In that sense it creates an impetus favoring a
planned L & MD program. Since succession planning is a long-term effort, it
provides valuable information for charting the long-term direction of a planned
L & MD program.

Carrying Out Succession Planning

In many organizations, a succession planning ritual is carried out at least once a year. There is no one right way to go about that ritual. One size does not fit all. Like other formal methods of L & MD, the most appropriate way to carry out the succession planning process depends on the organization's culture, traditions, and top management philosophies.

With that caveat in mind, we can still describe several key steps that are workable in most settings.

First, top managers should appoint someone to spearhead and coordinate the succession planning program. A good choice is the L & MD director, L & MD coordinator, or HR director. The person chosen for this role must be tactful and discrete. Any violation of trust may lead to a complete loss of credibility for the individual and the program. Since the CEO bears ultimate responsibility for organizational succession, he or she should appoint the individual to spearhead the effort. Great care should be taken at the outset to ensure that, if succession matters will be kept secret, the individual chosen as program coordinator must not learn of succession plans personally affecting him or her.

Second, the L & MD director or coordinator should work to clarify the purpose, policy, and procedures to guide succession planning in the organization. The program coordinator should meet with the CEO—and with all top managers in the organization, subsidiary, or division—to answer such questions as:

- What should be the program's purpose?

- What results are desired from it?

- What positions should be included—or excluded—from consideration? Should the program focus solely on high-level positions, as is common, or should it extend into the nonexempt ranks so as to include possible replacements for supervisors or team leaders? Should the program include or exclude the talent pool found in contingent workers, temporary workers, vendors, suppliers, distributors, and even competitors?

- How often should succession planning be carried out?

- Who should be involved in identifying and developing possible successors? More specifically, how much say should the job incumbent have in reaching this decision? How much say should others have?

- What forms or other data-gathering methods should be used in the process, and on what criteria should they be based?

- How will confidentiality of the process—and its results—be ensured? What is the organization's philosophy on confidentiality? Who should have access to succession planning results?

- How open should the process be? Should prospective successors be told that they are listed in a succession plan—or not told?

Third, the succession planning coordinator should work in consultation with others to draft a proposed succession planning policy, procedures, and forms to be used. (Examine the model succession planning policy and procedures provided in Exhibit 7-1 as a starting point for developing them in your organization.) Forms commonly used in succession planning include:

- A *personal history form* to describe the background of each key position incumbent as well as a *personal history form* to describe the backgrounds of possible successors.
- A *succession planning chart*, based on the organization chart, highlighting key positions to be filled and individuals identified as possible successors.
- A *performance appraisal form* for each key job incumbent and each possible successor.
- A *future potential appraisal form* for each possible successor.
- An *individual development form* indicating developmental steps to be taken to help each designated successor qualify for the position to which he or she has been linked. Sample forms appear in Exhibits 7-2, 7-3, 7-4, 7-5, and 7-6.

Once drafted, the policy, procedures, and forms can be sent out to top managers for comment. This approach is best because it minimizes the amount of executive time which must be spent in meetings. If issues emerge that cannot be ironed out in this way, meetings may be held to arrive at consensus.

Fourth, the succession planning coordinator should review procedures regularly so they keep pace with organizational and environmental change. When first unveiled, succession planning procedures should be explained and the importance of the process should be emphasized. The CEO should unveil the process to dramatize its importance. A kickoff meeting or retreat led by the CEO can be followed up by briefings or training to describe detailed procedures to the users.

If the L & MD director has been asked by the CEO to be available to offer one-on-one counseling to senior managers as they plan individual development activities—and that is highly advisable—the CEO should say so in a kickoff meeting and encourage that interaction as necessary.

Fifth, the L & MD director should follow through once forms have been submitted to ensure that progress is being made on individual development plans. For instance, he or she may wish to phone key managers or pay them visits to review succession plans for their areas of responsibility and offer them specialized advice about ways to develop management employees or individuals possessing exceptional leadership potential. As positions become vacant, he or she may also be called on to help locate successors by using confidential succession planning information loaded on a personal computer.

Sixth, the L & MD director or coordinator should establish some means by which to measure program effectiveness as needs for management or leadership talent arise. To that end, some means must be devised by which to track the "hits" and "misses" of the succession planning program. He or she should

Exhibit 7-1
A Sample Succession Planning Policy

Purpose	To ensure replacements for key job incumbents and leaders in executive, management, technical, and professional positions in the organization. This policy covers middle management positions and above in (*name of organization*).
Desired Results	*The desired results of the succession planning program are to*: • Identify high-potential employees capable of rapid advancement to positions of higher responsibility than they presently occupy. • Ensure the systematic and long-term development of individuals to replace key job incumbents as need arises due to deaths, disabilities, retirements, and other unexpected losses. • Provide a continuous flow of talented people to meet the organization's management needs. • Meet the organization's need to exercise social responsibility by providing for the advancement of protected labor groups inside the organization.
Procedures	*The succession planning program will be carried out as follows*: • In January of each year, the L & MD director will arrange a meeting with the CEO to review results from the previous year's succession planning efforts and plan for the present year's process. • In February, top managers will attend a meeting coordinated by the L & MD director in which: • The CEO will emphasize the importance of succession planning and review the previous year's results. • The L & MD director will distribute forms and establish due dates for their completion and return. • The L & MD director will review the results of a computerized analysis to pinpoint areas of the organization in which predictable turnover, resulting from retirements or other changes, will lead to special needs for management talent.
Procedures	*The succession planning program will be carried out as follows*: • The results of a computerized analysis will be reviewed to demonstrate how successfully the organization has been attracting protected labor groups into high-level positions and to plot strategies for improving Affirmative Action practices. • In April, the forms will be completed and returned to the L & MD director. If necessary, a follow-up meeting will be held. In any case, the information will be deposited in a secure database for retrieval as need for management talent arises. • Throughout the year, the L & MD director will periodically visit top managers to review progress in developing identified successors throughout their areas of responsibility. • As need arises, the database will be accessed as a source of possible successors in the organization.

Exhibit 7-2
A Sample Personal History Form

Please fill in the information requested below.					
Biographical Information					
Name		**Job Title**		**Date of Birth**	
Organization		**Reports to**		**Date Appointed to Present Position**	
Date Hired		**Salary Level/Grade**			
Interests					
Completed Education					
Graduation Date	**Degree**		**Major**		**University/College**
Education in Progress					
Licenses/Accreditations/Professional Designations					
License/Accreditation	**Designation**		**Institution**		**Date Completed**
Employment History (with present employer)					
Job Titles	**Key Duties**			**Started**	**Ended**
Employment History (with previous employers)					
Job Titles	**Key Duties**			**Started**	**Ended**
Succession Candidates					
Succession Candidates			**Year Prepared**		

Exhibit 7-3
A Sample Succession Planning Chart

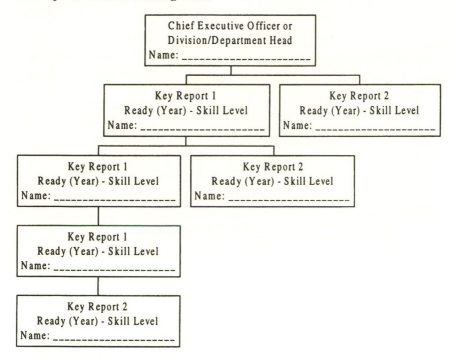

keep track of positions that were actually filled from within based on succession planning results. Positive comments about the program from executives should be put in writing so they may be shared with skeptics as testimonials.

Problems Affecting Succession Planning

Several problems may be encountered in succession planning programs. To overcome them, keep several points in mind.

The first point to remember is that succession planning is only one part of a comprehensive L & MD program. It is not the only part. It is not intended to head off all need for external recruiting. Nor is it intended to encourage promotion-from-within when alternative staffing methods will more effectively infuse new ideas into the organization and prevent inbreeding. But succession planning does encourage the development of internal talent, which may occur less predictably without a succession planning program designed to identify, assess, and prepare individuals for the future.

A second point to remember is that no successor is permanently designated as an "heir apparent." Successors may change from year to year. They may also change when external environmental conditions, competitive pressures, con-

Exhibit 7-4
A Sample Performance Appraisal Form

Employee's Name
Date of Appraisal
Appraiser
<div align="center">**Part I. Position Description**</div>
Directions: In the space below, describe the responsibilities of the individual performing this job. (*These responsibilities should be relatively stable and enduring.*) State these responsibilities in terms of the most typical activities performed in the position. Use additional paper if necessary.
Position Description:
<div align="center">**Part II. Performance Objectives**</div>
Directions: In item 1 below, describe specific, measurable objectives that are to be achieved on a continuous and regular basis by the individual in his or her position. (Base these objectives on the responsibilities set forth in Part I of this Appraisal Form.) In item 2 below, describe unique, measurable and one-time only objectives to be achieved over the course of the next appraisal period. Use additional paper if necessary.
Item 1--Position Responsibilities Stated in Measurable Terms
2. What specific, measurable responsibilities should the individual achieve in his or her position on a continuous and regular basis?
Item 2--Unique, Measurable, and One-Time Only Objectives to Be Achieved During the Next Appraisal Period
<div align="center">**Part III. Review Meetings**</div>
Directions to the Appraiser: Meet with the individual over the course of the appraisal period to provide guidance and suggestions for achieving requirements of the position and one-time objectives for the year. In the space below, make clear when these discussions occurred and what results or agreements stemmed from the discussions. Use additional paper if necessary, enclosing it in this appraisal booklet. (Enclose separate sheets if you hold more than one review meeting.)
Review Meeting Summary
Date   **Time**   **Results**
<div align="center">**Part IV. Performance Review**</div>
Directions: In the space below, assess how well the individual achieved performance objectives for his or her position during the appraisal period. Compare results at the end of the appraisal period to the position responsibilities and one-time objectives (set forth in Parts I and II of this form) established at the beginning of the appraisal period. Base the review on this comparison. Use additional paper if necessary.
4. Performance Review (Compare results to objectives)
<div align="center">**Part V. Management Skills**</div>
Directions for Appraisers: For each general management skill listed below, describe the employee's performance over the appraisal period. Appraise management employees only on skill areas applicable to them.

1	Planning
2	Controlling
3	Organizing
4	Budgeting

Exhibit 7-4 (continued)

5	Appraising		
6	Communicating		
7	Developing employees/oneself		
8	Making decisions		
9	Managing projects effectively		
10	Staffing the unit/department		
11	Respresenting the organization effectively		
12	Influencing others		
13	Making changes		
14	Dealing with changes		
15	Other skills (Specify)		
Employee Comments			
Approvals			
Employee	Date	Signature	
Appraised by	Date	Signature	
Authorized by	Date	Signature	
Effective Date:			

sumer preferences, position demands, or strategic plans also change. They should certainly change when individuals, otherwise designated as possible successors, experience dramatic setbacks in performance in their current positions. (Success in the existing job is a critical prerequisite for advancement to more responsible positions.)

A third point to remember is that key policymakers should decide upon a philosophy about candor in the succession planning program. In other words, should designated successors be told of their status? There is no simple answer to this question. Advantages and disadvantages can be cited on both sides of the question. If successors know their status, they may feel advancement is guaranteed and exemplary performance in their present positions does not have to be sustained. That is an argument against candor. The reverse can also be true: designated successors, if told of their status, may approach their present positions with renewed vigor and take an active role in developing themselves for future challenges facing them. That is an argument favoring candor.

A fourth point to remember: if designated successors are alerted to their status, they should never be queried about what developmental steps they should take to prepare for advancement. The rationale for this general rule is simple enough: they are not positioned to judge what they need. Only position incumbents, top

Exhibit 7-5
A Future Potential Appraisal Form

Employee's Name	Date of Hire
Date of Appraisal	Date of Appointment to Present Position
Appraiser	Position Level

Part I. Present Position Description/Performance

Directions: In the space below, describe the current responsibilities of this job and how well the job incumbent has been performing those duties over the last year.

Part II. Future Position Description/Performance

Directions: In the space below, describe the responsibilities of this job as you believe they should exist in five years if they are consistent with the organization's strategic plan and pressures exerted by external competition. Then describe how well the job incumbent is *presently* equipped to perform those *future* duties.

Part III. Development Needs

Directions: In the space below, describe the job incumbent's development needs by setting forth areas of difference between his or her present position description/performance (Part I) and future position description/performance (Part II).

Part IV. Developmental Plan

Directions: In the space below, describe how the individual should be developed to meet the needs outlined in Part III. Center attention on developmental activities that may occur over the next one to three years.

Need	How Should the Need Be Met?	Notes

Approvals

Employee	Date	Signature
Appraised by	Date	Signature
Effective Date		

Exhibit 7-6
A Sample Individual Development Plan

Employee's Name	Date

I. Objectives
What are the employee's *learning needs*, and what *learning objectives* will best help meet those needs over the next year?
Learning Objectives

II. Strategies/Methods
What learning strategies or methods will help the employee achieve the learning objectives outlined in Part I above?
Learning Strategies/Methods

III. Resources
What *resources*—time, money, material staff, or equipment—does the employee need to achieve the learning objectives listed in Part I by means of the strategies or methods listed in Part II?
Resources

IV. Evaluation Methods
How will the employee's achievement of learning objectives be measured? Describe evaluation and measurement methods for each learning objective.
Learning Objectives   *Evaluation and Measurement Methods*

Approvals		
Employee	Date	Signature
Appraised by	Date	Signature
Effective Date		

managers, and the L & MD director should be consulted on this issue. Key position incumbents have a proven track record. They are likely to be valuable resources for identifying strategies to help designated successors narrow the gap between the knowledge/skills they possess in their present positions and those needed for success in future positions. Top managers should be consulted because they have the best grasp of the organization's strategic plan, which implies new performance requirements over time. The L & MD director should also be consulted about possible L & MD methods that can be used to narrow gaps in knowledge or skill.

MANAGEMENT OR LEADERSHIP CAREER PLANNING PROGRAMS

When used as a formal L & MD method, a *management or leadership career planning program is a systematic means of identifying information about posi-*

tion requirements in an organizational setting, communicating that information to employees, and encouraging them to establish and work toward realistic career goals. In one sense, a management or leadership career planning program is a mirror image of a succession planning program because it is driven from the bottom up rather than (like most succession planning programs) from the top down. While the responsibility for career planning always remains an individual's responsibility,[2] career goal-setting can be greatly improved when the organization clarifies position requirements and career paths.

The Importance of Management or Leadership Career Planning

Few contemporary observers dispute that changes in labor market conditions are occurring more rapidly than ever before. Indeed, labor markets are growing more uncertain as organizations go bankrupt, downsize, relocate, move offshore, and undergo other changes. Careers and staffing arrangements have grown complex and dynamic.

Against this backdrop, management or leadership career planning is becoming more important. Employees at all levels of an organization's decision-making pyramid are no longer confident that, as in times past, they can start working for one employer and remain there for a lifetime. To serve their own best interests, they must keep their skills finely honed so that they can compete in the labor market—on a moment's notice, if need be. For this reason, they must plan their careers consistently, incessantly, and even obsessively.

How Do Management or Leadership Career Planning Programs Differ?

Management or leadership career planning programs, like career planning programs geared to other groups, fall into three general categories: (1) *formal programs* in which the organization takes active steps to encourage career planning and provide information about position requirements and career paths; (2) *informal programs* in which individuals are provided with general, but not organization-specific, career planning information and carry out career planning activities on their own; and (3) combination programs in which the organization takes active steps to encourage career planning while individuals take the initiative for their own career planning efforts.

When Should Management or Leadership Career Planning Be a Programmatic Focus of L & MD?

Use management or leadership career planning as a programmatic focus of L & MD when it is necessary to increase the participation, involvement, and ownership of individuals in their L & MD activities. Career planning helps individuals see that L & MD activities are, in fact, vehicles for helping them realize their career goals. In addition, career planning helps individuals reach a better understanding that the responsibility for their lives and careers rests with them and not with their immediate organizational superiors, organizations, or co-workers.

Designing and Implementing Management or Leadership Career Planning Programs

The appropriate steps to take in establishing a management or leadership career planning program depend on what kind of program it is—formal, informal, or combination.

A *formal career planning program* is carefully planned. It begins with a few specific questions: (1) What should be the program's purpose? (2) What job classifications, groups, or functional areas should receive special attention? (3) Who should participate in program operations? Often, the highest priorities are devoted to groups experiencing higher-than-average turnover and to programs designed to encourage cultural, racial, and sexual diversity in the organization's ranks.

Subsequent steps in designing and implementing a formal career planning program include identifying organizational needs, selecting target groups, evaluating existing career patterns, selecting appropriate change efforts, effecting appropriate change, and assessing results.[3] Successful programs involve employees, their immediate organizational superiors, and top managers.

A *pilot program* is often a starting point for a formal career planning program. It is a small-scale effort directed at specially targeted departments or occupational groups. Immediate organizational superiors are encouraged to take an active role in program development, are briefed on program particulars, and are encouraged to promote career planning activities among workers reporting to them. Few organizations will choose to direct career planning programs to management employees alone, though some may choose to pilot a career planning program in the management ranks and later extend the program to other worker groups.

It is common to begin a pilot program by

- Clarifying management position requirements (if position descriptions do not exist or are outdated) or competencies distinguishing exemplary from fully successful performers.

- Forecasting future position requirements or competencies required.

- Clarifying key differences between higher-level and lower-level management positions.

- Establishing vertical career paths showing desirable or typical progressions from lower- to higher-level positions.

- Establishing horizontal career paths showing desirable or typical "position broadening" that can occur within an existing position.

Participants in formal career planning programs are frequently trained on career planning methods and furnished with the resources appropriate for setting career goals and taking career action in the context of their organizations (see the sample outline of the training program in Exhibit 7-7). Those who counsel others on career issues may also receive special training on effective career counseling methods.

An *informal management or leadership career planning program* may also begin with needs assessment. However, the focus is on the individual rather than on the organization. Often, L & MD directors, L & MD coordinators, or HR specialists spearhead the effort. Then career planning materials are gathered and made available. Workers are able to check out these materials for their own use—or for counseling selected individuals on career issues.

Many organizations have experienced considerable success with in-house career planning programs. Of special note are *bottom-up programs* in which workers learn to conduct career planning discussions and establish written career plans with their immediate organizational superiors. Unlike performance appraisal discussions focusing on past job performance, career planning discussions focus on future career goals and methods of realizing them. All levels of the organization's workforce—not just management employees—may be involved in these voluntary (rather than mandatory) programs. Special career planning forms help workers to formulate what career goals to pursue, identify how to achieve those goals, and set the agenda for a meeting to discuss their career goals with their immediate organizational superiors (see the sample form appearing in Exhibit 7-8).

Problems Affecting Management or Leadership Career Planning Programs

No L & MD method is foolproof. This principle applies as much to management or leadership career planning programs as it does to other L & MD programs.

One problem with management or leadership career planning programs is that they rely heavily on the element of trust between employees and their organizational superiors. Employees must be truthful about their career goals and plans. But several issues undermine such truthfulness. For instance, workers may have their hearts set on career goals *outside* their present employer—for example, they may aspire to become owners of small businesses, independent entrepreneurs, consultants, stay-at-home parents, or caregivers for elderly relatives. Employees may worry that candor about such goals may undermine their future career prospects with their present employer. While most employees trust their immediate superiors, a disquieting minority does not.

Exhibit 7-7
**A Sample Training Course Outline on Career Planning for Management
Employees and Leadership Prospects**

Purpose	To review key issues and practices in career planning for management employees and leadership prospects of the organization
Objectives	*Upon completing this course, participants should be able to*: 1. Define career planning 2. Explain the importance of career planning 3. Point out the importance of the current job as it affects career planning 4. Describe how to assess personal strengths and weaknesses 5. Identify personal values in career planning 6. Describe career options in the organization 7. Chart personal career goals 8. Draft and communicate a written career plan

Course Outline	I. Introduction
	  A. Describe
	    1. The course title
	    2. The purpose of the course
	    3. The objectives of the course
	    4. The structure of the course
	  B. Ask participants to summarize their personal goals for the course
	
	II. What is career planning?
	  A. Definition of career planning
	  B. Importance of career planning
	  C. The importance of taking personal responsibility for career planning
	
	III. How does the present job fit in to career planning?
	  A. Surfacing key issues affecting the present job
	  B. Surfacing key values
	  C. Understanding the importance of the present job as it affects career plans
	
	IV. What about the future?
	  A. What are your present strengths and weaknesses?
	    1. Definitions of strengths and weaknesses
	    2. Methods of identifying strengths and weaknesses
	    3. Individual activity
	  B. What trends affect career planning?
	    1. National trends
	    2. Industry trends
	    3. Organizational strategy
	    4. Present/future career paths
	    5. Effects of strengths/weaknesses on future career prospects
	
	V. How is career planning carried out?
	  A. Stating goals
	  B. Establishing time frames and choosing methods
	  C. Communicating goals and building alliances
	  D. Writing down the career plan

Exhibit 7-7 (continued)

Course Outline	VI. Conclusion
	A. Evaluate
	1. Personal career plans
	2. The course
	B. Establish
	1. Methods of self follow-up
	2. Methods of follow-up with immediate organizational superiors

Nor is candor a troubling issue for employees alone: their immediate organizational superiors may face barriers to it as well. For instance, they may be unable to share what they know about the organization's plans to offer early retirement incentives or eliminate lines of business—all issues that may affect individual career decisions. They may also be prohibited by policy, philosophy, or tradition from sharing what they may know about an individual's prospects for the future as tentatively outlined in succession plans.

There is no simple solution for overcoming these problems. The best advice is to clarify the parameters of career planning programs. Perhaps individuals can be limited to considering career goals in one organization. A key assumption may have to be that the program is based on "all other things being equal"—meaning that there will be no major changes in the organization's or individual's plans.

A second problem with management or leadership career planning programs is that they can create legal liability or build unrealistic employee expectations unless carefully handled. Employees' immediate organizational superiors must be trained to avoid making oral or written promises that they cannot keep. Top performing employees may grow disenchanted if they feel betrayed on promises of promotions. Such promises may also be construed as legally binding contractual agreements. Statements like these should be avoided:

- "If you do all these things we have discussed, then you will be promoted."

- "You can't be fired here."

- "If you maintain good performance in this organization, the chance is zero that you will be laid off."

- "Don't worry about your future. I'll see to it that you receive the next promotion."

Instead of making sweeping and dangerous statements like these, managers should emphasize the tentative nature of organizational goals and plans, explaining that they are always subject to change due to the effects of a dynamic, competitive environment. Immediate organizational superiors should promise only what they are certain they can deliver.

Exhibit 7-8

A Sample Leadership and Management Career Planning Form

Name of Employee *(Last, First, Middle Initial)*	
Budget Center	
Job Title	
Immediate Supervisor *(Last, First, Middle Initial)*	
Start Date	**Date Appointed to Present Position**

General Instructions to Management Employees and Leadership Prospects

The purpose of this form is to help you structure your thinking about your career plans. Complete the form, attaching additional paper if you feel it is necessary. Then forward a copy of this form to your immediate supervisor and schedule a meeting with him or her to discuss your career plans. It is not mandatory for you to complete this form or to meet with your immediate supervisor about it. If you meet with your immediate supervisor to discuss career issues, please forward a copy of this form to the Human Resources Department for use in identifying company Leadership and Management Development needs.

Part I. Assessing Personal Career Goals and Interests

What would you like to be doing in this organization in 3–5 years?

Part II. Identifying Jobs Within the Organization Which Match up to Personal Career Goals

What jobs in the organization do you feel will help you become what you want to be in the future? How well do you feel they will make use of your special talents and skills? What are those talents/skills? What would you like to know about those jobs?

Part III. Assessing Personal Strengths and Weaknesses Relative to Necessary Qualifications for the Jobs

How well qualified do you feel you are at present to do a job you would like to do in the future in this organization? In what ways do you feel especially well prepared now to do this job? In what ways do you feel less than well prepared?

Part IV. Expressing Interest in Promotion, Transfer, or Increasing Technical Competence to the Supervisor and to the Human Resources Department

What career advice would you especially like to get from your immediate organizational superior? from the HR Department? What information would help you establish clear career goals and work toward preparing yourself for the future?

Part V. Identifying Conditions Inside or Outside the Organization Which May Change Necessary Minimum Job Qualifications

How might changing conditions inside or outside the organization affect what you need to know or do to achieve your career goals? How might changing organizational policies, procedures, work methods, or organizational conditions affect what you need to know or do to prepare for meeting your career goals in the organization?

Part VI. Prepare a Personal Action Plan to Narrow Gaps Between the Individual's Present Knowledge, Skills, and Experience and Those that are Necessary to Meet the Minimum Qualifications for the Job?

What can you do over the next year to equip yourself with the knowledge, skills and experiences you need to prepare for achieving your long-term career goals? Consider such activities as forming a mentoring relationship with someone who is doing what you want to do or who is familiar with how to advance in a given occupational field; seeking approval from your supervisor to work on short-term assignments that are related to your career goals; seeking long-term work assignments on your present job which are related to your long-term career goals; seeking a lateral transfer, temporarily or permanently, so as to provide experience in line with long-term career

Exhibit 7-8 (continued)

goals; seeking approval from your immediate supervisor to do more work similar to what the individual is presently doing (job enlargement); seeking approval from your immediate supervisor to take on additional duties which require more responsibility (job enrichment); preparing an independent study plan to learn more about a new subject, occupation, or discipline (career diversification); identifying meetings, seminars, conferences, workshops, or other organized events where you can learn new skills or knowledge pertinent to your career goals in the organization; teaching seminars, presenting at conferences, or otherwise learning by doing the work. Meet with your immediate supervisor and establish specific objectives for the next year in the space below.

Part VII. Follow-Up
How well do you feel you have been making progress in realizing your career goals in the organization? What significant strides have you made?

Approvals	
Signature of Employee	Signature of Employee's Supervisor
Date	Date

INTERNAL GROUP TRAINING PROGRAMS

Businesses in the United States spend large sums each year on supervisory, management, executive, and leadership training. A substantial portion of this training is provided by in-house staff only. Higher and additional percentages are achieved when in-house staff is coupled with outside vendors in joint ventures.

Many topics treated by in-house training staff focus on supervisory and management issues. The most common training courses offered in-house center on performance appraisals, leadership, hiring/selection, interpersonal skills, team building, delegation skills, and employee training methods (train-the-trainer). Each year other internal group training programs are offered on topical issues or trends. For example, at this writing many organizations are also offering internal group training on customer service, TQM, and team building. Rothwell's 1998 survey on L & MD identified top trends affecting L & MD programs in the future. These are described in the respondents' own words below.

Trends Affecting L & MD Programs

> *Question: What major trends inside or outside your organization* do you feel will affect efforts in your organization to develop management and/or leadership talent? List them in order of importance below, with 1 = most important. (*Examples might include restructuring, installation of team-based management, or others.*)

Trends Ranked #1

- Growth—explosive
- Merger

- Move to team-based delivery of services
- Top executive's plan to implement a corporate university
- Downsizing of management staffs
- New head of HR department will start next week
- Culture transition to team-based organization
- Retirement of key managers
- Funerals
- Need to increase organizational effectiveness—doing more with less requires effective leaders who can instill a sense of accountability, vision, and empowerment in staff at all levels
- Availability of tailored corporate university
- Changes in the practice of law. Demands are very different nowadays. They are scared about the changes.
- Culture change → help it
- Extremely fast growth pace of our concept—we are doubling our size every year
- Acquisitions or expansion efforts will drive need
- "Constant" corporate reorganizations and corporate turnover of leadership roles
- Succession planning
- The inability to find candidates outside the organization with the specific skills I need
- Search for final stage of venture capital
- Customer pressures
- Impact of managed care on health care delivery
- We've been acquired by two companies who will split us up next year
- Pace at which we are growing (promoting those with little supervisory experience.)
- Ownership change and shift in corporate culture
- Rapid expansion—extremely fast-paced growth, not enough time to properly train and develop
- Reinventing government
- Deregulation of electric utility industry
- Reduced funding due to reduced income—due to competition
- Continued reduction of funding by the Department of Energy
- Business growth and complexity
- Keeping up with the need for more managers (we've recently acquired a company 3 times our size and the top executives have been shifting talent in an effort to "seed" the new portion of the business)
- Budget. I think increases in budget will be the first thing we see as importance increases
- Flattening of organizations—need for fewer managers
- More action learning or self-discovery processes to create longer-lasting impact
- Job-based simulations

- We've been without a president for several months, when a new one is in place, that may affect our management development efforts
- ISO 9001
- Retirements—lack of bench strength
- Talent shortages
- Downsizing, cost-cutting
- Tight workforce—lack of available talent
- Demand to retain and develop technology talent
- Potential for affiliation/merger with another organization
- Increased competitive pressure
- Competition from other employers who do focus on developing management/leadership
- Competition for talent

Trends Ranked #2

- Talent pool, ability to develop
- Hire versus train
- Growth—demand for increased management skill
- Strategic objectives which focus on redesign, re-engineering
- Cost reductions
- Acquisitions of new lines of business
- Installation of "Team Manufacturing" system
- Increasing turnover due to tight labor market
- Retirements
- Incredibly competitive labor market
- New Managing Partner is making it an issue and they are worried about the impact
- Turnover → hurt it but show cause for succession management
- State of economy means we are experiencing increasing difficulty in finding high-caliber management candidates and retaining them
- Retirements of many seasoned managers/executives
- Pressure for constant improvement without celebration of improvements accomplished
- The need to foster loyalty to my organization other than via salary compensation
- Beta test of developing software
- Technological changes
- Transition from technical expertise as a rationale for promotion to focus on leadership skills
- Philosophical change of upper management to staff offices with more personnel
- Dealing with budget constraints
- Reorganization of municipal utilities to municipal authorities

- Lack of support from management
- The ability of internal organizations to obtain funding from other sources outside the Department of Energy
- Competition for talent
- Expanding geographically—were just in California, now we are nationwide
- Media. We are moving toward other methods versus standard classroom action
- Greater responsibility by individuals for personal development outside normal working plans and/or time
- Self-directed work teams
- Lack of cross-functional experiences
- Desire to create a more diverse senior management team
- Move toward high-performing work teams
- High turnover
- Change in senior executive leadership
- Shift to more high-tech services being offered by our company
- Budgetary constraints
- Retirement 12/99

Trends Ranked #3
- Retain
- Need for succession planning
- Need for broader knowledge *and* more depth
- Anticipated increase in number of employees
- Competition for market share
- Cost of programs
- On-the-job retirements while waiting for a funeral
- Incredibly competitive industry. We have to have the *best* staff developing their people to optimum potential in order to survive
- It's new to the firm and lawyers don't like risk taking
- Stagnation → hurt it → nowhere for talent to go but out
- Due to 1 and 2 above—retention can be a problem because concept is complex, hours are long, labor pool bad → increased stress levels!
- Tying compensation or bonus to stock price performance
- Software launch
- Grooming prospective supervisors
- Rapid process of change
- Resolving labor/management issues
- Staff restructuring
- Changes in company structure—law of champions

- Importance of survival versus development embraced by those in charge of budgets
- Company commitment to development
- Increased cycle time or need for greater speed, shorter lead times for everything
- Growth
- Interest in building a more flexible adaptive leadership team
- Increased "business focus" versus "Good Old Boy" network
- Profitable year to allow for additional training monies
- Rapid growth of our company requires more people in leadership positions
- Geographic barriers (e.g., several offices in three states/regions)
- Industry competitiveness, mergers/acquisitions, international expansion

Defining Internal Group Training

Internal group training is often planned, designed, delivered, and followed up systematically so as to narrow the gap between what individuals know or do and what they should know or do to (1) Prepare for changes in their jobs or responsibilities, (2) Qualify for vertical or horizontal advancement, (3) Orient themselves to new work roles upon promotion, (4) Keep their knowledge or skills up-to-date. It is *systematic* because there is a direct relationship between the processes of identifying performance problems, assessing training needs, writing performance objectives, selecting training methods, delivering training, and choosing evaluation approaches.

Internal group training for management employees or those exhibiting exceptional leadership potential is prepared and/or conducted by members of the organization—often by the L & MD director, L & MD coordinator, or internal training and development specialists. Its chief advantage is that it can be uniquely geared—in a way that is difficult, time-consuming, and expensive for external training vendors—to the organization's culture, philosophy, work requirements, and procedures so as to increase the possibility that what is learned will be applied on the participant's job.

However, recent writers on L & MD have pointed out that much of the substantial investment businesses make in internal group management or leadership training each year is of questionable value because on-the-job results are often difficult to see or measure. Another reason: it is difficult to ensure that the on-the-job work environment supports and allows for application of what is learned.

When Should Internal Group Training Be a Programmatic Focus of L & MD?

Use internal group training as a solution only when performance problems stem from deficiencies of knowledge, skill, or attitude. More specifically, internal group training is an appropriate focus for L & MD when

- The organization is large enough to have a steady stream of individuals entering and progressing through the ranks

- Groups of people share common (macro) learning needs

- On-the-job training is not likely to produce desired results at all or else is not likely to produce those results quickly enough

- Consistency of training content across learners is important

Internal group training takes advantage of economies of scale. It reduces the time and effort necessary to train individuals on similar issues or organizational policies, procedures, or requirements. It is thus advantageous for its consistency in training groups of people and its efficiency in training them in a shorter time span than would typically be possible if individuals were trained one-on-one.

But internal group training is not appropriate when performance problems stem from causes other than deficiencies of knowledge, skill, or attitude. Nor is it appropriate when the organization is too small to warrant internal group training, individuals experience widely diverse learning needs, on-the-job training is more cost-effective, or methods other than internal group training will be less expensive in achieving desired changes in individual performance.[4]

Planning Internal Group Training

Of all L & MD methods, internal group training lends itself best to systematic instructional planning. Recall from Chapter 4 that theories of *curriculum design*—that is, approaches to planning instruction or learning—vary widely. A management or leadership training curriculum is essentially an instructional plan that ties together management or leadership training and helps individuals who make transitions into, through, or out of the organization's ranks. Some subject-centered curricula are too rigid, forcing all learners to participate in the same experiences, like the sequence of course titles outlined in Exhibit 7-9. They imply a one-size-fits-all mentality, increasingly eschewed by recent writers on L & MD because it is at odds with recent trends pointing toward increasingly individualized work place learning. Other approaches to curriculum design produce more flexible learning plans that allow for individualization of planned learning experiences and accommodate individual learning styles. Such instruction is more effectively planned through individualized development plans.

Often, L & MD specialists aim to strike a balance between standardized (rigid) and individualized (flexible) training. After all, everyone who is promoted, transferred, or hired into a new position will share certain common learning needs. But they will also experience uniquely individualized or job-specific learning needs. What is necessary, then, is a plan for group instruction to satisfy macro learning needs *and* a plan for individual instruction to satisfy micro learning needs.

While there are various ways to plan internal group training experiences,

Exhibit 7-9
A Sample Leadership and Management Training Curriculum

Job Category	Course Titles	Length
Presupervisory/ Supervisory	• Orientation to the Role of Supervisor	1 Day
	• General Principles of Supervision	1 Day
	• Principles of Labor Relations	1 Day
	• Setting Performance Objectives	1 Day
	• Conducting Performance Appraisals	1 Day
	• Facilitating Health, Wellness, and Safety	1 Day
	• Handling Stress	1 Day
	• Leading Meetings	1 Day
	• Managing Conflict	1 Day
	• Listening Skills	1 Day
	• Written Communication Skills	1 Day
	• Interviewing Skills	1 Day
	• Dealing with Employee Performance Problems	1 Day
	• Understanding the Supervisor's Role in Strategic Plans	1 Day
Premanager/ Manager	• Orientation to the Role of Manager	1 Day
	• Managing People	1 Day
	• Managing Quality	1 Day
	• Establishing and Managing Workteams	1 Day
	• Managing Time	1 Day
	• Solving Problems and Creative Thinking	1 Day
	• The Manager as Career Coach and Career Counselor	1 Day
	• Strategic Thinking, Planning, and Managing	1 Day
Pre-Executive/ Executive	• Orientation to the Role Executive	1 Day
	• Annual Briefing on Legal Trends Affecting the Industry	1 Day
	• Annual Briefing on Strategic Thinking, Planning, and Managing	1 Day
	• Annual Briefing on Industry Trends	1 Day

depending on the approach to curriculum design that is selected, one ambitious approach is to follow a twelve-step instructional systems design model for management or leadership training.[5]

The first step in the instructional systems design model is distinguishing between issues appropriate for training and issues more appropriate for other methods. To that end, start out by asking several questions: (1) Is the problem caused, in whole or part, by a learning need? (2) Does a group of workers share a learning need? (3) Is the learning need likely to persist over time as new people enter—and progress through—the ranks? (4) Does the organization have the time, money, and expertise required to offer internal group training to address the learning need? If the answer to question 1 is ''no,'' then some method other than internal group training should be used to meet the need (see Exhibit 3-1). If the answer to question 2 is ''no,'' then group training is inappropriate. The learning need calls for individualized training. If the answer to question 3 is ''no,'' then it is a one-time need that may be met more cost-effectively by sending people outside the organization. If the answer to question 4 is "no," then internal group training is not likely to work. An external vendor may have to be used, or else workers may have to be sent outside the organization for external training.

If all answers are "yes," then internal group training is appropriate. Move on to the second step in the instructional systems design model: assessing the learning needs of management employees or other individuals demonstrating exceptional leadership potential. (This issue was treated in Chapter 3.)

The third step in the instructional systems design model is assessing relevant learner characteristics. Before designing internal group training, you must know something about the learners:

- Who are they?
- What do they already know about the issue?
- What problems are they facing?
- How much do they want to learn about the issue?
- What are their individual learning styles?

Just as products or services should be geared to meet the needs of an identifiable market, internal group training should be tailored to meet the learning needs of an identifiable group of targeted learners. Learner characteristics should influence the way that learning experiences are designed.

The fourth step of the instructional systems design model is assessing the work setting(s) in which the learning will be subsequently applied. Before designing internal group training, find out about the work setting:

- What conditions in the work setting may impede management employees (or others demonstrating leadership potential) from applying what they learn in internal group training?
- What conditions in the work setting will encourage management employees (or others demonstrating leadership potential) to apply what they learn in internal group training?
- Are sufficient time, money, staff, and other resources available to permit learners to apply what they learn?

Just as products or services should be positioned so they can be sold and should be designed to meet the requirements of the users, so too should internal group training be tailored to fit the conditions in which the learners will perform. If a problem exists with the work setting, then separate action should be taken to correct the problem.

The fifth step in the instructional systems design model is analyzing the work performed. Before designing internal group training, you must know about the work performed by the targeted learners:

- What do they do?
- How do the targeted learners perform the work?
- How is the subject of the training related to the work, work methods, work procedures, and problems confronting those performing the work?
- What knowledge and skills are needed now to perform the work?
- What knowledge and skills will be needed to perform the work competently in the future?

Management or leadership training should be tied to the present and/or future work performed by the targeted learners.

The sixth step in the instructional systems design model is preparing performance objectives and measurement methods. A *performance objective*, synonymous with *instructional* or *learning objective*, is perhaps best understood as a statement of the results desired. When a performance objective is met, a training need is satisfied. Objectives are thus designed to narrow or close a gap between existing and desired performance. A *measurement method* is a means of assessing a performance objective. It answers this question: ''how well was the performance objective achieved by the learner?''

Start the process of designing internal group training by transforming statements of needs into performance objectives. With the results of a needs assessment in hand, begin drafting performance objectives to clarify what participants in training should know, do, or feel *at the end* of the learning experience. Stated another way, think of a performance objective as a description of what people should (1) Be able to *do* when they get up and leave the room after completing an internal group training experience, (2) *How well* they should be able to do it, (3) *Under what conditions* or *with what resources* they should be able to perform. Perhaps an example will help to clarify these issues. Suppose you are designing an internal group training course on job interviewing for supervisors. Begin course preparation by first investigating how supervisors conduct interviews and how they should conduct them. Pinpoint the gap between what is presently being done and what should be done. Then prepare performance objectives and measurement methods to describe and measure what the targeted learners should know or do when they complete the training.

State performance objectives in this way: *Upon completing this training, participants should be able to*: [*Begin with a verb and clarify the conditions in which the task will be performed and the means by which success will be measured.*]

Some writers on instructional design suggest that pre- and post-test items should be developed directly from performance objectives before training materials are selected, prepared, or selected and modified.[6] While most people think of test items as written questions posed in true-false, multiple choice, essay, or other formats, they may also take the form of role plays, simulations, or practically oriented work demonstrations.

The seventh step in the instructional systems design model is clarifying the training delivery techniques to be used. At this writing, over 600 management or leadership training delivery techniques have been identified.[7] Many training delivery techniques are popular. Among them are the following:

- Videotapes
- Lectures
- One-on-one instruction
- Role plays
- Audiotapes
- Games/simulations
- Slides
- Films
- Case studies
- Self-assessment and self-testing instruments
- Noncomputerized self-study programs
- Video teleconferencing
- Teleconferencing (audio only)
- Computer conferencing

Exhibit 7-10 lists these techniques, explains when they are appropriate, and summarizes their key advantages and disadvantages. Some techniques may be used by themselves for individualized training, but many techniques are often combined when delivering internal group training. The most popular combination: video and lecture.

The eighth step in the instructional systems design model is selecting, designing, or selecting and modifying internal group training materials. Once performance objectives have been stated and delivery methods have been chosen, it is time to select, design, or modify instructional materials. We use the term *select* to mean sourcing from existing printed, published, distributed, or otherwise available material; we use the term *design* to mean preparing instructional materials from scratch for internal use; and we use the term *modify* to mean revise to suit the unique needs of one organization or one group of learners.

Selecting materials is more common now than a decade ago because training material—so-called *off-the-shelf material*—is readily available for purchase from many commercial publishers, video distributors, software vendors, and other sources. For instance, the American Management Association has a catalog containing many self-study management courses that can be adapted for group delivery or used, as intended, for self-study. Other sources of material include Human Resource Development Press, John Wiley, and Jossey-Bass/Pfeiffer. Published books and articles can also be made into training materials, although

Exhibit 7-10
Techniques for Delivering Internal Group Training

Method	Appropriate Uses	Key Advantages and Disadvantages
Videotape	Meeting learning objectives tied to visual identification	• **Advantage(s)**: Captures attention through the senses of sight and sound • **Disadvantage(s)**: Does not work well for introducing complex theories or giving hands-on practice
Lecture	Meeting learning objectives tied to facts or theories	• **Advantage(s)**: Efficient method for communicating information; familiar to most people from their school experiences • **Disadvantage(s)**: Depends heavily on skills of presenter; can be boring; listeners can hear faster than speakers can talk
One-on-one instruction	Meeting learning objectives tied to comprehending and applying facts, theories, principles, and motor skills	• **Advantage(s)**: Permits immediate feedback; transfer of learning is not a problem because the learner is usually positioned in the work site when he or she receives instruction • **Disadvantage(s)**: Can be disorganized and unstructured
Role Play	Meeting learning objectives tied to comprehending and applying facts, theories, principles, and motor skills	• **Advantage(s)**: Builds learner involvement; provides means by which learners can practice what they learn • **Disadvantage(s)**: May be difficult for learners to engage themselves in artificial roles and experiences
Audiotape	Meeting learning objectives that rely on the sense of hearing	• **Advantage(s)**: Relatively inexpensive to produce; lends itself well to use in automobile commutes • **Disadvantage(s)**: Difficult to use as a stand-alone medium because the learner's attention will wander in group presentations in which audiotapes are used
Games/ Simulations	Meeting learning objectives tied to comprehending and applying facts, theories, principles, and motor skills	• **Advantage(s)**: Build learner involvement; provide means by which learners can practice what they learn • **Disadvantage(s)**: May be difficult for learners to act within the rules of games or live up to the spirit of simulations
Slides	Meeting learning objectives tied to visual identification	• **Advantage(s)**: Easy, inexpensive to prepare when computer software assistance is used; eye-popping colors intensity visual stimulation • **Disadvantage(s)**: Cannot be used effectively without special equipment or without a darkened room
Film	Meeting learning objectives tied to visual identification	• **Advantage(s)**: Captures attention through senses of sight and hearing • **Disadvantage(s)**: Does not work well for introducing complex theories or giving hands-on practice; increasingly obsolete when compared to more conveniently used videotapes
Case Study	Meeting learning objectives tied to comprehending and applying facts, theories, principles, and motor skills	• **Advantage(s)**: Builds learner involvement; provides means by which learners can practice what they learn • **Disadvantage(s)**: May be difficult for learners to identify and/or solve problems without more details than are typically provided in most case studies
Self-Assessment and Self-Testing Instruments	Meeting learning objectives tied to self-discovery and affect (feeling-oriented) issues, such as "personality type"	• **Advantage(s)**: Provoke individual insight; motivate people to learn • **Disadvantage(s)**: Expensive; difficult to validate issues

Exhibit 7-10 (continued)

Method	Appropriate Uses	Key Advantages and Disadvantages
Noncomputerized Self-study Programs (such as correspondence study)	Meeting learning objectives tied to facts, theories, or principles	• **Advantage(s)**: Easy to use; easy to distribute • **Disadvantage(s)**: Difficult to write; difficult to keep current
Video	Meeting learning objectives tied to senses of sight and hearing	• **Advantage(s)**: Captures attention • **Disadvantage(s)**: Does not work well for introducing complex theories or for giving hands-on practice
Teleconferencing	Meeting learning objectives tied to facts and theories	• **Advantage(s)**: Relatively inexpensive to present • **Disadvantage(s)**: Difficult to use as a stand-alone medium because the attention of learners will wander in group presentations, much as it will during audio-tape presentations
Traditional computer-based training	Meeting learning objectives tied to facts, theories, or principles	• **Advantage(s)**: Easy to use; fast • **Disadvantage(s)**: Hard to keep learners interested; may be unstructured and poorly organized; requires special equipment to use
World Wide Web–based training	Meeting learning objectives tied to facts, theories, or principles	• **Advantage(s)**: Easy to access with the appropriate equipment and browser; fast • **Disadvantage(s)**: Hard to keep learners interested; may be unstructured and poorly organized; requires special equipment to use; social needs of learners may not be taken into account unless planned

copyright restrictions should be scrupulously observed. Computer-based or World Wide Web–based training is also available on a broad range of topics from many organizations.

To select materials, L & MD specialists should rely on their performance objectives as a guide for undertaking a search. They should start out with two key questions: (1) What are learners supposed to do? and (2) What materials or activities will help them achieve the objectives? They can then undertake a search for previously written books, articles, videotapes, audiotapes, research, and activities to help achieve the performance objectives.

Designing materials, while costly and time-consuming, is a third and popular alternative. It is appropriate when the training content is to be centered around unique practices of one organization and when it is important to use actual forms, procedures, or methods used in one organization. For instance, L & MD specialists may tailor training to suit one organization's policies and procedures regarding employee performance appraisals, employment interviews, or progressive discipline.

To design internal group training materials, L & MD specialists usually begin with an outline called a *syllabus*. Each performance objective becomes the basis for each part of the course outline. The outline can stand alone, sufficient as a *lesson plan* to guide subject matter specialists who serve as instructors. Alternatively, the outline can become the basis for a detailed lesson plan to guide

Exhibit 7-11
A Sample Lesson Plan Format

Procedures	Lesson Outline
• Hand out an *Attendance Sheet*	• Give the course title: *The Career Counseling Workshop*
• Display V-1, *"The Purpose of the Course"*	• Give the purpose of the course:
	Course Purpose
	To introduce supervisors, managers, and executives to effective career counseling methods
• Display V-2, *"The Objectives of the Course"*	• Give the objectives of the course:
	Course Objectives
	Upon completing this course, participants should be able to:
	• Define *career counseling*
	• Explain the value of career counseling
	• Describe key steps in a model of the career counseling process
	• Demonstrate each step in the model of career counseling
	• Identify personal values in career planning

prospective instructors who are not necessarily experts on the subject. A detailed lesson plan is advantageous because it ensures consistency in training across groups. It can also become the basis for video or audio scripting—or preparation of other media. A sample lesson plan format appears in Exhibit 7-11.

Modifying materials is the middle ground between selecting and designing instructional materials. First, L & MD specialists must locate materials from inside or outside the organization. Then they must modify the materials for instructional use to ensure they will help achieve identified performance objectives. Finally, they should have the materials reviewed by subject matter experts (SMEs) from inside or outside the organization to ensure they are accurate, current, and appropriate.

The ninth step in the instructional systems design model is planning and monitoring the instructional design process. Few L & MD specialists would advise leaping directly from preparing training materials to delivering the training, though novices may be tempted to do just that. It is better to test and revise materials before offering the training. Instructional materials may be tested in several ways. (Strategies for testing materials are described in Chapter 10.)

The tenth step in the instructional systems design model is conducting the training. Few L & MD specialists can dispute the importance of delivery, since all previous steps in planning instruction culminate at that time. Effective classroom delivery is a more complex subject than it appears to be. Many books have been written about it. Here are a few useful tips for conducting successful internal group training sessions:

- Plan and rehearse the session carefully beforehand
- Arrange the facilities in a way appropriate to the experience
- Make sure you have the right number of handouts
- Arrange to have needed equipment on hand, checking well before a training session begins to make sure the equipment is in working order
- Start the session by giving the title of the course, reviewing its purpose, describing the performance objectives, and summarizing what topics will be treated in the session
- Provide information about needs assessment results so participants will understand the gap between *what is* and *what should be*
- Introduce yourself and ask participants to introduce themselves when they do not already know each other
- Provide an opportunity for participants to surface issues of importance to them, perhaps by going around the room and asking them, "What do you hope to learn about today, and why?"
- Ask questions frequently—about one every 2–3 minutes
- Maintain effective eye contact with the participants
- Vary your voice tone
- Move out with participants rather than lurking behind a podium
- Avoid disputes with argumentative participants so you will not dampen group spirit and thereby reduce participation
- Provide a forum to discuss obstacles that keep participants from applying on the job what they learn in training
- Ask participants to surface suggestions or strategies for overcoming obstacles that keep them from applying what they learn
- Ask participants to offer suggestions for improving the training session—and take their advice

The eleventh step in the instructional systems design model is evaluating training results. There are four levels of evaluation: *participant reactions, participant learning, participant performance*, and *organizational results*.[8] Evaluation will be covered at greater length in Chapter 10.

The twelfth and final step in the instructional systems design model is following up to ensure that what is learned in training is applied by learners on the job. After all, off-the-job learning will be of minimal value in improving performance if people do not apply what they learn. Really part of evaluation,

Exhibit 7-12
A List of Methods to Improve Transfer of Learning from Internal Group Training to the Job

Before Training Delivery	• Involve targeted participants and their immediate organizational superiors in the instructional design process • Feed needs assessment results back to prospective participants and their immediate organizational superiors so as to stimulate interest and create an impetus for change • Visit the work site and identify obstacles that will prevent transfer of learning • Plan incentives for transfer of learning
During Training Delivery	• Ask the immediate organizational superiors of targeted participants to speak on the importance of the topic during the training session • Ask learners to surface barriers to transfer of learning and devise strategies to overcome them • Ask the learners' immediate organizational superiors to attend training so as to increase the learners' accountability for applying what they learn
After Training Delivery	• Build measures of application into job descriptions and performance appraisals to encourage transfer of learning • Visit the work site of past participants in training and ask them how well they have been applying what they learned • Send written surveys to learners in order to ask them how well they have applied what they learned—and what obstacles to application they encountered • Send written surveys to the immediate organizational superiors and/or subordinates of the learners about six months after participation in a planned learning experience in order to assess how much change they perceive in the learner

we have chosen to give *transfer of learning*—sometimes called *transfer of training*—special emphasis. The reasons: it is critically important and is too often neglected. If genuine improvement is to flow from internal group training, the change effort must not cease when a classroom course adjourns; rather, the change effort must begin then. At every stage in designing and delivering internal group training, L & MD specialists should be thinking about what they (and others) can do to encourage the transfer of learning from the training environment to the job environment. A few methods that can be helpful for this purpose are provided in Exhibit 7-12. Refer to that list, noting what methods are already being used in your organization and what additional methods could be used to increase the likelihood of learning transfer.

Problems Affecting Internal Group Training

Several special problems are common when planning and assessing internal group training for management employees or for individuals demonstrating leadership potential.

One problem is that internal group training is sometimes designed and offered inappropriately. For that reason, L & MD specialists should resist pressure to chase the latest fads. Always ask people several questions when they propose a new training course: (1) What performance problem will it solve? (2) How is the training related to the organization's strategic plan? (3) What will happen if the training is *not* designed and delivered? Weigh the answers carefully.

A second problem is that internal group training may be neglected due to time and staffing constraints. In the last few decades, downsizing and layoffs have produced massive restructuring in the white-collar and middle management ranks. One result is that fewer people are carrying out jobs than once were. That has led to less flexibility in staffing schedules so that every person is needed at the work site. L & MD specialists may thus find it difficult to induce prospective management participants to attend internal group training when it is needed and appropriate. To solve this problem, use two strategies: first, appeal directly to the immediate organizational superiors of prospective participants to enlist their support; second, make training available in multiple formats—such as self-study, video, or audio—so that extremely busy learners can take material home (if need be) rather than take time out during the hectic work day to attend class.

A third problem is that needs assessment is not properly handled. Far too few organizations take steps to distinguish learning from nonlearning needs and to identify what learners really must know, do, or feel at the end of their learning experiences. That means much time and money is wasted in delivering misdirected training.

The best way to overcome this problem is to make a concerted effort to assess needs for internal group training experience. Avoid shortcuts. Instead, make a real effort to bring a return on investments of time and money.

A fourth problem is that management or leadership training is not always tied, as it should be, to the organization's strategic plan or identifiable business needs. To solve this problem, double check every proposed internal group training course against the organization's strategic plan. If the training cannot be justified on that basis, then it should not be offered. Twelve specific methods have already been identified to link up planned learning efforts with strategic plans, and these methods can be applied to L & MD.[9]

EXTERNAL GROUP TRAINING PROGRAMS

External group training is instruction that is planned, designed, delivered, and evaluated by external vendors, university faculty, or community college staff. It is not tied to the degree requirements of a university and is not uniquely geared to change or accommodate one organization's culture, philosophy, work requirements, or procedures. Its purpose is to broaden individuals by exposing them to new viewpoints.

Examples of external group training include seminars offered off-site by professional associations, industry groups, nonprofit organizations, and for-profit

consulting firms. Some community colleges offer "individual enrichment seminars" but do not grant college credit to participants. Seminars of this kind are
widely and frequently advertised in newspapers, direct-mail brochures, radio
announcements, direct-phone solicitation, and other methods.

When Should External Group Training Be a Programmatic Focus of L & MD?

Use external group training when

- The organization is too small to have a steady stream of individuals entering and
  progressing through the management ranks
- Groups of people do not share common learning needs
- Internal group training is not likely to produce desired results quickly enough
- The organization's workers need exposure to new ideas
- Individuals have unique learning needs that are best met outside the organization
- Consistency of training content is not important

External group training is advantageous for meeting short-term individual
learning needs or rectifying individual performance problems. But it is generally
not appropriate when the organization is large enough to warrant internal group
training, when more than a few individuals experience similar learning needs,
when on-the-job training is more cost-effective, or when alternative methods
will prove to be less expensive.

Planning External Group Training

Although L & MD specialists often think of a management or leadership
training curriculum as limited to internal programs, it can also include external
programs. For example, some organizations send all newly promoted or about-
to-be-promoted individuals to special seminars sponsored by industry associations, professional associations, or universities.

To plan and execute external group training, L & MD specialists may choose
to follow a six-step model. The first step of that model is distinguishing issues
appropriate for external group training from those more appropriate for other
methods. For instance, external group training should not be chosen as an alternative to disciplining wayward workers who are neglecting their responsibilities. Nor should it be used as a vehicle to clarify work expectations when
immediate organizational superiors have neglected their responsibility to do so.
External group training is also inappropriate as a means by which to provide
rewards for exemplary performers by giving them fancy vacations in exotic
locations.

The second step in the model is assessing training needs of management employees or, more broadly, those who demonstrate exceptional leadership potential. Use external group training to broaden individual horizons, giving workers the opportunity to meet new people, share ideas with people from outside their organization, or experience new insights. Be sure what the worker "needs" before researching and selecting an appropriate seminar.

The third step in the model is researching external seminars and sponsors or contract to have seminars developed. Literally thousands of seminars are offered each year. Some organizations rely on them increasingly, substituting them for internal group training. But finding one to meet the unique needs of one worker can pose a real challenge for those unaware of where or how to look. Assuming that the learning needs of management employees or prospective leaders have been identified, track down possible external seminars that may be appropriate.

Once you have identified the titles of seminars that *appear* to meet the unique individual or group learning needs of management employees or prospective leaders in your organization, contact vendors to request detailed information, such as performance objectives, topic outline, evaluation results, names and addresses of past participants who can be contacted directly, and a biosketch listing the instructor's credentials. Then compare this information to the learning needs of management employees or prospective leaders in your organization. Assess how well the seminar matches up to the needs. If in doubt, send only one or two people to the first seminar—or attend yourself—and use that experience to decide whether others should be sent.

You may wish to use the same basic approach to research a vendor to design a program tailored for internal group training. Once qualified vendors are identified, contact them for more information about the training they offer and their credentials. If possible, travel to other organizations to watch them in action. If that is not feasible, at least call your counterparts in other organizations to find out what the vendors did and what results were obtained from their efforts. Then compare what you hear to what your organization needs.

Always prepare a written contract to specify exactly what you expect the vendors to do. Spell out everything you expect. Be sure to make clear what penalties will be imposed on vendors who miss deadlines or do not meet other project requirements. Then have a competent lawyer review the contract before it is executed. The fourth step in the model is selecting and sending participants off-site, as appropriate, to meet identified needs. In short, identify and prioritize who should attend the external seminar. As you do so, realize that many external seminars are designed to tempt a spur-of-the-moment response. If an attractive direct-mail brochure lands on the desks of workers experiencing an immediate learning need, they will often behave like compulsive and less-than-critical consumers. Many assume that any seminar will be better than none.

But few organizations can afford the luxury of sending their workers trekking off to parts unknown, often at significant expense, without being sure that the learning experiences will genuinely benefit them. One way to solve this problem is to check the references of a seminar's sponsoring organization to obtain detailed information about training content before investing time, enrollment fees, or travel expenses.

The fifth step in the model is ensuring that participants are clear about why they have been selected to attend seminars, are willing to take initiative to learn, and are held accountable for results upon their return. To ensure a real payoff from external group training, be sure that participants meet with their immediate organizational superiors before they attend. That meeting should clarify why they are being sent and what they should learn. If accountability is established first, participants can aggressively press seminar instructors to ensure their learning needs are met. When the participants return to their organizations, they can then be debriefed to determine what they can be held accountable for applying on their jobs.

The aim should be to establish a basis of accountability so that the organization's investment in external seminars has a payoff. Above all, management employees or prospective leaders should *not* be sent to attend external seminars in glamorous locations as a form of vacation time or a reward for work well done. If they are, the value and credibility of external seminars are diminished and scarce organizational resources are squandered.

The sixth step in the model is evaluating results. Once workers have returned from attending external group training, they should be asked to evaluate the results. In this way, the organization can determine what benefits, if any, were realized.

No single approach exists to evaluate the results of external group training. Many methods are used. Some organizations require participants to write and circulate an essay to others about what they learned; some organizations require participants to complete a written questionnaire, similar to the questionnaires handed out at the end of internal group training sessions; some organizations require participants to train others about what they learned. Any one of these approaches can be helpful, depending on the desired results.

Problems Affecting External Group Training

Of all L & MD methods, external group training lends itself least effectively to systematic planning. There is one major reason why: external seminars—what those in the training trade call *public seminars*—are rarely designed to meet the unique learning needs of one individual, group, or organization. In many cases their value is suspect because the information they provide is not necessarily compatible with one organization's culture, philosophy, competitive conditions, or work expectations.

One partial solution to this problem: L & MD specialists should establish a means of evaluating public seminars before workers attend them. Another partial solution: require prospective participants to meet before and after the seminar with their immediate organizational superiors. The pre-attendance meeting should focus on clarifying why individuals are being sent and what they are expected to learn; the post-attendance meeting should clarify what they learned and how they can apply it to their jobs.

EXTERNAL EDUCATION PROGRAMS

External education is directly tied to the degree or certification requirements of a high school, adult educational institution, university, or college. Like external group training, external education is usually conducted off-site—though external educational experiences can sometimes be brought on-site before working hours, during lunch time, or after hours by special arrangement with educational institutions. It is not uniquely geared to change or to accommodate one organization's strategic plan, culture, business philosophy, work requirements, or procedures. Nor is it designed, delivered, or evaluated by the L & MD director, L & MD coordinator, or L & MD staff.

The purpose of external education is to broaden individual horizons by exposing people to new ideas from outside their organizations. In this respect it is similar to external group training. But it is also generally more effective in helping individuals realize their career goals by helping them qualify to advance in a present occupation, change occupations, or prepare for outplacement. A major difference between external group training and external education is that training focuses on helping individuals qualify for jobs with one employer, but education focuses on the general betterment of individuals. By giving individuals educational credentials such as degrees, external education may provide a means to make individuals occupationally mobile across employers.

Examples of external education include courses taught through educational institutions, executive MBA programs, night school programs, correspondence study, or "university without walls" programs. Often publicized through catalogs and schedules published by educational institutions, job-related courses typically qualify for employer reimbursement through educational assistance programs—a common employee benefit in many organizations.

When Should External Education Be a Programmatic Focus of L & MD?

External education is appropriate for L & MD when

- The organization is too small to have a steady stream of individuals entering and progressing through management ranks or its leadership talent pool is small

- The prospect of earning a degree increases motivation to learn

- Individuals have unique learning needs that are best met outside the organization

- Long-term individual skill development is desirable

- The organization's management employees or other prospective leaders need to broaden their horizons by coming in contact with new ideas from other organizations, industries, or cultures

• Maintaining consistency across training or educational content is not essential

External education is particularly advantageous for meeting long-term individual needs. Like external group training, however, it is generally not appropriate as a substitute for internal group training when

• The organization is large enough to warrant internal group training

• Individuals experience similar learning needs

• The need exists to use learning experiences to change or accommodate the organization's strategic plan, culture, business philosophy, work requirements, or procedures

• On-the-job training is more cost-effective, or

• Other approaches to performance improvement will prove to be less expensive or more appropriate for achieving desired individual changes

Unique exceptions are tailor-made MBA programs, common in some European countries, and internal group training programs that meet the requirements for recommended college credit in the United States through the Program on Non-collegiate Sponsored Instruction (American Council on Education, One Dupont Circle, N.W., Washington, DC 20036; Phone: 202–939–9430).

Planning External Education

When planning external education for management employees or for other prospective leaders, L & MD specialists confront three key questions: First, should external education be tied to other programs? Second, should external education be tied to succession plans so as to help prepare talent to meet the organization's needs? Third, should external education be tied to management or leadership career planning programs in a way designed to help individuals realize their career goals? Depending on the answers to these questions, methods of planning external education may vary.

If external education is treated as a stand-alone program, then a policy on organizational tuition reimbursement or prepayment should be prepared and communicated to employees. This policy should describe the purpose of the tuition reimbursement or pre-payment program, stipulate allowable charges (tuition, fees, books), provide a means by which to distinguish between job-related and non-job-related courses, clarify how employees apply for tuition reimbursement or prepayment, establish yearly or lifetime limits on tuition reimbursements or prepayments available to individuals, and clarify procedures to claim tuition reimbursement (such as a minimum grade of C or better in courses). The policy should also explain whether the employer will permit course attendance or study during work hours, how the employer will handle tuition reimbursement or pre-payment if the employee terminates in the middle of a course, how educational achievement is viewed when the employer makes decisions regarding promotions, transfers, or salary increases, and what academic counseling services (if any) the employer will offer.

Some employers distinguish between two types of educational programs: (1) those requested by employees; and (2) those requested by the employer. Those requested by employees are voluntary or discretionary; those requested by the employer are involuntary or mandatory. *Voluntary courses* are taken for individual improvement, are attended on the employee's own time, and are subject to minimum grade requirements for tuition reimbursement. On the other hand, *involuntary courses* are taken to help satisfy job requirements or rectify identified performance deficiencies. Employees may attend them on the employer's time. They may also be considered necessary for continued employment. Tuition for these courses is often pre-paid and qualifies for complete reimbursement of all necessary and contingent expenses.

If external education is tied to a succession planning program, then a possible starting point is preparation of an individual development plan (see Exhibit 7-6) designed to narrow the gap between what prospective successors already know and what they should know to qualify for advancement. In this respect, external education becomes a vehicle by which to meet future position requirements. However, since external educational experiences rarely take into account one organization's strategic plan, culture, business philosophy, work requirements, or procedures, they must often be supplemented with other planned learning experiences designed to help individuals qualify for advancement.

If external education is tied to a management or leadership career planning program and is intended to help individuals identify and meet their career goals, then a typical starting point is the preparation of a written career plan that links up career goals to individual learning needs. In this respect, external education becomes a vehicle to help individuals realize their career aspirations.

Problems Affecting External Education

Keeping people from leaving an organization is difficult to do. But many top managers, and L & MD specialists, worry that the substantial costs of external education will only increase the occupational mobility of management employees or other prospective leaders but not produce payoffs in job performance to the employer who subsidized the education.

To address this issue, some employers institute a payback policy. Workers who participate at employer expense in substantial educational programs—such as Ivy League or Big 10 Executive MBA programs—are asked to reimburse their employers for educational subsidies if they terminate their employment before a specified time following matriculation. However, legal authorities do not agree how enforceable these agreements are. Can a payback agreement be enforced as a contract? If terminating employees refuse to pay back funds, what recourse does the employer have? Is the employer willing to sue or turn the account over to a collection agency? These and similar issues make employee education programs difficult to administer.

JOB ROTATION PROGRAMS

A management job rotation (MJR) or leadership job rotation (LJR) program is a planned effort to develop management trainees, supervisors, managers, executives, or others with leadership potential by placing them in new jobs and work settings under the guidance of new organizational superiors for extended timespans. Job rotations have been widely used to develop workers. A survey study conducted by Saari, Johnson, McLaughlin, and Zimmerle (1988) of 1,000 organizations—611 of those surveys were returned—revealed that "40% [of the responding organizations] report using job rotation."[10]

The aim of management or leadership job rotations is to help individuals increase their portfolio of knowledge and skills. Since learning occurs on the job, the transfer of learning does not pose the same looming concern that it does for off-the-job learning experiences such as internal group training, external group training, or external education. Job rotation programs may also be combined with other forms of training and education.

When Should Management or Leadership Job Rotation Be a Programmatic Focus of L & MD?

Job rotation is perhaps the best suited of any formal L & MD method to increase the organization-specific knowledge of management employees or others with leadership potential. After all, it gives them firsthand experience with different functions, operations, people, and situations. It is highly appropriate to:

- Broaden individuals, giving them in-depth exposure to areas outside the functions or occupational specialties into which they were originally hired and advanced. As best-selling authors Naisbitt and Auburdene note, one way to re-invent the corporation is to "move people laterally to develop well-roundedness."[11] That is what job rotation is all about.

- Build the credibility of future leaders. As authors Kouzes and Posner write, "people are more likely to follow you if they have confidence that you understand their area, the organization, and the industry."[12] Job rotation builds that credibility.

- Assuage career burnout. As Leonard Nadler and Zeace Nadler explain, "some good employees find that after several years of doing the same job, they lose their interest and motivation, and though they are not interested in leaving the organization, they are seeking different job challenges within the organization."[13] Job rotation can create a new challenge to stimulate individuals.

- Test how well high-potential management employees (HiPos) or other prospective leaders adapt to change, solve problems, and learn how to learn. By rotating management employees or prospective leaders through different positions, decision makers gain insight about how flexible they are and how well they perform under different conditions.

- Give management employees or other prospective leaders exposure to new cultures and ways of doing business. Many large international corporations find that, by rotating their leadership talent internationally, they are able to develop crucial sensitivity to the unique cultural and business conditions that affect corporate operations outside the United States.

- Give management employees or other prospective leaders exposure to new models of effective leadership and different management styles. Management employees or other prospective leaders who rotate gain firsthand experience with different management styles and are able to observe firsthand the effects of these styles.

In a survey study on management job rotation programs we conducted—117 of 500 questionnaires were completed and returned, making the overall response rate 24.3 percent—we found that organizations sponsoring a planned MJR program do so primarily for the following reasons, listed in order of importance:[14] developing individuals for increased responsibility, increasing the pool of promotable talent, improving the organization's ability to respond to technological change, and helping individuals realize their career plans within the organization. These reasons were ranked by respondents as slightly more important than such other reasons as increasing the productivity of employees, contributing to effective implementation of the organization's strategic plan, improving the organization's ability to respond to environmental change, providing general training to individuals inside the organization, or improving employee morale.

Planning and Carrying Out Management or Leadership Job Rotation Programs

Plan a job rotation program by following a six-step model. As a first step, determine the program's purpose, scope, and methods of selecting participants. By *purpose* we mean what the program is intended to achieve. By *scope* we mean what areas of the organization are to be included and/or excluded. By *methods of selection* we mean how individuals are chosen to participate.

Management employees or others with leadership potential should not be rotated if decision makers have not clarified the program's purpose. After all, rotations can be anxiety-producing for participants, their spouses, and children— especially when international travel is involved. Moreover, rotations can be expensive if the organization pays all relocation fees, ensures that participants do not assume the burden of higher home mortgages when arriving at new work sites, assists participants in selling their homes, and provides employment assistance for working spouses.

The purposes of rotation programs may vary. But just *how much* are they intended to

- Help broaden individual horizons?
- Build leadership credibility?
- Assuage career burnout?
- Test high-potential management employees or others demonstrating exceptional leadership talent?
- Expose management employees or other prospective organizational leaders to new cultures and ways of doing business?
- Expose management employees or other prospective organizational leaders to new models of effective leadership and management styles?

The purpose(s) must be clarified so rotations can be established accordingly.

The scope of the program is also important. Some division or department managers institute *limited-scope* rotation programs restricted to their own workers. The purpose is usually to ensure cross-training and development across employees in one part of the organization only. On the other hand, decision makers in some organizations institute *broad-scope* rotation programs encompassing some or all employees. The aim is to ensure leadership and management development on a larger scale, help realize succession plans, and improve the selection process for employees with leadership potential who are aspiring to more responsible positions.

Finally, the method of selecting participants is also important. In some organizations rotation programs are purely *voluntary*. When a vacancy occurs, workers with leadership potential are given an opportunity to rotate. They may even choose assignments. In other organizations, rotation programs are *mandatory*, and individual choice is thus restricted. Management employees or others with leadership potential are told to rotate. They have little choice to refuse if they wish to keep their jobs. Finally, rotations may be *competitive*. High-potential employees compete on the basis of their abilities, and "winner(s)" receive organizational investments of time, money, and effort.

In the survey of management job rotation programs, we found that voluntary and competitive rotation programs are used by organizations slightly more often than mandatory programs.[15] Voluntary rotation programs are advantageous because participants are willing to rotate to increase their opportunities in the organization and assume greater or newer challenges. But, unfortunately, a disadvantage is that they do not always attract those who can benefit most from rotation. Mandatory rotation programs avoid that problem but risk the loss of otherwise promising employees when working spouses or school-age children oppose being uprooted, militating against the rotation on the home front.

A second step in establishing a management or leadership job rotation program is identifying functions and activities which individuals will learn through rotations. It does not make much sense to rotate individuals without having a good idea about what they should learn through their moves. For this reason, it is important to establish performance (learning) objectives for *each* rotation. The objectives may simply take the form of the functions, activities, duties, or responsibilities performed by the present job incumbent; or, they may include new, one-time objectives unique to rotating employees only.

To establish performance objectives for a rotation, start by preparing an up-to-date position description listing all the major responsibilities of the job incumbent. Show the description to the job incumbent—or else ask the incumbent to write it. Then compare the description to the responsibilities previously performed by the rotating employee. Identify responsibilities new to the rotating employee, establishing them as the performance objectives for the rotation. In this way, a rotation leads to gradually increasing knowledge and experience for participants, presenting them with new challenges to broaden their horizons.

A third step in establishing a management or leadership job rotation program is enlisting the support of participants and affected employees. When establishing a job rotation program of this kind, you must grapple with several issues. Among them: (1) How can the support of participants be enlisted and maintained? (2) How can the support of affected employees—especially those reporting to rotating management employees—be established and maintained? (3) What problems or difficulties with rotations can be foreseen and overcome?

Participant support is most important to establish in mandatory rotation programs, since voluntary and competitive rotation programs assume that support from the participant already exists. Three methods may be used, separately or in combination, to build that support: (1) an incentive program geared to encourage participation; (2) moral suasion; and (3) a support program.

In our survey of management job rotation programs, we found that relatively few special incentives are offered to individuals on rotation.[16] For instance, not one respondent to the survey indicated that their organizations make it a policy to offer special leave, before or during rotations, as an incentive; only a few respondents indicated that management employees on rotation in their organizations are given a special leave after the rotation or are awarded a one-time bonus; and fewer than one-fourth of our respondents cited as routine the practice of promoting managers on rotation upon arrival at their new work sites. However, the survey respondents did indicate that more than half of management employees on rotation receive:[17]

- Assurance of possible promotion if the rotation is successfully completed (100 percent of respondents agreed that this practice affects high percentages of management employees on rotation in their organizations).

- Assurance that the rotation will be viewed favorably when an appropriate position becomes available (83.3 percent of respondents agreed that this practice affects high percentages of management employees on rotation in their organizations).

- Assurance of possible salary consideration (66.6 percent of respondents agreed that this practice affects high percentages of management employees on rotation in their organizations).

• A special one-time salary increase (50 percent of respondents agreed that this practice affects high percentages of management employees on rotation in their organizations).

The responses thus seem to indicate that employees bear the burden to demonstrate their ability on rotation first, at which point they may become eligible for rewards. Incentives offered before or during rotation are less uncommon than rewards bestowed afterward for proven, successful performance.

Moral suasion is a second way to encourage participation in management or leadership job rotations. Individuals to be rotated meet with their immediate organizational superiors, who offer persuasive career advice. Without making legally binding promises or false assurances, an immediate organizational superior explains the purpose of the rotation; what the employee is expected to learn from it; how long the rotation will last; where the rotation will be geographically located; who is employed at that location; why interaction with them may be useful to the employee's development; when the rotation should begin; why the employee was chosen for the rotation; and how the employee will be trained, coached, or otherwise guided before and during the rotation. At this time the individual should also be informed by his or her immediate organizational superior regarding what assistance, if any, the organization will provide to support (1) a geographical move, (2) problems created by uprooting spouse and family, (3) learning a new culture or language (if an international assignment), and (4) other issues of importance to the employee. In some cases it may be appropriate to establish several meetings: the first between employee and immediate organizational superior; the second including spouse and children. If the rotation will not require extensive travel, the employee's new organizational superior—the person to whom the employee will report while on rotation—may be included in these discussions as well.

A third way to encourage participation in management or leadership job rotations is a support program, meaning an organized and systematic effort to address the concerns of the whole person—and, indeed, a whole family—affected by a management or leadership rotation. Components of such a support program may include any or all of the following: training to help rotating employees adjust to new job responsibilities; training to help adjust to new work environments; training to help adjust to new, immediate organizational superiors; assistance in finding a comparable home in another location; assistance in selling the family home; training to help individuals and their families learn about other cultures; assistance to help uprooted spouses find employment in new locations; assistance in helping children make the transition; or, assistance with elderly parents.

A fourth step in establishing a management or leadership job rotation program is preparing learning contracts for each rotation. Adult learning theorist Malcolm Knowles has been an outspoken advocate of contract learning.[18] A learning contract is an action plan to guide the learning of one individual or group. At minimum it should set forth:

- *Performance objectives* (what should the person know or do upon completion of a planned learning experience?)
- *Instructional methods* (how should learning experiences be carried out?)
- *Evaluation techniques* (how should the learner's achievement of instructional objectives be measured?)

A sample learning plan, used in conjunction with succession planning, was provided in Exhibit 7-6. The same form can be modified as a learning contract for a management or leadership job rotation. A learning contract provides an excellent starting point for a management or leadership job rotation. It establishes accountabilities, clarifying what the learner is to know or do upon completion of the rotation.

In our research study of management job rotation programs, we found that individual learning contracts are prepared for all rotating management employees by 30 percent of all organizations with management job rotation programs.[19] Moreover, 17.4 percent of the organizations take steps to make these contracts mutually agreeable to employees and their immediate organizational superiors.

A fifth step in establishing a management or leadership job rotation program is training and coaching to support individuals and work groups affected by a job rotation program. Preparing for a rotation is important, but supporting and coaching employees on rotation is vital to success. After rotations begin, management employees or others on rotation should receive training to help them learn new job duties, receive coaching on how to deal with difficult but predictable problems arising on the new job, and receive frequent feedback at predictable checkpoints in time so they are kept apprised of how they are doing.

Some method should also be established to foster acceptance of individuals on rotation by their peers and their new work group. People naturally feel anxious when they start to work for a new, immediate organizational superior, since they are unsure how his or her expectations will match up with those to which they have become accustomed. It is for this reason that changes in leadership are sometimes viewed as a way to introduce change itself. To ease the natural concerns of employees about this switch in leadership, those on rotation should meet right away with their work groups and review their basic expectations. They should also meet individually with the highest-performing and most seasoned veterans of the work group to ask for their advice, suggestions, and support. Such approaches, if followed, will garner support and ease the transition.

The sixth step is evaluating the effectiveness of management or leadership job rotation programs and individual participants. Since evaluation ties together plans and actions, it is widely used to compare the developmental results of rotations and/or individual performance to objectives established at the outset.

Indeed, in our research study on job rotations, most respondents agreed with the statement that "an individual performance evaluation is prepared after each rotation."[20] More specifically, respondents from 16 of 23 organizations sponsoring management job rotation programs indicated that such evaluations are conducted with 51 to 100 percent of management employees on rotations.

Two separate issues may be subject to evaluation on rotations: *developmental issues* and *performance issues*. Both issues are important; both may be evaluated. Developmental issues have to do with how well individuals satisfy the performance objectives of their rotations; performance issues have to do with how well individuals satisfy the requirements of the jobs into which they rotate.

Some organizations make no distinction between a standardized performance appraisal conducted at regular intervals with all workers and a special rotation appraisal conducted at the middle or at the end of a management or leadership job rotation. But it is possible to make that distinction. Special rotation appraisals may be filled out on forms specifically designed for this purpose. Often, they are quite simple (see Exhibit 7-13). But they do provide a means by which to give individuals feedback on their performance, stimulating their further development and providing the organization with a valuable record of how well they have been performing. To improve the likelihood of further development stemming from this feedback, some L & MD specialists prefer to ask rotating employees to *self-evaluate* so as to provide information that can then be compared to—and coupled with—the appraisal performed by their immediate organizational superiors while on rotation (see an example of a form for a self-evaluation in Exhibit 7-14).

Problems Affecting Management or Leadership Job Rotations

Rotation programs go awry when they are not adequately planned. If individuals are just shifted around without explanation, then they quickly become disenchanted, since moves are anxiety-producing for them and their families. Likewise, if the purpose of a rotation program is not clearly spelled out, then it is not clear to participants—or their immediate organizational superiors—why it's worthwhile for them to invest time in the program. And if no time is devoted to training, coaching, and evaluating, then the developmental value of rotations will not be great.

To overcome these problems, then, it is important to follow the steps outlined in this chapter in order to establish the rotation program on a sound footing. Of chief importance is determining and communicating the program's purpose, scope, and methods of selecting participants. It can also help to train the immediate organizational superiors of those on rotation so they are sensitized to the importance of regular feedback and coaching provided by them.

Exhibit 7-13

A Sample Performance Evaluation Form for a Management or Leadership Job Rotation Program

Name of Employee	
Job Title	
Budget Center	
Start Date	**Date Appointed to Present Position**
Immediate Supervisor	
Directions	
Use this form to evaluate an individual's performance and development while on a Management or Leadership job rotation. Simply answer the questions appearing in each part below. Then share the completed evaluation with the employee and schedule a meeting with him or her. When you are finished, forward the original copy of the evaluation to the HR Department for inclusion in the employee's HR file. Attach more paper, if necessary.	
Part I. Rotation Objectives	
What were the learning or job performance objectives of this rotation? *(Attach a copy of the Learning Plan, if it spells out the objectives. Otherwise, describe them below.)*	
Part II. Areas of Strength	
What strengths did the employee demonstrate during this rotation? Describe them below. Be as specific as possible, citing examples when appropriate.	
Strength	**Example**
Part III. Areas for Improvement	
What areas for improvement did the employee demonstrate while on this rotation? Describe them below. Be as specific as possible, citing examples when appropriate.	
Areas for Improvement	**Example**
Approvals	
Signature of Employee	**Date**
Signature of Employee's Supervisor	**Date**
Effective Date:	

POSITION ASSIGNMENT PROGRAMS

A *position assignment program* is designed to increase the knowledge or skills—or change work attitudes—of workers through short-term, on-the-job assignments. Position assignments are usually temporary. Individuals are exposed to new work duties, responsibilities, tasks, projects, or people for short time spans. In this respect they differ from job rotations in which individuals move into new positions with new duties, new co-workers, and a new supervisor.

Position assignments may stand alone or may be paired up with succession planning programs; management or leadership career planning programs; internal group training programs; external group training programs; external educa-

Exhibit 7-14
A Sample Self-Evaluation Form for a Management or Leadership Job Rotation Program

Name of Employee	
Budget Center	
Job Title	
Start Date	**Date Appointed to Present Position**
Immediate Supervisor	

Directions: Use this form to evaluate your own performance and development while on a Management or Leadership job rotation. Simply answer the questions appearing in each part below. Then share the completed evaluation with your immediate organizational superior and schedule a meeting with him or her. When you are finished, forward a copy to the HR Department for inclusion in your HR file. Attach more paper, if necessary.

Part I. Rotation Objectives

What were the learning or job performance objectives of this rotation? *(Attach a copy of the Learning Plan, if it spells out the objectives. Otherwise, describe them below.)*

Part II. Areas of Strength

What strengths did you feel you demonstrated on this rotation? Describe them below. Be as specific as possible, citing examples when appropriate.

Strength	**Example**

Part III. Areas for Improvement

What areas for improvement did you recognize from this rotation? Describe them below. Be as specific as possible, citing examples when appropriate.

Areas for Improvement	**Example**

Approvals	
Signature of Employee	**Date**
Signature of Employee's Supervisor	**Date**
Effective Date	

tion programs; or job rotation programs. A position assignment helps others judge how well individuals may function in other positions for which they are being considered or groomed, as in the case of assigning individuals to ''fill in'' for vacationing job incumbents whose responsibilities are at a higher level than those temporarily taking their places.

When Should Position Assignments Be a Programmatic Focus of L & MD?

Position assignments may be deliberately crafted to

• Recruit or select new talent by trying out individuals on carefully chosen, critical activities of a possible future job.

- Cross-train supervisors, managers, or executives on activities in other parts of an organization, division, or department.

- Prepare individuals for advancement to more technically complex duties in the same job (*horizontal advancement*) or in a more responsible job (*vertical advancement*).

- Develop individuals by helping them cultivate new insights or improve working relationships across an organization.

What are some examples of position assignments? To list a few:

- Asking nonexempt employees to fill in for vacationing exempt employees

- Asking exempt employees to serve as backups or stand-ins for their immediate organizational superiors during vacations or other periods of absence

- Trading duties across exempt or nonexempt incumbents in a work unit, department, or division to spread around knowledge and skills

- Delegating some high-level duties, on a short-term basis, to individuals in lower-level positions for a developmental purpose

- Giving individuals special projects on new areas of the organization, new product lines, new equipment, or new people so as to assess—or build—their skills

- Sending individuals on field trips to collect information from competitors or organizations renowned for their effective practices

- Having individuals serve as organizational representatives to suppliers, distributors, customers, or other stakeholders

- Sending individuals on college or technical recruiting trips

As many as 88 such assignments have been linked to managerial success.[21]

Planning Position Assignments

More than one way may be used to plan a position assignment program. The "right" approach depends on the program's purpose. Of course, a program may have more than one.

If the aim is to cross-train management or leadership talent, then start by identifying all responsibilities in an organization, division, department, or work unit. You might think of this process as akin to writing a job description for an entire unit, department, division, or organization. Then link the activities/responsibilities to people already performing them. Finally, schedule times so those who do not customarily perform them may gain exposure to them through observation, participation, or firsthand experience. (Use Exhibit 7-15 for an example of a Worksheet for planning departmental management or leadership cross-training or cross-exposure.)

But if the aim is to educate one individual in preparation for promotion, modify the approach to make it more specific to the position for which he or she is being groomed. Prepare a current job description for the position. Verify

Exhibit 7-15
A Worksheet for Planning Departmental Management or Leadership Cross-Training or Cross-Exposure

Directions: Use this Worksheet to plan management or leadership cross-training or cross-exposure in *one* department. In column 1 below, list the responsibilities performed by management or leadership employees. (If necessary, simply list all duties appearing on position descriptions for management or leadership employees in the department.) In column 2, list the names and titles of individuals *not* presently performing the tasks or carrying out the duties. In column 3, describe how and when the management or leadership employees listed in column 2 will be cross-trained or cross-exposed to these tasks or duties. (Leave column 3 blank if it is decided not to cross-train or cross-expose an individual to a task or duty.) In column 4, make notes about the results of the cross-training or cross-exposure experiences. Add paper as necessary.			
Column 1	**Column 2**	**Column 3**	**Column 4**
Responsibilities	**Names**	**Methods**	**Outcomes**
What duties and responsibilities are performed by all management employees in the department?	**Who does not perform the duty?**	**When and how will employees listed in column 2 be cross-trained or cross-exposed to tasks or duties they are not presently performing?**	**What were the results of the cross-training or cross-exposure experience?**

it with the incumbent to ensure that all duties, activities, and responsibilities listed on the description are actually performed. Interview the incumbent's immediate organizational superior to determine whether any *changes* are contemplated in those duties and activities. If so, list them. Group together related activities or duties and prioritize them from most to least important. In this context, *important* may mean *critical to job success* or *most often performed*. Then assess how well the individual who is being groomed for advancement is *presently* able to perform each duty listed. Handle this assessment process like a performance appraisal, even though the individual is not presently doing the job. Finally, prioritize areas in which the individual requires development, identifying appropriate position assignments that can help the person to meet the responsibilities of the new position (see Exhibit 7-16).

If the aim is simply to educate or develop individuals through short-term assignments, apply the same approach described in the preceding paragraph—but make one important modification. Instead of focusing on "duties to be performed in the next position," focus instead on "new insights" to which the individual should be exposed.

Problems Affecting Position Assignments

Position assignments go awry when they are not adequately linked to future needs or when they are not planned. Managers who prize development may enjoy giving people assignments designed to "stretch" (broaden) them. But those assignments will not be useful or helpful if they are not related to future

Exhibit 7-16

A Worksheet for Preparing an Individual for Promotion Using Short-Term Work Assignments

Directions: Use this Worksheet to help plan for preparing an individual for promotion using short-term and on-the-job work assignments. In column 1 below, list the tasks, duties, or responsibilities of the targeted position for which the individual is being prepared. (Make any anticipated changes in the duties of the position, as necessary.) In column 2, check (✓) whether the individual is—or is not—already prepared for performing the task, duty, or responsibility. In column 3, focus attention only on those tasks, duties, or responsibilities for which the individual needs to be prepared. Describe when and how the individual should be prepared using short-term position assignments linked to the tasks, duties or responsibilities. Add paper as necessary.	

Column 1	Column 2		Column 3
Tasks/Duties	**Prepared Now?**		**Short-Term Work Assignments**
What tasks, duties, or responsibilities are performed in the targeted position? (List them below)	**Yes (✓)**	**No (✓)**	**When and how should the individual be prepared for tasks, duties, or responsibilities for which he or she has not already been prepared? (Describe below)**

organizational or individual needs. Position assignments should not be given for their own sake; rather, they should be linked to identifiable needs.

Poor planning can also torpedo the best-intentioned position assignments. Before the position assignment begins, the employee's immediate organizational superior should clearly formulate what the management employee or leadership prospect should know, do, or feel by the end of the assignment, how he or she will learn during the assignment, and how success or failure will be evaluated. Without planning and direction, results will be uncertain.

To overcome these problems, then, it is important to

- *Identify the purpose of the position assignment and the needs it is intended to meet.* What is it that individuals should learn from the assignment?
- *Spell out the desired outcomes.* Establish performance objectives for position assignments to clarify what people should know or do upon completion.
- *Communicate expectations.* Be sure that immediate organizational superiors meet with management employees or leadership candidates before a position assignment begins to explain why the assignment is being given and what lessons they should strive to learn. Then be sure that follow-up meetings are later held to double check that desired results are being achieved.

SUMMARY

In this chapter we reviewed the following *formal L & MD methods*:

- Succession planning programs
- Management or leadership career planning programs

- Internal group training programs
- External group training programs
- External education programs
- Job rotation programs
- Position assignment programs

These L & MD methods, while seemingly unrelated, all lend themselves to centralized planning, administration, and oversight.

NOTES

1. W. Rothwell, *Effective Succession Planning: Ensuring Leadership Continuity and Building Talent from Within* (New York: AMACOM, 1994).

2. W. Rothwell and H. Sredl, *The ASTD Reference Guide to Professional HRD Roles and Competencies* (2nd ed.), 2 vols. (Amherst, MA: Human Resource Development Press, 1992).

3. Z. Leibowitz, C. Farren, and B. Kaye, *Designing Career Development Systems* (San Francisco: Jossey-Bass, 1986).

4. W. Rothwell and H. Kazanas, *Mastering the Instructional Design Process: A Systematic Approach* (2nd ed.) (San Francisco: Jossey-Bass, 1998).

5. Ibid.

6. Ibid.

7. A. Huczynski, *Encyclopedia of Management Development Methods* (London: Gower, 1983).

8. D. Kirkpatrick, *Evaluating Training Programs: The Four Levels* (San Francisco: Berrett-Koehler, 1994).

9. W. Rothwell and H. Kazanas, *Human Resource Development: A Strategic Approach* (rev. ed.) (Amherst, MA: Human Resource Development Press, 1994).

10. L. Saari, T. Johnson, S. McLaughlin, and D. Zimmerle, "A Survey of Management Training and Education Practices in U.S. Companies," *Personnel Psychology*, Vol. 41, p. 735.

11. J. Naisbitt and P. Auburdene, *Reinventing the Corporation: Transforming Your Job and Your Company for the New Information Society* (New York: Warner Books, 1985), p. 51.

12. J. Kouzes and B. Posner, *The Leadership Challenge: How to Get Extraordinary Things Done in Organizations* (San Francisco: Jossey-Bass, 1987), p. 285.

13. L. Nadler and Z. Nadler, *Developing Human Resources* (3rd ed.) (San Francisco: Jossey-Bass, 1989), pp. 65–66.

14. W. Rothwell and H. Kazanas, "Issues and Practices in Management Job Rotation Programs as Perceived by HRD Professionals," *Performance Improvement Quarterly*, Vol. 5, No. 1, pp. 49–69.

15. Ibid.

16. Ibid.

17. Ibid.

18. M. Knowles, *Using Learning Contracts: Practical Approaches to Individualizing and Structuring Learning* (San Francisco: Jossey-Bass, 1986).

19. Rothwell and Kazanas, "Issues and Practices in Management Job Rotation Programs as Perceived by HRD Professionals," pp. 49–69.

20. Ibid.

21. M. Lombardo and R. Eichinger, *Eighty-Eight Assignments for Development in Place: Enhancing the Developmental Challenge of Existing Jobs* (Greensboro, NC: The Center for Creative Leadership, 1989).

Chapter 8

Planning and Using Informal Methods

Informal L & MD methods grow out of the daily interaction between workers and their immediate organizational superiors. They are often spontaneous and are tailored to meet unique individual needs in a way that is not true of formal L & MD methods. In this chapter we turn to such informal L & MD methods as:

- On-the-job management or leadership training
- On-the-job management or leadership coaching
- Management or leadership mentoring or sponsorship
- Management or leadership self-development
- Management or leadership self-study

These methods are similar in that they do not lend themselves to centralized planning, administration, or oversight; rather, they are better handled at the work site and overseen by the learners, their immediate organizational superiors, or their co-workers. Informal L & MD methods are mainstays of L & MD, and they have existed in one form or another for many years.

However, informal L & MD methods are not always as fully utilized as they could be. There are many reasons why that is true. One reason is that workers are promoted from within but are only rarely trained on how to train, educate, or develop their peers or those reporting to them. As a result, they lack a belief in the value of L & MD. Moreover, they have no skills to carry it out. A second reason: supervisors, managers, and executives are not necessarily rewarded for training, educating, or developing others. Often, getting the work out is judged to be more important than developing employee skills. One predictable result is that, as needs for leadership talent surface, it is apparent that nobody has been gradually and systematically prepared to assume the new responsibilities posed by predictable—let alone unpredictable—changes. Then decision makers are faced with limited options: developing individuals on a short-term basis, hiring from outside, transferring from inside, or thrusting ill-prepared people into the jobs. These problems can be avoided if management employees or leaders are better trained to use, apply, or encourage such informal L & MD methods as on-the-job management or leadership training, on-the-job management or leadership coaching, management or leadership mentoring or sponsorship, management or leadership self-development, or management or leadership self-study.

ON-THE-JOB MANAGEMENT OR LEADERSHIP TRAINING

On-the-job management or leadership training, which we shall hereafter abbreviate simply as OJT, is an apt starting point for discussing informal L & MD methods. OJT is frequently used in many organizations, regardless of industry. OJT is often preferred because it is fast and inexpensive. Moreover, it can be easily individualized.

Defining OJT

OJT occurs on or near the work site. It is the most common form of training offered to workers in organizations today. Indeed, the American Society for Training and Development estimates that employers spend between three and six times more on OJT each year than they spend on internal group training.[1] OJT is important because it has the potential to reduce the unproductive breaking-in period for newly hired, newly transferred, or newly promoted leaders.

The terminology associated with OJT is not consistent. But it is helpful to distinguish between two types of OJT: *unstructured* and *structured*.[2]

Unstructured OJT means *unplanned training at the work site*. As problems arise on the job, employees are given quick instructions and shorthand guidance about how to handle them. After many months or years of encountering problems and receiving guidance, workers are eventually able to handle most problems as effectively as their immediate organizational superiors, who frequently function as their trainers.

Unstructured OJT is not systematically planned to meet learner needs; rather, it is organized around day-to-day experience. This approach is a leisurely one in which workers require many years to be trained. It is increasingly ineffective in light of the rapidly changing conditions in modern-day organizations, but it has been used for time eternal. We have elsewhere called it *learning by osmosis*,[3] linking it to the process of osmosis in Biology by which single-cell entities acquire food by being placed in close proximity to it. In learning by osmosis, people are expected to learn by being placed in close proximity to the knowledge, skills, and attitudes they are expected to absorb.

Structured OJT means *planned training at the work site*. Employees are given planned instruction designed to

- Clarify what they are supposed to do and/or what results they are to expected to achieve
- Introduce them systematically to important policies, procedures, laws, and regulations affecting what they do
- Brief them about employees, working conditions, equipment, and other important matters in the area they are to oversee as supervisors, managers, or executives

Structured OJT is akin to *job instruction training* (JIT), an approach first devised during World War I to increase the effectiveness of training given to shipbuilders. Unlike unstructured OJT, JIT is formally planned and organized in the working setting and makes use of lesson plans or outlines to guide on-the-job learning, training schedules, and planned feedback to learners about their performance. It is appropriately conducted on the work site so that problems of transfer of learning are minimized. A chief advantage of structured OJT is that the learning and working environments are similar, facilitating transfer of learning and speedy application of what is learned. Another advantage is that, when workers are trained by their immediate organizational superiors, they can be held accountable for applying on-the-job what they learned in training. That is not always easy or possible when others do the training or the training occurs off-the-job.

When Should On-the-Job Management or Leadership Training Be a Programmatic Focus of L & MD?

Structured OJT should be used when an organization's management is willing to:

- Commit the time to carry out training properly
- Devote the resources of time, money, staff, and equipment to it
- Assign knowledgeable, experienced, and competent people to carry it out
- Minimize the daily distractions of the work environment so employees have sufficient time to be trained
- Train people on principles of structured OJT so they know how to carry it out

On the other hand, OJT should not be used when these conditions cannot be met *or* when training will pose a hazard to employees or other people or undercut the credibility of those being trained.

Planning and Delivering On-the-Job Management or
Leadership Training

Structured OJT is usually not approached as a program sponsored by an organization; rather, it is planned and delivered at the work site, one-on-one, between a worker and his or her immediate organizational superior. However, a centralized L & MD function can be helpful by training management employees how to be effective trainers for their exempt and nonexempt employees.

A ten-step model may be followed when planning and delivering structured OJT for management employees or for other leaders. When planning structured OJT for employees, the first step is to ask their immediate organizational superiors to conduct a thorough job analysis or job breakdown. That is the traditional starting point for structured OJT in technical jobs. It also works for training in management or professional jobs. However, special approaches may have to be used for analyzing managerial work or work requiring leadership. Management activities and work outputs differ markedly from their technical counterparts.

One result of a thorough job analysis or job breakdown is an updated job description. It provides a statement of the major purpose of the job and information about essential functions, the estimated time devoted to these functions, nonessential functions, the estimated time devoted to those functions, knowledge and skills required to perform the job effectively, and information about what knowledge and skills are necessary to qualify for the job.

The second step of the model is preparing an individualized training schedule to make employees productive in their work as quickly as possible. Without a plan of some kind, training will take a back seat to the daily pressures of getting the work out. One way to avoid that problem is to use the updated job description as a starting point for developing an individualized training schedule. Immediate organizational superiors should first group together related functions of the job. They should then prioritize the functions for training.

Then they should describe (1) How employees will be trained on each responsibility/duty, (2) By whom employees will be trained, (3) When each step of on-the-job training will be completed, (4) How training results or outcomes will be measured so that the employees' levels of ability can be assessed. Use the Worksheet appearing in Exhibit 8-1 as an aid for this purpose.

The third step in the model is explaining the training schedule to employees so they understand the desired results to be achieved from the training and the sequence of training events. When adults enter a new job or undertake new duties, they frequently experience anxiety. They are unsure of what the change will mean to them, and they are usually reluctant to appear foolish. For these reasons, then, it is often wise to begin their training with a brief overview of what they can expect. This approach builds learners' self-confidence and self-esteem. Moreover, gestalt learning theorists suggest that people learn most effectively from whole-to-part, beginning with an overview (a map of everything

Exhibit 8-1

A Worksheet for Planning Structured On-the-Job Training for Management Employees or Other Leaders

Directions: Use this Worksheet for planning structured on-the-job training for management employees or other leaders. In column 1 below, list all essential job functions on which the employee is to be trained. In column 2, indicate priority for training. (A ranking of **1** means **highest importance**.) In column 3, describe *how* the employee will be trained. In column 4, describe *by whom* the employee will be trained. In column 5, indicate *when* the on-the-job training should be completed. In column 6, indicate *how training results or outcomes will be measured* so that the employee's level of ability can be assessed. Add paper to this Worksheet as necessary.

Column 1	Column 2	Column 3	Column 4	Column 5	Column 6
Activities	Priority	How will training be done?	Who will perform the training?	When should the training be completed?	How will the results of training be assessed?

to be learned) and followed up by detailed examinations (a step-by-step description of each part of the map). Begin the training, then, by giving the learners an overview of what they are expected to learn and how the training will proceed.

The fourth step in the model is providing a detailed explanation of each key duty, activity, or desired outcome of the job—or at least pointing the learners to sources from which they can receive detailed explanations. The employees' immediate organizational superiors, who often serve as the trainers, should implement the training schedule by going through it in an organized fashion, preferably treating related activities at the same time so that learners can structure what they hear and take notes as necessary. The trainers should begin by explaining each key duty, activity, or outcome, always making clear *why* it is important. (If immediate organizational superiors do not have the time to conduct the training personally, they should assign knowledgeable people to substitute for them.)

Learners should never be treated as mere passive receivers of information. Indeed, they can be assigned to investigate a duty, activity, or issue on their own so they take an active part in their own learning. What is learned through investigation is usually remembered better than what is merely explained. To use this approach, pose a series of questions about an issue for the learners to investigate and direct them to the right sources to find the answers. Then ask them to report back for follow-up when they have found the answers.

The fifth step in the model is identifying and providing instructions about applicable organizational or governmental policies, procedures, regulations, or other mandates that influence how the duty or activity is to be carried out. Many management duties and activities are affected by organizational policies or procedures and government laws or regulations. As management employees receive structured OJT, they should thus be familiarized with applicable organizational policies or procedures and government laws or regulations affecting what they do.

The sixth step of the model is explaining detailed points related to each activity or duty. Employees' immediate organizational superiors should then explain, in detail, each activity or duty the worker is to perform. The individualized training schedule should indicate what activities to discuss.

The seventh step in the model is showing employees how to perform the duty or activity—or pairing them up with those already successfully performing. In management work or in leadership roles, some activities lend themselves to demonstrations; others do not. For instance, if management employees must use the computer, they can certainly be given a demonstration of that. But if they are to conduct job interviews or carry out disciplinary interviews, they may have to learn by watching experienced people carry out those activities. Nor do demonstrations lend themselves to all tasks, such as decision making. Instead, management employees may have to ask questions to find out the steps in reaching a decision. (See Exhibit 8-2 for a list of questions that can help surface the reasons or mental steps by which a decision is reached.)

The eighth step of the model is letting management employees perform the duty. However, trainers must also watch the results. The true test of structured OJT is how well learners can perform. After explaining the duty and demonstrating it, the employees' immediate organizational superiors should then let the learners perform the duty or task—but should also watch the results.

The ninth step of the model is providing detailed feedback about how well management employees perform, praising what is properly done, and offering encouragement for what should be improved. Praise should be offered when a duty or activity is properly performed; encouragement and additional guidance should be offered when it is not properly performed.

The tenth and final step is putting management employees on their own to perform what they have learned. However, they should receive concrete feedback at regular intervals so they know how well they are doing.

Problems Affecting On-the-Job Management or Leadership Training

The major problems with OJT have to do with management or leadership attitudes and lack of training to perform OJT properly. Management attitudes are a source of problems because some managers do not believe that structured OJT is worthwhile. They favor a sink-or-swim approach. Because they suffered through that experience, they believe others should, too. There is no simple solution to that problem. Attitudes are difficult to change. But, with time and proper incentives, employees' immediate organizational superiors can learn that it is worthwhile to devote time to structuring OJT.

Exhibit 8-2
Questions to Ask about Decision Making

Directions: Use this list of questions as a means to help you learn how to go through the mental steps of a process. Pose the questions to one or more people who are widely recognized in the organization as excellent performers in this area of decision making. Record the answers to the questions for future reference and for comparison with answers provided by other excellent performers.	
1	Today I would like to ask you some questions about how you go about deciding (*what? Describe the topic you are asking about.*) I'd like you to think back to the last time you had to make a decision on this issue. Begin by describing for me the circumstances of that situation. How did you go about reaching the decision you reached? Explain the steps in reaching the decision.
	Description of Situation:
	Step-by-step Description of Reaching Decision:
2	What issues are most important to keep in mind when reaching a decision in a situation like the one you described?
3	How would I know when it is appropriate to make a decision on this issue? In other words, how do I recognize when the steps you described should be used?
	Cues to the Need for Decision Making:
4	In your opinion, what mistakes in decision making would be the easiest for a novice to make? How could these mistakes be avoided?

Most Likely Mistakes	Ways to Avoid Mistakes

Another problem is lack of training. Knowing how to train does not come naturally. It requires knowledge and skill in its own right.

ON-THE-JOB MANAGEMENT OR LEADERSHIP COACHING

A *coach* is one who provides on-the-spot guidance, instruction, and feedback. On-the-job coaching and on-the-job training are closely related terms. In practice they often overlap. Sometimes they are used synonymously. But we use the term *on-the-job management* or *leadership coaching* to mean guidance, feedback, and counseling provided in the work setting to management employees or to other leaders, typically by their peers or immediate organizational superiors. It ranges from simple advice to mandated direction and is chiefly used to stimulate individual creativity or improve on-the-job performance. It may be unplanned or planned.

When Should On-the-Job Management or Leadership Coaching Be a Programmatic Focus of L & MD?

Use on-the-job management or leadership coaching when there is need to improve job performance, and management employees feel it is their responsibility to develop those reporting to them.

Planning and Delivering On-the-Job Management or Leadership Coaching

Few management employees or other leaders receive training on how to coach others effectively. But mounting interest in self-directed workteams and employee involvement programs has produced a groundswell of interest in the role of coach, counselor, and facilitator. Indeed, the skills that a management employee or leader needs in participative or empowering organizations differ dramatically from those needed in authoritarian organizations.

Various models of coaching have been proposed. While differing in complexity, they do share common characteristics. Perhaps the best way to distinguish them is by how detailed they are.

Oral coaching is usually spontaneous. It occurs on the spot, immediately before or after action is taken. Oral coaching requires the immediate organizational superior to pay close attention to what an employee is about to do (or has done) and to make a deliberate effort to offer useful comments on it. For instance, the employee's immediate organizational superior praises what is done right and ignores—or issues mild reprimands about—what is done wrong. More attention is paid to finding people performing properly than finding them performing improperly.

To praise orally on the spot and thereby reinforce good performance, the employee's immediate organizational superior should follow a simple model. To describe the model, let us show it in the context of a simple example of how it is applied.

The immediate organizational superior should:

Coaching Model for Issuing Praise	*Application of the Model*
1. Describe briefly what the employee did.	1. "I have noticed that you have been working overtime on that project."
2. Praise the employee's efforts, expressing gratitude.	2. "I really appreciate your efforts."
3. Emphasize the importance of the employee's efforts.	3. "I'm sure you realize that, if we do not receive the business that this project means for us, our profits will suffer this year."

4. Summarize the positive consequences of the employee's efforts in terms of what they mean to the organization, the immediate organizational superior, or the work group.

4. "Your efforts will mean our owners will be pleased with our performance this year, and that could mean a bonus for all of us."

Note that *personal* expressions of gratitude or praise, like the one shown in the example, are more powerful than *impersonal* ones. An example of a personal expression of gratitude is this: "I really appreciate what you are doing. Thank you." Such a simple comment can have a powerful effect, reinforcing good performance. In contrast, an impersonal expression of praise takes this form: "Everyone really appreciates your effort!" This comment could be heard as distant, cold, and removed. It may have minimal effect—or even a negative effect.

To correct orally on the spot, the employee's immediate organizational superior should follow a different model. To describe the model, let us show it in the context of another example. The immediate organizational superior should:

Coaching Model for Correcting Problem Performance

1. Describe clearly what the employee should improve.

2. Emphasize the importance of the employee's efforts.

3. Summarize the consequences of the employee's efforts.

4. Express confidence in the employee's ability to do it right.

Application of the Model

1. "I have noticed that you have not been working overtime on the project that is behind deadline."

2. "I'm sure you realize that, if we do not receive the business that the project means for us, our profits will suffer this year."

3. "More vigorous effort will mean that our owners will be pleased with our profit performance this year, and that could mean a bonus for all of us!"

4. "I am confident in your willingness to 'pitch in,' doing whatever it takes to get that project back on track."

Note that this approach does not attack the person; rather, it focuses on what needs to be done to achieve desired results. It preserves harmonious working relationships between employees and their immediate organizational superiors while helping employees understand what to do to improve performance. In this respect, coaching becomes a method of offering advice, direction, and counseling.

But oral coaching does not always work. Some people are unwilling or unable to listen, experiencing difficulty in accepting compliments or taking criticism.

In these cases, oral coaching may eventually have to be followed up by written coaching.

Written coaching is planned. It requires very close attention to the details of what the employee has been doing. Indeed, the employee's immediate organizational superior should collect specific examples of what the employee has been doing right—or wrong.

To praise employees in writing and thereby reinforce good performance, their immediate organizational superiors should use the same basic approach that is used orally. On the other hand, a written reprimand should adhere to the organization's disciplinary policies and procedures. While there are various philosophies and approaches to discipline, most share common characteristics: first, individuals are warned orally; second, they receive written documentation; third, they are suspended; and, fourth and finally, they are discharged.

Written documentation typically answers seven specific questions:

1. What has the employee been doing?
2. What should the employee be doing?
3. Why is the gap between *what is* and *what should be* important?
4. What are the consequences of the gap?
5. What advice can the employee's immediate organizational superior offer to help the employee narrow or close the gap?
6. How long will the employee's immediate organizational superior allow for the employee to narrow or close the gap?
7. What future disciplinary action will be taken if the employee's performance or behavior does not improve by the date agreed upon or if the behavior does not cease?

The authors of this book have found that many employers are reluctant to take these steps—even when warranted—because they dislike emotional confrontations with people. But, if these questions are answered in writing and provided to a management employee or other organizational leader, they can often have a profoundly positive effect on performance.

An appropriate way to approach problem performance is to prepare written documentation first, answering the questions above. Then share it with the employee, asking him or her to go to a quiet place to read the documentation. Then reconvene after 10 to 30 minutes and ask the employee for opinions. (Give the employee the opportunity to respond in writing, attaching comments to the documentation if necessary.) Above all, follow up as planned to coach the employee, making every effort to help the person improve.

Problems Affecting On-the-Job Management or Leadership Coaching

Few people can dispute that an employee's immediate organizational superior exercises significant influence over individual development. What employees' immediate organizational superiors say can, and does, exert tremendous influence over what employees say and do. It is through the power of this interaction that coaching works.

But the status of employees' immediate organizational superiors can influence the value of coaching. If the immediate organizational superior is a high-potential, high-performing employee, then individual coaching carries substantial weight and credibility—and can influence perceptions throughout the organization. The reverse is also true: if the immediate organizational superior is a low-potential or plateaued performer, then individual coaching may be less useful or effective.

MANAGEMENT OR LEADERSHIP MENTORING OR SPONSORSHIP

The term *mentor* was first used to refer to Nestor, the teacher of Odysseus' son Telemachus in Homer's *Odyssey*. A mentor is thus a teacher whose primary goal is to prepare another person for a successful life or career.

In modern organizational settings, mentors offer advice to others about career, work, or personal issues. Unlike coaches, who are usually the immediate organizational superiors of those they coach, mentors need not be. Indeed, employees choose their own mentors based on traits they admire or wish to emulate. Research has revealed that outstanding performers share one trait in common: most can point to one or more mentors who helped shape them personally or professionally.

A *sponsor* is different from a mentor. Sponsors are positioned one or more levels above their *mentees* on the organization's chain of command. Sponsors protect their mentees and advertise their achievements. Sponsors also challenge their proteges by seeing that they receive choice assignments to showcase their talents.

Mentoring and sponsorship take two forms in organizations: *informal* and *formal*. Informal mentoring or sponsorship is not administered by the organization; rather, individuals seek out people they admire and ask for their advice or help. A special chemistry exists between these people. Each gains from the relationship: the mentor satisfies a deep-felt need to help and develop others; the protege benefits from the advice of one who is more experienced, more politically savvy, and more acutely aware of competitive or organizational conditions.

Formal mentoring or sponsorship programs are administered by the organization. An HRD representative or an L & MD specialist links mentor or sponsor and protege. Usually, some effort is made to match them based on their personalities, areas of interest, experiences, or other matters. Their first meeting is by appointment. Mentors or sponsors may even be given special training on how to enact their roles and provided with suggested questions as icebreakers with their proteges. Thereafter, they may continue their relationship, though they are not forced to do so.

When Should Mentoring or Sponsoring Be a Programmatic Focus of L & MD?

Use mentoring or sponsorship to supplement other L & MD methods. Mentoring and sponsorship can be most effective when tied to

1. Succession planning programs as a tool to develop management employees or other leaders in the organization as replacements for key positions
2. Management or leadership career planning programs as a means to provide management employees or other leaders with personalized career counseling from those who have already climbed the career ladder successfully
3. Internal group training programs, external group training programs, and external education programs to help people learn how to apply on-the-job what they learned off-the-job
4. Job rotation programs as a means to explore new approaches to be used on new jobs with new people and new problems
5. Position assignment programs as a means of exploring approaches to use in handling special problems, situations, or people

Planning and Implementing Mentoring and Sponsorship Programs

By definition, most mentoring and sponsorship occurs spontaneously. It is thus unplanned and informal. To improve the mentoring or sponsorship capabilities of management employees or other leaders, however, organizations can offer internal group training on these subjects and encourage management employees or other leaders to become mentors. Effective mentors and sponsors share certain characteristics; successful mentees also have distinctive characteristics. These characteristics can be enhanced by training on mentoring (see Exhibit 8-3).

Problems Affecting Mentoring and Sponsorship Programs

Three special problems may arise with mentoring and sponsorship. One nettlesome problem has to do with mentoring or sponsorship between individuals of different sexes. Mentoring and sponsorship relationships are often intimate ones. When such relationships exist between two people of different sexes, people may talk, asserting that more exists in the relationship than mere friendship or mentoring. This problem is sometimes called the *development dilemma.*[4]

There is no simple solution to this problem. One approach is to encourage

Exhibit 8-3
A Sample Training Course Outline on Techniques of Effective Mentoring and Sponsorship

Purpose	To introduce supervisors, managers, and executives to effective mentoring or sponsorship techniques
Objectives	*Upon completing this course, participants should be able to:* 1. Define mentor 2. Define sponsor 3. Explain the value of mentoring and sponsorship 4. Describe key steps in a model of the mentoring and sponsorship process 5. Demonstrate each step in the model 6. Identify personal values

Course Outline	I. Introduction
	   A. Describe
	      1. The course title
	      2. The purpose of the course
	      3. The objectives of the course
	      4. The structure of the course
	   B. Ask participants to summarize their personal goals for the course
	
	II. What is Mentoring and Sponsorship?
	   A. Definitions
	   B. Importance of Mentoring and Sponsorship
	   C. The Role of the Immediate Organizational Superior in Mentoring and Sponsorship
	
	III. What Skills Are Needed for Effective Mentoring and Sponsorship?
	   A. Supporting Mentoring and Sponsorship Relationships
	   B. Encouraging Individuals to Approach Others for Advice and Help
	   C. What Are the Skills of a Mentor or Sponsor?
	      1. Description of Skills
	      2. Role Plays
	   D. Valuing Diversity: Same-Sex and Different-Sex Mentoring/ Sponsorship
	      1. Description of Key Issues
	      2. Role Plays
	      3. Discussion, Follow-Up and Debriefing
	
	IV. Conclusion
	   A. Evaluate
	      1. Participants' Mentoring and Sponsorship Skills
	      2. The Course
	   B. Establish Plans to Improve and Practice Mentoring and Sponsorship Skills

mentoring and sponsoring relationships between same-sex individuals only. Another, perhaps better approach, is to train management employees or other leaders on mentoring and sponsorship. As part of this training, they should learn about ethical issues in same-sex and different-sex mentoring and sponsorship relationships. Through training, people can learn to overcome prejudice.

A second problem has to do with dependence in mentoring or sponsoring relationships. As people gain experience, they eventually outgrow their mentors and sponsors. They may pick new ones. In some cases, the protege's success eventually eclipses the mentor's, posing a unique problem for their relationship. They must learn to part on amicable terms.

A third problem has to do with preparing for the future. Mentors and sponsors rely heavily on what they have learned from their experience. That is as it should be. But the past in which they developed posed unique challenges, different from those which the future holds in store. Proteges must learn that mentors and sponsors can be helpful, reflecting their own experience and their own values. But mentors and sponsors are not always helpful in predicting the future and suggesting strategies to address new, unique challenges posed by it.

For this reason, proteges must recognize that there are limits to the value of mentoring and sponsorship arrangements. The past is not always the harbinger of the future. Proteges must make their own efforts to predict, and grapple with, future challenges.

MANAGEMENT OR LEADERSHIP SELF-DEVELOPMENT

To a considerable extent, all L & MD is self-development. After all, individuals are the final arbiters of their own learning needs. And without individual motivation, no learning will occur.

Self-development refers to independent efforts undertaken by adults to improve themselves and grapple with the work-related and life-related challenges they confront. Research by Cyril Houle in the 1950s revealed that adult learners can be classified into three groups:[5] (1) *goal-oriented learners*, who set out to achieve pre-defined objectives from their learning activities; (2) *activity-oriented learners*, who set out to increase their social contact through learning; and (3) *learning-oriented learners*, who seek personal challenge and growth.

Houle's student Allen Tough extended the investigation of learning, finding that adults are typically motivated to learn by problems confronting them in their work or their lives. Learning is organized around "projects . . . defined as a series of related episodes, adding up to at least seven hours. In each episode more than half of the person's total motivation is to gain and retain fairly clear knowledge and skill, or to produce some other lasting change in himself."[6] Tough found that most adults spend more time than they realize on learning projects of this kind: "Almost everyone undertakes at least one or two major learning efforts a year, and some individuals undertake as many as 15 or 20.

... It is common for a man or woman to spend 700 hours a year at learning projects."[7]

More recent studies of self-development and self-initiated learning have focused on *learning style* or *cognitive style*, meaning the optimal way that individuals approach learning and learning situations. Individuals vary in their learning styles. While descriptions of learning styles vary, one well-known scheme was devised by David A. Kolb. According to Kolb, individuals may be categorized into four dominant categories:[8] (1) *Convergers*, whose learning style focuses on technical, but not interpersonal, issues; (2) *Divergers*, whose chief sensitivity is to values, meanings, and feelings; (3) *Assimilators*, whose strength is devising abstract models; and (4) *Accommodators*, who thrive on action, risks, and adapting to situations. If individuals are aware of their learning styles, they can take advantage of their learning abilities to effectively master new situations and develop themselves.

When Should Self-Development Be a Programmatic Focus of L & MD?

Self-development should always be a programmatic focus of L & MD. If it is not, individuals will not be truly committed to learning, and will expect others to take responsibility for their development—and perhaps their lives and careers as well. Unfortunately, too many people expect their employers and their immediate organizational superiors to take that responsibility.

Planning and Carrying Out Self-Development Activities

By encouraging the use of individual development plans, organizations can help individuals plan and carry out self-development activities. Using that approach, management employees or other leaders negotiate work-related learning projects or learning episodes each year with their immediate organizational superiors. In this way it is possible to achieve a marriage of interests between the organization and the individual.

To use this approach, an L & MD specialist can simply make a learning contract form and an outline of recommended procedures available. It is then up to employees and their immediate organizational superiors to set aside time for planning learning projects. The process can stand alone, or it can be directly tied to such activities as management or leadership performance appraisal, succession planning, or work planning.

Alternatively, the process can be entirely voluntary. Employees may complete an individual development plan in conjunction with a career planning form. In this way, learning is linked to career plans, prompting individuals to undertake learning activities designed to turn their career goals into realities.

If employees and their immediate organizational superiors agree to send copies of completed learning contracts to the L & MD director or L & MD coordinator, they can be combined to identify common learning needs shared by many people. Then the L & MD director or L & MD coordinator can function as resource person and enabling agent to help meet those needs.

Many activities may enhance self-development activities. To list just a few:

- Read about new topics
- Attend lectures
- Go to trade shows
- Talk to other people about unfamiliar topics
- Tackle a tough problem
- Think over different approaches to implementing a solution
- Talk to people at different levels of experience about what they have learned
- Lead a charity drive or a church group
- Teach or train others on something you know
- Take a self-assessment test
- Talk to a child about a complex subject
- Paint a picture
- Write a poem
- Write an article
- Write a memo
- Write a book
- Learn new software
- Wander through a library
- Take a walk in a scenic location
- Talk to a person from another culture
- Take a trip to another country
- Examine your supervisor's job description and assess what you can and cannot do
- Talk to your spouse about areas in which you could stand to improve
- Talk to a parent about your childhood
- Talk to a parent about your life
- Attend a play and write a critique
- Write a letter to yourself about areas of your life that you could improve
- Fill out a performance appraisal on yourself
- Watch someone do something you have always wanted to do
- Seek out people who are experts on a subject of interest to you and talk to them about it
- Delegate a difficult job task, coaching another person on how to do it
- Read a literary classic and critique it
- Take a course at a local school on a subject of interest to you

- Seek out someone in another organization doing the same job you do and talk to him or her about how to deal with job problems

Problems Affecting Self-Development

Self-development is heavily influenced by *present* or *pending* problems confronting learners. For instance, people who are about to go to Spain are highly motivated to learn about it. Likewise, couples soon to become parents are highly motivated to learn about babies, and an individual about to be promoted becomes highly motivated to learn about the new job.

Learning of this kind is decidedly *problem-driven*. It is affected by *recency bias*, the tendency to focus on recent or pending problems or issues. Longer-term matters are too often de-emphasized. It is this short-term emphasis that can lead self-development astray. If learners take no time to reflect on the long term, they will be not be able to establish and work toward meeting long-term career goals. They become compulsive consumers of learning activities rather than thoughtful, analytical pursuers of continuous individual improvement and growth.

Perhaps the best way to avoid this negative side effect of self-development is to establish a means of checking signals about learning projects with such others as immediate organizational superiors, mentors, sponsors, coaches, L & MD specialists, or other knowledgeable people. If learners cannot explain how specific learning projects are tied to their career goals or work-related performance improvement goals, then the value of those projects can be examined to ensure that they are not neglecting others with greater potential for long-term payoff.

MANAGEMENT OR LEADERSHIP SELF-STUDY

There are many ways to undertake learning. Individuals may initiate their own self-development learning projects, prompted by immediate problems they are encountering. In a related manner, they may choose to learn through organized methods—such as pursuing correspondence study, reading job-related or career-related materials, viewing videotapes, or listening to audiotapes on their own. Learning materials abound. For the motivated person, it is only a matter of finding the time to locate and use them. *Self-study* refers to efforts made by individuals to improve themselves by organized study and by grappling with work-related and life-related challenges they confront.

When Should Self-Study Be a Programmatic Focus of L & MD?

Self-study is appropriate for management employees or other leaders who are

- Motivated to learn on their own
- Patient enough to take the time to research materials to help them meet their needs

- Interested in learning a subject in depth rather than remaining comfortable with a shallow understanding sufficient just to get by

- Comfortable with structured learning material, such as correspondence study, that probably does not directly answer pressing questions or solve pressing problems

- Creative and capable of coming up with their own solutions to problems rather than relying uncritically on what others think

- Capable of devoting time to researching materials and studying them

Self-study is rarely appropriate when any or all these conditions cannot be met.

Planning and Carrying Out Self-Study Activities

Since self-study is usually individually initiated and individually implemented, the role of the organization must necessarily be supportive rather than directive. If a decision is made to pursue self-study as a programmatic focus of L & MD efforts, then L & MD directors or L & MD coordinators can take several steps to support the efforts. They may:

1. Survey or interview individuals about self-study activities of interest or value to them, making sure to determine the underlying reasons for this interest

2. Identify common needs across individuals, when they exist, to provide economical approaches to meeting self-study needs

3. Identify materials and activities to support self-study efforts

4. Provide administrative support, such as completing and turning in paperwork for correspondence courses, helping individuals enroll, and interfacing with sponsors of courses or other materials

5. Help individuals evaluate the value of their self-study efforts and assess how they may apply to their jobs what they have learned

Use the Worksheet appearing in Exhibit 8-4 to identify self-study activities that may be of interest to sponsor in your organization; and, read the case study appearing in Exhibit 8-5 to see how one organization successfully used two different self-study methods for L & MD.

Problems Affecting Self-Study

The same key problem affects self-study that affects self-development: learning becomes *problem-driven* and is *affected by recency bias*, with the possible result that learners take no time to reflect on the long term. Likewise, the same approach used to overcome this problem with self-development may also be

Exhibit 8-4
A Worksheet for Identifying Self-Study Activities on Value for an Organization

Directions: Give this Worksheet to a management employee and ask him or her to use it as a starting point for a discussion between the employee and his or her immediate organizational superior about self-study activities that could be particularly valuable for the employee. (These activities can range from those conducted during working hours to those conducted outside of working hours.) Ask the management employee to take notes on the answers to the questions posed on this Worksheet.

Questions to be posed by the management employee and answered by the management employee's immediate organizational superior:

1	What learning activities were particularly helpful to you in preparing you for your present job? Include *any* activity of value to you—not necessarily training, education, or development activities sponsored by the organization—but also such others as leading a church group, serving on the board of directors of a local charity, working with a local school, or raising children. Try to confine your answer to only one or two learning activities that were *most* helpful to you.
2	What learning experiences would you suggest for me? Please make some suggestions, explain why you believe they would be helpful to me from the organization's perspective, and offer advice about what I should try to learn from them.

used with self-study: a means of cross-checking self-study learning projects should be established with organizational superiors, mentors, sponsors, coaches, L & MD specialists, or other knowledgeable people. In this way, the payoffs from these efforts may be considered at the outset before substantial investments of time or money have been committed to them.

SUMMARY

In this chapter we reviewed the following *informal L & MD methods*:

- On-the-job management or leadership training
- On-the-job management or leadership coaching
- Management or leadership mentoring or sponsorship
- Management or leadership self-development
- Management or leadership self-study

These methods share one important similarity: they do not lend themselves well to centralized planning, administration, or oversight; rather, they are better handled at the work site and overseen by the learners, their immediate organizational superiors, or their co-workers.

Exhibit 8-5

A Case Study of Successful Use of Self-Study in L & MD

Todd Lendquist is the L & MD Director at Ace Office Supplies, a manufacturer and distributor of office products. Ace employs over 1,500 people—approximately 350 of them are management employees—at its corporate headquarters in Duluth, MN. Ace is not unionized.

Two years ago, Todd was in a quandary: Whenever he issued a schedule of management training classes, many people signed up to attend. But few actually showed up to the classes. Todd felt that, while the perceived need for the classes was high, the corporation's downsizing effort had made it exceedingly difficult for company team leaders, supervisors, managers, and executives to find time during working hours to attend internal group training.

So Todd decided to try something different: He would make the learning efforts more geared to self-study than to group study. To that end, he conducted a needs assessment and used the results to identify and prioritize topics of perceived value to management employees. He then scheduled a large meeting room for his use, on a long-term basis, about one-half-hour before working hours began. Todd rented videotapes, none longer than 20 minutes, on topics of interest that were identified through the survey. He also ordered breakfast to be brought into the meeting room. Todd called this series the "Great Brown Bag Breakfast Management Video Training Effort."

Todd prepared handouts before the meeting, showed the video, and then held a brief discussion after the video. The first 10 minutes consisted of an introduction and an opportunity for networking among participants. The next 20 minutes consisted of the video showing. The final 30 minutes consisted of discussion, question-and-answer, and an occasional simple exercise. Every session ended with a simple activity for participants to take back to their jobs and apply. Todd decided that no session would last longer than 60 minutes. The first 30 minutes were held on the individual's time; the last 30 minutes were held on company time.

The survey results revealed that the most important topics were perceived to be Total Quality Management (TQM), employee involvement, and on-the-job training. Todd then sent out a schedule of sessions on these topics by electronic mail and office carrier. He notified all team leaders, supervisors, managers, and executives of the schedule—and all topics that he would cover.

Todd was astounded by the results. On the first showing, 300 of the company's 350 management employees signed up to attend—and 120 showed up. Todd decided to make the "Great Brown Bag Breakfast Management Video Training Effort" a long-term program. He also planned to use its sessions to build interest in longer classroom sessions he offers.

After a year of these sessions, Todd began to notice that the same people attended every week. One day he set aside some time in a session to ask them about others who never attend. Using the information he learned from their remarks, Todd established the "Great Management Training Library Check-Out and Take-Home Store." Todd purchased the most popular videos he had shown at the Brown Bag Breakfast and made them available to management employees to check out, take home, and watch on their own time. He also purchased audiotapes, books, self-assessment questionnaires, and computer software on the same topics.

Again, Todd was astounded by the results. Many people who never attended a Brown Bag Breakfast contacted Todd so they could check out material for the two-week loan period.

Using these two simple methods—Brown Bag Breakfasts and a Video Check-Out Library—Todd increased the amount of training offered to management employees by several hundred percent.

NOTES

1. A. Carnevale and L. Gainer, *The Learning Enterprise* (Alexandria, VA: The American Society for Training and Development and the U.S. Department of Labor, Employment and Training Administration, 1989), p. 25.

2. W. Rothwell and H. Kazanas, ''Structured on-the-Job Training (SOJT) as Perceived by HRD Professionals,'' in W. Rothwell, ed., *Emerging Issues in HRD Sourcebook* (Amherst, MA: Human Resource Development Press, 1995).

3. Ibid.

4. B. Ragins, ''Barriers to Mentoring: The Female Manager's Dilemma,'' *Human Relations*, Vol. 42, No. 1, pp. 1–22.

5. C. Houle, *The Inquiring Mind* (Madison, WI: University of Wisconsin Press, 1961).

6. A. Tough, *The Adult's Learning Projects* (2nd ed.) (Toronto, ON: Ontario Institute for Studies in Education, 1979), p. 6.

7. Ibid., p. 1.

8. D. Kolb, *Experiential Learning: Experience as a Source of Learning and Development* (Englewood Cliffs, NJ: Prentice-Hall, 1984).

Chapter 9

Planning and Using Special Methods

Special L & MD methods are neither formal nor informal. They may be planned or unplanned. But they are distinctive because they are cutting-edge or controversial methods. In this chapter we turn to several of them:

- Adventure learning
- New Age Training (NAT)
- Action learning

ADVENTURE LEARNING

Sometimes called *outdoor learning, adventure learning* is a popular and trendy method that traces its origins to the personal fitness craze, interest in the outdoors, and the ecology movement. However, it is not a uniformly accepted L & MD method. Indeed, some "critics charge that outdoor management training is nothing more than an excuse for busy managers to take 'vacations' on company time."[1]

But adventure learning can be more than an excuse for getting away from the maddening job pressures of the 1990s. Its appeal does not appear to be short-lived, as might be expected of a flash-in-the-pan fad. It poses an exciting alternative to learning in stuffy classrooms or hectic work places. It is also truly *experiential* because it is decidedly short on theory but long on application.

Defining Adventure Learning

Adventure learning is set in the outdoors or wilderness. Its aim is to lead individuals to examine their values and lead group members to reach new conclusions about how they work together and depend on each other.

Adventure learning experiences can be divided into three categories: (1) *short-term*; (2) *intermediate-term*; and (3) *long-term*. They can also be further divided into those focusing on *individual* or *group/team* change.

A *short-term adventure learning experience* is a mere outdoor jaunt. It lasts only a few minutes. L & MD specialists use it much like a role play, simulation, or case study to break monotony and reinforce a lesson begun in a classroom session. It need not be set in a wilderness; rather, it can be set in other outdoor locations—such as in a municipal park, on a tennis court, next to a tree, by a street light, or even in a parking lot. Descriptions of short-term adventure learning experiences of this kind appear in Exhibit 9-1.

An *intermediate-term adventure learning experience* ranges in length from several days to a week. There are two kinds: (1) *the stand-alone program*; and (2) *the management retreat.*

In a stand-alone program the learning experience is not tied to background readings or introductory lectures; rather, participants begin and end their learning experience outdoors. For instance, they take a camping trip together. Learning experiences have been planned, however. They are specifically designed to evoke new ideas. These experiences may use ropes, logs, or rafts.

Stand-alone programs are frequented more often by supervisors and nonexempt workers than by middle managers or executives. The participants are usually part of the same work unit, work group, or work team. At this writing, the costs range from $300 to $2,800 per participant and are usually set in a local park rather than in a wilderness.

A management retreat is a special subcategory of the intermediate-term adventure learning experience. Retreats are held in such pastoral settings as resorts or parks. Participants may be individuals, stranger groups, family groups, or work groups. *Stranger groups* consist of people who have never met before and will never meet again; *family groups* consist of spouses and/or children; and, *work groups* consist of a manager—often a top manager—and all those reporting to him or her. Individuals attend to learn about themselves; stranger groups learn about themselves and how they relate to others (group dynamics); family groups help people learn how they interact with significant people outside the work place and are akin to marriage encounters; and, work groups help people learn how they interact among significant people in their work places.

Learning activities during stand-alone programs vary widely. They may include group meetings in a lodge or less formal activities such as gardening, woodchopping, yoga, meditation, massages, hot baths, saunas, and swimming.[2]

A *long-term adventure learning experience* lasts a week or more. Participants camp outdoors, usually in the wilderness. Learning experiences have *not* necessarily been planned. As participants partake of all the excitement and dangers of life in the wilderness—such as whitewater rafting, mountain climbing, sailing, and other hazardous ventures—they learn about themselves and their group. The aim is to lead a group to develop strong cohesiveness and camaraderie. Experiences of this kind are frequented more often by executives or middle managers

Exhibit 9-1
Short-Term Adventure Learning Experiences

Activity 1	**Objective**	To reflect on the status of a group
	Materials Required	A long piece of rope or twine; scissors or penknife; tape
	Time Required	Allow 10–20 minutes
	Setting	Move from an indoor setting (such as a classroom) to an outdoor setting (such as a sidewalk, parking lot, or municipal park)
	Procedure	• When discussing teamwork, suggest that a small group can learn best by doing something together. • Ask group members to count off in threes or fours and appoint a spokesperson. Leave the work setting or classroom and go outdoors. • Ask each group to illustrate how the group interacts by depicting the group as it appears to them. Tell each group to use a piece of rope for that illustration. Make the scissors, penknife, or tape available to each group, as needed.
	Discussion Questions	1. Ask the spokesperson of each group to explain what the group's illustration means. How has the group depicted itself, and why has the interaction been illustrated in the way it was? 2. Ask members of each group to describe how they believe the group *should* appear. (Allow them a few minutes to repeat the activity.) 3. Ask participants *how* they may *change* their groups (or themselves) so that the group appears as they believe it *should* appear in response to item 2 above.
Activity 2	**Objective**	To build camaraderie and team spirit
	Materials Required	Whiffle ball, plastic bat, catchers' mitts
	Time Required	Allow 60 minutes
	Setting	Move from an indoor setting (such as a classroom) to the nearest baseball diamond. (If no baseball diamond is available, secure permission to use a parking lot or other open space available nearby.)
	Procedure	• When discussing teamwork, suggest that people can gain insight about how well they interact by playing a team sport. • Ask the group to count off in twos. Leave the work setting or classroom and go outdoors. Ask the groups to play baseball (or whiffle ball) together.
	Discussion Questions	1. After the game is over, ask the winning team what their impression is about what it feels like to "lose." 2. Ask the losing team how they feel. 3. Ask the two groups to compare how they interacted during the game and how they interact at work. What similarities do they note? What differences do they note?

than by supervisors or nonexempt workers. The costs at this writing also range from $300 to $2,800 per participant.

When Should Adventure Learning Be a Programmatic Focus of L & MD?

Adventure learning is not for the faint-hearted. Although growing into more than a fad, the most rigorous adventure learning experiences do pose unique hazards to participants that are seldom cause for concern in learning experiences centered in classrooms or work sites. After all, in what other learning experiences do L & MD specialists have to worry about participants falling off a mountain, drowning in a babbling brook, or getting lost in the woods?

Adventure learning is uniquely suited to meeting *affective* (feeling-centered) learning objectives. It can also be used to support more than one programmatic focus of L & MD. For individuals it helps to:

• Clarify problems, concerns, or desires
• Reveal how they relate to groups (generally) or their family members or co-workers (specifically)
• Lead to deep reflection about personal or career problems

For groups it helps to:

• Intensify cohesiveness and feelings of interconnectedness
• Reveal group dynamics stripped of the (sometimes shallow) courtesy found in work places
• Build camaraderie
• Lead to new insights about more effective ways of working together

Generally, however, adventure learning is not appropriate for meeting *cognitive* (knowledge-centered) objectives. Nor is it appropriate for helping people increase their technical knowledge.

Planning and Offering Adventure Learning

Short-term adventure learning experiences can be readily planned and offered to supplement internal group training and on-the-job training. Activities similar to those shown in Exhibit 9-1 may be readily adapted for many uses. If managed effectively, they will usually be greeted enthusiastically by participants.

But intermediate-term and long-term adventure learning experiences are another matter. Rarely will an L & MD director, L & MD coordinator, or L & MD specialist be qualified to plan and deliver them. (An exception, of course, is the L & MD director who has previously managed such programs for a

Exhibit 9-2

A Worksheet for Planning Adventure Learning Experiences

Directions: Use this Worksheet to help you structure your thinking about the objectives of an Adventure Learning experience before participants take part in it.	
1	What is the purpose of the experience? Why do you feel that an adventure learning experience is the best way to achieve that purpose?
2	What should participants feel or appreciate more upon their return from the experience?
3	Describe precisely what activities will best achieve the objectives described in question 2 above. Examples of possible activities might include: log-rolling, backpacking, mountain climbing, rafting, sailing, boating, rope climbing, hiking, jogging, camping, fishing, or hunting. Describe the events in any special sequence you feel should occur.

Date/Time	Activities	How are the activities related to the objectives?

4	How should the adventure learning experience be evaluated?
5	How should the lessons learned by the participants in the adventure learning experience be transferred back to their jobs? By what means can the likelihood of such transfer of learning be increased?

consulting firm.) That means an external vendor will be needed to design, operate, and follow up the adventure. Many vendors specialize in adventure learning. That external vendor becomes the *trip facilitator*.

Always approach a prospective external vendor with clear-cut performance objectives in mind for adventure learning. If you don't, you will probably waste valuable time—and perhaps incur additional expense—figuring out what results should stem from the adventure learning experience. Be sure that the activities planned match up to the identified learning needs. If they don't, the experience will probably turn into nothing more than a pleasure trip. Decision makers will later shake their heads, wondering what returns the organization received for this substantial investment. The credibility of the L & MD function may also suffer as a result.

A better approach is to begin by considering these questions:

- What should participants feel at the end of the experience?
- Who should participate?
- How will adventure learning contribute to meeting participants' needs?
- Why is adventure learning preferable to other L & MD methods for meeting those needs?

Once these questions have been answered—use the Worksheet appearing in Exhibit 9-2 to sort out key issues—then approach consulting firms specializing in adventure learning. Ask for advice about the best adventure learning design to meet the identified needs and achieve the specified learning outcomes. Use an evaluation form for vendors of adventure learning experiences (see Exhibit 9-3) to help in this process.

Before an intermediate-term or long-term adventure learning experience begins, identify the participants. Hold a briefing session for them. If possible, have them complete an expectations activity, like the one appearing in Exhibit 9-4, as an aid in planning the experience. Finally, have them sign a release form, reviewed and approved in advance by the organization's legal counsel, to absolve the organization of liability stemming from injuries or fatalities that may occur during the experience. Update emergency information about the participants so that appropriate people may be contacted as necessary.

At the time the adventure learning experience begins, the trip facilitator should explain its purpose, desired outcomes, and any special responsibilities of the participants. Be sure, too, that the role of the trip facilitator or scout is clarified. It should not be assumed that everyone understands the purpose of the trip, the objectives to be achieved, or the role of the group leader(s).

If the adventure learning experience includes such specific challenges as logrolling, rope climbing, whitewater rafting, the trip facilitator should be sure to debrief participants after *each* experience so as to catch them in a teachable moment. More specifically, they should be asked to *process their feelings*, meaning they should describe what they feel before they have recovered from the intensity of the moment. They should be asked to clarify what they have learned from the experience about themselves, other individuals in the group, or the group as a whole. The trip facilitator should allow them to learn from each other, intervening only when one person attacks another. Personal attacks will only undermine group cohesiveness.

After the trip is concluded, the trip facilitator should hold a debriefing session with participants. They should be asked to share what they feel they learned. Those insights should be recorded for future playback. If necessary, experiences of previous groups may also be shared. Participants should be asked to address questions like these: (1) What did you learn? (2) How do you feel about yourselves and others in the group? (3) In your opinion, how did the adventure learning experience contribute to helping you meet your learning needs? The participants should then be asked to record their insights on a videotape segment or in a letter, indicating how they can apply on-the-job what they learned from the experience.

Problems Affecting Adventure Learning

Adventure learning presents unique challenges. Not everyone feels comfortable participating in such experiences. Some people do not find the outdoors particularly appealing; some have family or personal commitments that complicate their ability to participate; some fear the dangers implicit in mountain climb-

Exhibit 9-3

An Evaluation Form for Vendors of Adventure Learning Programs

Directions: Use this form to evaluate vendors of adventure learning programs. Fill out the vendor's name, the date, and the name(s) of those evaluating the vendors' program(s). For each question posed in column 1 below, check (✓) _yes_ or _no_ in column 2. Then comment on the response—or the vendor—in column 3. Finally, rank the vendor in comparison with others in the box below the vendor's name on page 1 of the evaluation form. Use 1 to designate the most desirable vendor. Use higher numbers to designate less desirable vendors.

Vendor's Name			**Date**	
Score			**Evaluator(s)**	

Column 1		**Column 2**		**Column 3**
Questions		**Yes** ☒	**No** ☒	**Comments**
1	Has the vendor stated the purpose of the adventure learning experience?	☐	☐	
2	Has the vendor stated the performance objectives of the adventure learning experience?	☐	☐	
3	Has the vendor adequately described what will occur on the adventure learning experience?	☐	☐	
4	Has the vendor supplied a rationale for the adventure learning experiences proposed for the client organization?	☐	☐	
5	Has the vendor provided a lesson plan or other description of events that will happen during the adventure learning experience?	☐	☐	
6	Do the activities recommended by the vendor appear to match up to the performance objectives of the client organization?	☐	☐	
7	Has the vendor identified where the trip will be held?	☐	☐	
8	Does the location appear to be appropriate for meeting the performance objectives of the adventure learning experience?	☐	☐	
9	Is it clear who the trip facilitator will be?	☐	☐	
10	Is the trip facilitator qualified by appropriate credentials in psychology or related disciplines to conduct an adventure learning experience?	☐	☐	
11	Does the vendor have a track record of facilitating adventure learning experiences?	☐	☐	

Exhibit 9-3 (continued)

Column 1		Column 2		Column 3
Questions		Yes ☒	No ☒	**Comments**
12	Is the vendor's accident rate low?	☐	☐	
13	Has the vendor adequately described safety precautions?	☐	☐	
14	Is the vendor able to supply testimonials from satisfied clients?	☐	☐	
15	Do the vendor's references check out?	☐	☐	
16	Has the vendor taken adequate precautions to minimize legal liability?	☐	☐	
17	Has the vendor provided a realistic estimate of all costs associated with the trip?	☐	☐	
18	Is the vendor's price competitive?	☐	☐	

ing, rafting, or other hazardous ventures. Participants' spouses may grow suspicious if male and female co-workers camp outdoors for some time. There is no simple way to meet these challenges. But here are a few suggestions:

- Consider the need for an adventure learning experience carefully.

- Do *not* pressure individuals who have qualms about participating. Let dissenters opt out.

- Take care to avoid making it appear that the learning experience is geared to one group, individual, or sex—or is designed to exclude anyone.

- Take care to discuss the idea with your organization's legal counsel well ahead of time, clearing it so that liability issues can be minimized. If they cannot be minimized, then don't proceed with the adventure learning experience.

NEW AGE TRAINING

Think of crystals, Astrology, Far Eastern philosophy, ESP, UFOs, meditation, and yoga. As you do, you enter the realm of the *New Age*. Critics charge that so-called New Age methods are silly or even potentially dangerous because they mislead gullible people.[3] Adherents point to the large number of true believers who give credence to horoscopes, UFOs, and ESP.

Exhibit 9-4
An Expectations Activity for Adventure Learning Experiences

Directions: Use this Worksheet to assess the expectations of prospective participants in an adventure learning experience. Before they embark upon the experience, administer the activity below to gauge their expectations.	
1	What do you feel is the purpose of this experience? Why is your employer sponsoring this experience?
2	What do you want to learn from this experience?
3	How supportive of this experience is your spouse or significant other of this experience? *(Mark an X above the scale below that best represents his or her level of support.)*

Actively opposes the experience	Somewhat opposed	Neutral/Is not aware of it	Somewhat supportive	Strongly supports

4 Indicate below what activities you are and are not willing to participate in during the adventure learning experience. *(Mark an X on the appropriate lines below)*

Willing to Participate	Activity	Unwilling to Participate
_____	Backpacking	_____
_____	Boating	_____
_____	Camping	_____
_____	Canoeing	_____
_____	Fishing	_____
_____	Gardening	_____
_____	Hiking	_____
_____	Hot bathing	_____
_____	Hunting	_____
_____	Jogging	_____
_____	Mountain climbing	_____
_____	Rafting	_____
_____	Rope climbing	_____
_____	Sailing	_____
_____	Swimming	_____
_____	Wood chopping	_____
_____	Yoga	_____
_____	Other	_____

5 How should this experience be evaluated? How will you define success?

Defining NAT

New Age Training (NAT) is the application of New Age beliefs and approaches to L & MD. Rather than one method, NAT makes use of many to help individuals or groups undergo change and learning. Most widely accepted for L & MD: Neurolinguistic Programming (NLP), suggestology, visioning, meditation, yoga, and imaging. Least accepted and most controversial for L & MD: crystals, Astrology, ESP, UFOs, certain abstruse Far Eastern philosophies of leadership, and instruction based on religion in the work place.

When Should NAT Be a Programmatic Focus of L & MD?

Try to avoid the least acceptable NAT methods—which we shall not discuss in this book. A more prudent course of action is to combine accepted NAT methods with other L & MD methods. For example, use visioning, meditation, yoga, or imaging methods to punctuate traditional classroom activities. That approach can be quite effective—and it minimizes possible controversy.

Planning and Offering NAT

If NAT methods are used in combination with more traditional methods, then planning and offering them is a relatively simple matter:

- Identify occasions when they may be appropriate. For example, visioning activities work well in creativity training, team-building sessions, or strategic planning meetings; imaging works well with creativity training; and yoga or meditation works particularly well at the beginning or ending of a group session by establishing a relaxed but alert climate.

- At the outset of the experience, explain its purpose and how it relates to what participants have learned or will learn.

- Give step-by-step instructions to participants. Do not assume they will know what to do.

- Follow up the experience with a brief discussion to clarify the results and reinforce how the method relates to what participants have learned or will learn.

See Exhibit 9-5 for examples of two NAT methods that may be effectively used in L & MD.

Problems Affecting NAT Methods

Like adventure learning and other cutting-edge approaches, NAT methods are by no means a panacea for L & MD. To cite two common problems: Some people may not wish to participate in the least accepted NAT methods on religious grounds, and some participants—or their families—may claim brainwashing by controversial NAT methods, and this may create a public relations nightmare and enormous potential legal liability for the organization. We do not recommend mixing L & MD with the least accepted New Age techniques because we feel that religion in all its forms is a very personal matter that is ill suited to the work place. But if you feel pressured by influential managers to use extreme measures, be sure to review the techniques you plan to use with the organization's legal counsel and alert supporters to potential risks beforehand.

Exhibit 9-5
New Age Activities

Visioning Activity	
Objectives	To help members of a group establish a unified vision of an idealized future they wish to realize
Materials Required	Flipchart paper; flipchart stand; marking pens; masking tape
Time Required	Allow 30 minutes
Procedure	*Create small groups of three or four people each. Ask each group to:* • Set up a flipchart • Elect a spokesperson • Work together to answer this question: "Envision the *ideal future*. What would it look like in this organization, division, department, work group, or team?" • Describe the characteristics of that ideal future in short, descriptive phrases and record them on the flipchart. As flipchart sheets are filled, tear them off the pad and use masking tape to affix them to the wall • Avoid critical statements or disagreements; rather, work together quickly in listing adjectives to describe the future, even if they seem to conflict • Summarize key points of agreement in your description, prioritizing what you most desire for the future
Discussion Questions	• Ask each group spokesperson: What were the key points of agreement? • Ask each group spokesperson: What priorities did your group decide on? What was the reasoning for those priorities?
Imaging Activity	
Objectives	To help members of a group relax and increase their collective creativity
Materials Required	None
Time Required	Allow 10–15 minutes
Setting Required	Meeting room or classroom
Procedure	*Ask participants to:* • Remain seated • Close their eyes • Envision a pastoral setting • Imagine that, as the facilitator counts backward from 10, you are entering the pastoral setting. You can feel wind at your back, see water lapping on the banks of a lake, and feel the heat from a soft, golden sun • Listen as the facilitator counts backward, beginning at 10 • When the facilitator reaches 1, tell the participants that they are entering the setting and will remain there for a few minutes

Exhibit 9-5 (continued)

Imaging Activity	
Discussion Questions	*Ask participants: Did you actually feel the wind, see the lake, and feel the heat of sunshine?*
	• How many fell asleep during the imaging session? (Ask for a show of hands.) Explain that sleep indicates complete relaxation • How might imaging help you relieve stress you face during the work day?

ACTION LEARNING

Historically, L & MD specialists have focused their attention on what might be called *content-oriented L & MD methods*. They are traditionally designed to communicate information, build skills, or change the attitudes of individual managers. Content-oriented L & MD methods are intended to improve efficiency ("doing things right"). One key assumption is that management employees (or other leaders) will improve performance if trained in what they are expected to do and how well they are expected to do it. Another common assumption is that the best, most reliable information about management comes from academic theories and research about management.

But increasing attention is being devoted to *action learning*.[4] Intended to improve effectiveness ("doing the right things"), action learning is designed to *discover* new ideas and approaches for application in unique cultures or organizational settings. It unleashes the creative abilities of individuals, groups, or organizations, making planned learning experiences a competitive weapon to uncover utterly new ways to address complex organizational problems. It assumes that participants in a planned L & MD program should learn from organization-specific and job-specific problems confronting them.

When Should Action Learning Be a Programmatic Focus of L & MD?

Most organizations use some action learning methods. Usually it is a question of how often—or how well—they are used. Organizations pursuing TQM or employee involvement will typically devote more time and effort to action learning, since it is particularly well attuned to participative decision making. Moreover, TQM focuses on continuous improvement—what the Japanese call *kaizen*—in a way consistent with the assumptions made by action learning methods that the world is dynamic and constantly changing.

Using Action Learning

Content-oriented L & MD methods traditionally rely on historical information—such as management or leadership theories. They are not necessarily tied to unique conditions in one organizational setting. Nor do they rely on learning materials adapted from problems confronting learners; rather, they may rely heavily on learning materials about management or leadership purchased externally.

Action learning methods are different. They use problems or issues affecting an organization, group, job, or individual as the basis for learning experiences. Management or leadership competencies are inferred, in part or whole, from information gathered from *outside* the organization through benchmarking, customer surveys, or similar data-gathering methods. Customers, suppliers, distributing wholesalers, and competitors become key sources of information about *what should be*. That information is then compared to what already exists in the organization (*what is*). The difference between *what is* and *what should be* creates a performance gap that can be narrowed or closed by leadership or management training, education, or development. The targeted participants of an L & MD program are actively involved in planning their own learning activities and seeking out new knowledge, skills, and attitudes important for organizational and/or personal success.

Two models may guide the use of action learning. One is the *situation-specific* model; the second is the *comprehensive* model. The situation-specific model emphasizes small group learning; the comprehensive model encourages ambitious, large-scale change and learning throughout an organization.

To use the situation-specific model, take the following steps:

1. Identify a problem confronting a group or team
2. Call together management employees and/or those with leadership potential—and, possibly, other stakeholders—who are affected by the problem, are knowledgeable about it, or have a stake in solving it
3. Ask the group to work together to analyze the problem, develop solutions, and create an action plan for improvement

The central idea is to surface information about problems and arrive at an action plan to solve the problems from people affected by them. Group problem solving is thus coupled with group action planning.

On the other hand, a six-step model is helpful in guiding comprehensive action learning that unleashes employee involvement and learning throughout the organization. The first step in the model is gathering information from outside the organization through benchmarking, customer-oriented research, or environmental scanning. L & MD specialists and line managers ask competitors what they are doing. They ask customers, suppliers, distributing wholesalers, and other stakeholders what the organization should be doing. Then they pose questions about the role of management or other leaders in solving problems or taking action.

Many methods may be used to gather information from customers, competitors, and other stakeholders. To cite just two: customer surveys and focus groups (see the sample focus group plan appearing in Exhibit 9-6). Benchmarking information about practices in other organizations may also be gathered by phone surveys, written surveys, and field trips. (The value of benchmarking as a tool in needs assessment was briefly described in Chapter 3.)

The second step in the model is gathering information about the organization. One approach: L & MD specialists emphasize strategic plans as a starting point to guide L & MD learning activities. Another approach: L & MD specialists and managers harness the power of employee involvement by surveying exempt and nonexempt employees about new ideas and/or the existing strengths and weaknesses of the organization's management or leadership talent. To this end, many data-gathering methods may be used. Among them: attitude surveys, upward performance appraisals, idea teams, and employee focus groups. This data-gathering effort should yield results that may be compared with externally collected benchmarking information.

The third step of the model is comparing *what is* to *what should be*. A committee—consisting of a top manager, middle manager, supervisor, and others—is formed to interpret the results obtained from steps one and two. The committee is a tool for involving people in the decision-making process. Visible top management support for this effort should be demonstrated by involving a key top manager—such as CEO or COO—on the committee.

The fourth step in the model is identifying performance improvement methods appropriate to narrow the gap between what is and what should be. Committee members focus their attention on this question: how can management or leadership performance be improved and developed continuously in the organization?

The fifth step in the model is designing planned learning experiences with the active involvement of the targeted participants. One way to do that: use of the *action research model*, the basis of OD, to guide instructional development and harness the power of group decision making. To apply that model, the learning facilitator or L & MD specialist:[5]

1. Surfaces perceptions of problems (such as those uncovered from steps 1–3)

2. Establishes a means to gather information about the problems from group members and diagnose those problems

3. Feeds back the information about the problems to group members

4. Validates the information about the problems with group members

5. Guides group members through the process of highly participative problem solving

6. Facilitates efforts of the group to establish objectives for change (what corrective action to take) and strategies for achieving the objectives (how to take the action)

7. Facilitates group action on problems

8. Monitors the effectiveness of the action taken by the group—and collects information about effectiveness from other sources

9. Provides feedback to the group about the effectiveness of the action taken

Exhibit 9-6
A Sample Plan for a Customer Focus Group

Objective	To elicit information about ways to improve customer service and quality through improved management practices
Materials Required	Flipchart pad; flipchart stand; marking pens; masking tape
Time Required	Allow 1/2 to 1 day
Procedure	• Select between 5 and 20 customers or constituents of your organization at random and pay their way to a central location. Explain that the purpose of the focus group is to improve customer service and quality through improved management practices. • At the beginning of the session, ask the participants to introduce themselves and say a few words about the business they do with your organization. • Then provide a description of your organization. Be sure to cover at least: · The history of the organization · Key external trends or regulatory issues affecting the industry and organization · The structure of the organization · The financial condition of the organization · The organization's future prospects and plans (as reported in annual reports and other public documents) · The organization's philosophy of doing business • Take a break. Then ask group members to count off in threes, fours, or fives to create three to five small groups. Furnish the groups with flipchart pads, flipchart stands, masking tape, and marking pens. Ask each group to appoint a spokesperson. Then ask each group to answer three key questions, list the answers on flipchart sheets, tear off sheets that are filled and tape them to a wall, and be prepared to discuss them: • From the collective experience of the group members as customers, what are the key strengths of the organization? (List them on the flipchart in order of importance. 1 = Most important.) • From the collective experience of the group as customers, what are the key areas in which the organization could improve? (List them on the flipchart in order of importance. 1 = Most important.) • Assume that management bears complete responsibility for the organization's key strengths and key areas for improvement. In what areas do you believe management employees in this organization need better training, education, and development? (List them on the flipchart in order of importance. 1 = Most important.) • Ask the small groups to report on their prioritized lists. Appoint someone to take complete notes from all small groups. • At the end of the session, thank all the groups for their help. Explain briefly who will receive the results and what will be done with them. • Thank the focus group participants for their help. (A modest gift of thanks is appropriate for each participant.) • Then, when the results are used in the organization, send a letter to the participants to point out how their input was used. Describe exactly what use was made of it and what improvements in customer service, quality, or management development resulted from it.

10. Facilitates group efforts to improve the corrective action and ensure continuous improvement—returning to step 1 of this process and starting over

The sixth and final step of the model is selecting L & MD methods and techniques to identify new knowledge, skills, and attitudes. In recent years many methods and techniques have emerged to assist groups in joint decision making and problem solving, and most lend themselves effectively to helping teams or groups surface problems and possible solutions.[6] They can also be used in assessing future conditions or pinpointing emerging trends affecting the work. They are thus well suited to action learning. Exhibit 9-7 summarizes several action learning techniques that have previously been used in OD change efforts.

Problems Affecting Action Learning

Action learning methods are highly appropriate for generating energy and unleashing employee involvement. The method is especially appropriate for building leadership competence. But action learning methods can be threatening to the standard-bearers of the status quo, who feel they erode the traditional power and decision-making authority of management. To work effectively, action learning methods must be supported by top managers.

SUMMARY

In this chapter we reviewed three *special L & MD methods*—adventure learning, new age training (NAT), and action learning. They may be planned or unplanned. They are distinctive because they are on the cutting edge of practice or are controversial.

NOTES

1. P. Buller, J. Cragun, and G. McEvoy, "Getting the Most Out of Outdoor Training," *Training and Development Journal*, Vol. 45, No. 3, p. 58.

2. J. Springer and J. Thomas, "An Experiment in Individual Leadership Development," *Performance and Instruction*, Vol. 31, No. 2, pp. 44–48.

3. M. Lipton, "New Age Organizational Training: Tapping Employee Potential or Creating New Problems?" *Human Resources Professional*, Vol. 3, No. 2, pp. 72–76.

4. J. Storey, "Management Development: A Literature Review and Implications for Future Research," *Personnel Review*, Vol. 18, No. 6, pp. 13–19.

5. W. French, "Organization Development: Objectives, Assumptions, and Strategies," *California Management Review*, Vol. 12, No. 2, p. 26.

6. A. Van Gundy, *Techniques of Structured Problem Solving* (New York: Van Nostrand Reinhold, 1981).

Exhibit 9-7
Action Learning Methods and Techniques

Approach and Purpose	Procedures
Survey Feedback *To surface problems or issues that interfere with effective management performance and to focus attention on solving them.*	• Draft or buy an attitude survey, economizing on items so as to zero in on the most important issues only. • Set up the survey so that information will be collected by division or work group. • Send out the survey, (ideally) having secured top management approval and support beforehand. Compile results. • Feed a summary of the results back to top management, emphasizing the three or four most important issues identified. • Feed the detailed results back to management employees in charge of each work group. • Facilitate feedback and joint action-planning in each work group. • Facilitate action-planning for the management employee in charge of the work group. • Follow up on the action planned and results subsequently achieved.

Process Consultation
To focus on barriers to effective one-on-one or interpersonal interactions.
	• Identify a management employee who is the target of complaints about belligerence or poor interpersonal skills—or, alternatively, any manager who would like to improve his or her interpersonal skills.
	• Meet with the management employee, explaining that his or her interpersonal skills could be improved if he or she is willing to learn.
	• "Shadow" the manager—that is, follow him or her around—to group or one-on-one meetings with subordinates, peers, or superordinates.
	• Take notes on the manager's interactions with others during meetings or other interpersonal interactions—more specifically, on how he or she
	
	  A. Interrupts others
	  B. Uses eye contact
	  C. Asks questions
	  D. Makes statements
	  E. Solicits and treats information about alternative, even dissenting, points of view
	  F. Solicits and treats information about the feelings of other people
	  G. Handles conflict
	
	• Provide immediate, concrete feedback to the manager about what he or she does in each meeting.
	• Solicit the manager's ideas on improving his or her methods of interacting with others.
	• Monitor and praise progress.

Exhibit 9-7 (continued)

Approach and Purpose	Procedures
Organization Mirroring *To surface perceptions about one organizational unit and its interactions with others*	• Identify a work group, team, department, or division that is negatively perceived by others in the organization—or, alternatively, simply wishes to improve its image. • Draft a survey to solicit information about A. The greatest strengths and weaknesses of the work group, team, department, or division B. Any special strengths or weaknesses perceived particularly about the leader of the work group, team, department, or division • Conduct the survey A. Inside the work group, team, department, or division B. Outside the work group, team, department, or division with other target groups—particularly those believed to have perceptions of the work group, team, department, or division that are sharply at odds with the group's • Feed the results back to A. The work group B. The leader of the work group • Use the results to establish action plans for improvement.
Third-Party Peacemaking *To mediate interpersonal conflict constructively*	• Identify two or more management employees who are having difficulty getting along—or simply wish to improve how well they interact. • Meet with the management employees, explaining that their interpersonal skills could be improved—and thereby potentially improve the interaction of their employees. • Ask them separately what issues are leading to conflict between them—or have created problems for each of them in the past. • Bring the management employees back together, summarizing the problems—or issues—they individually surfaced. • Encourage the management employees to establish specific goals to improve their interaction. • Gain a commitment from each management employee to focus on issues, not personalities, in the future.

Part IV

Evaluating Leadership and Management Development Methods and Programs

This concluding part focuses on evaluating L & MD. We introduce Chapter 10 by defining evaluation. We also describe different types of evaluation, key obstacles to evaluation, methods to overcome those obstacles, and a step-by-step approach for conducting a program evaluation.

Chapter 10

Evaluating Methods and Programs

If you ask L & MD directors to identify one area of their planned L & MD programs which could stand significant improvement, you are likely to hear answers like these:

- "Evaluation. We have trouble demonstrating that real changes resulted from L & MD programs. And we have no compelling way to show how L & MD efforts are affecting the organization's 'bottom line' or strategic plan."
- "There must be better ways to show the value of our efforts than by circulating results of participant evaluations from classroom sessions. But, how is that done with a small staff and tight budget?"

These feelings are pervasive in L & MD, making the topic of evaluation a perennial favorite for articles and professional presentations.

But just what is evaluation? Why is it important? What barriers stand in the way of performing it successfully? What are the steps in carrying out a program evaluation? This chapter addresses these questions. As a starting point, read over the introductory case study which follows. It dramatizes the high stakes involved in evaluating L & MD programs and methods.

INTRODUCTORY CASE STUDY

John Terpa is L & MD director for the Walsh-Healey Company, a multinational conglomerate employing 73,000 people at 908 locations worldwide. Before he was hired, John was employed as a training professional at another conglomerate. He has been in his present job for eight years, having started a comprehensive, centralized L & MD function from scratch.

John has been very successful in setting up the L & MD function at Walsh-Healey. With a modest staff of just ten people at corporate headquarters in Mobile, Alabama, he has been able to offer a dizzying array of L & MD options to help Walsh-Healey's management employees and those with leadership potential to develop themselves. Through John's function the company offers classroom courses, teleconferences, video-based instruction, computer-based instruction, audiocassettes, and much more.

In the early days of John's employment, managers from company work sites had to crawl on airplanes and take expensive trips to corporate headquarters to participate in planned L & MD efforts. But over the last few years John eliminated the need for much travel by localizing L & MD efforts and by using distance learning methods such as teleconferencing. Exhausting travel is no longer a necessity. At present, only executives travel to corporate headquarters for lengthy planned learning experiences, and they do so only because it is preferred by top executives.

John has encouraged the appointment of an L & MD coordinator at each work site. John and his staff work directly with local L & MD coordinators to identify needs and select appropriate L & MD methods. John uses corporate staff to help identify and manage vendors for company work sites. John's corporate L & MD function also serves as a braintrust and troubleshooter, offering expert assistance to company work sites and sending in helpers to focus on difficult L & MD–related matters of local concern.

The Walsh-Healey company has recently undertaken a TQM effort. Top managers want to see several direct outcomes from the effort:

- Increased quality in the products made and services offered by the Walsh-Healey company
- Increased involvement of employees in decisions affecting them
- Successful implementation of self-directed work teams
- Fewer layers of management
- Employees trained on methods of problem solving that may be applied on their jobs
- Improved customer service
- A reduced, but more highly trained and highly involved, hourly workforce comprised of people who find their jobs challenging

John has been directed by the CEO to work directly with an outside TQM consultant to help achieve these goals.

An early step will be to identify the customers of John's own function, identify "world-class" L & MD functions in other organizations against which to compare Walsh-Healey's L & MD function, measure customer satisfaction with the products and services offered by the L & MD function, and establish efforts for continuous improvement in L & MD at Walsh-Healey.

While involved in this important effort, which John enthusiastically supports, he received a phone call from Walsh-Healey's Budgeting Department. That department was recently charged by the company's chairman with the important responsibility of "cutting costs and expenses in all nonessential areas in order to make Walsh-Healey more competitive in an increasingly competitive global marketplace."

John is told by phone that he will have to slash his budget by at least 20 percent for the remainder of the year. Management and supervisory training are special targets for reduction. John is asked to cut expenses by 35 percent for those programs. (Recent increases in those programs are directly attributable to the TQM initiative.)

Using information about the contribution of L & MD to Walsh-Healey's profitability, John wants to show that such a budget cut is ill-advised—particularly during implementation of TQM at Walsh-Healey.

Question: Put yourself in John's situation. How could you demonstrate that a 20 percent budget cut in L & MD is ill-advised? (See the recommended solution to this case in Exhibit 10-6 at the end of this chapter.)

WHAT IS EVALUATION?

Evaluation is the process of assigning value and making critical judgments. In L & MD, evaluation examines (1) *What changes* resulted from an L & MD program or L & MD methods, (2) *How much change* resulted from an L & MD program or L & MD methods, (3) *What value* can be assigned to those changes, and (4) *How much value* can be assigned to those changes. In short, evaluation means assessing how much and how well L & MD programs or methods contribute to improving organizational, group, or individual performance.

Four Types of Evaluation

In 1960, Donald Kirkpatrick introduced a simple model to distinguish between different types of instructional evaluation.[1] Since that time Kirkpatrick's model has been widely adopted, used, modified, and (on occasion) criticized.[2] It provides a useful way to conceptualize the evaluation of L & MD.

There are four levels to Kirkpatrick's hierarchical model:[3] (1) Participant reaction, (2) Participant learning, (3) Participant performance, and (4) Organization results. Each level of Kirkpatrick's hierarchical model has its own purpose, strengths, weaknesses, and guidelines for development.

Participant Reaction

Participant reaction is the first and lowest level of evaluation. It measures participant feelings about one planned learning experience. The most common form of evaluation, it is easy to administer and provides immediate feedback about instructors, facilities, materials, and L & MD methods. Participant reaction is measured through results of end-of-course "happiness surveys," informal interviews with participants, and group discussions.

To devise an effective participant reaction, you should:

1. Clarify what issues are to be evaluated
2. Prepare a questionnaire, interview form, or discussion guide for end-of-course use to evaluate the identified issues
3. Administer the survey, conduct interviews, or collect information about participant reactions in other ways
4. Compile the evaluation results
5. Feed back the evaluation results to stakeholders

Unfortunately, participant reactions are subjective. They do not measure participant learning, participant performance, or organization results. (A sample participant evaluation appears in Exhibit 10-1.)

Participant Learning

Participant learning is the second level of Kirkpatrick's hierarchy of evaluation. It measures how much participants changed as a result of a learning experience. Evaluations of participant learning furnish more objective information than evaluations of participant reactions.

Participant learning is typically measured through paper-and-pencil tests, demonstrations, role plays, and other methods. To devise effective measures of participant learning, you should:

1. Write test items—or choose other evaluative methods—based on performance objectives
2. Examine test items or other evaluative methods for clarity, validity, and reliability
3. Administer the evaluation instrument or methods to a small pilot group of individuals to ensure they are clear, valid, and reliable
4. Administer the test items/evaluative methods to learners before, during, and/or after planned L & MD experiences

Measuring participant learning requires special skill in designing tests and other evaluation measures. It thus lies beyond the reach of novices, and it does not provide much useful information about participant performance or organization results.

Participant Performance

The central question underlying the third level of Kirkpatrick's hierarchy of evaluation is this: How much *on-the-job change* resulted from L & MD expe-

Exhibit 10-1
Participant Evaluation

Directions: This evaluation form is intended to gauge your reactions to this course. Place an **X** above the appropriate space on the line following each question below. Then write a narrative in response to questions 10 through 12 below.

Purpose, Objectives, and Organization

1	How well was the purpose of this course stated?

Not at All	Not Sure	Very Clearly

2	How well were the objectives of this course stated?

Not at All	Not Sure	Very Clearly

3	How well was the organization (structure) of the course described?

Not at All	Not Sure	Very Clearly

Instructor

4	How effective was the instructor in presenting the course?

Not at All Effective	Not Sure	Very Effective

5	How effective was the instructor in making the course interesting?

Not at All Effective	Not Sure	Very Effective

6	Would you recommend this instructor to others?

I would absolutely not recommend this instructor to others	Not Sure	I would absolutely recommend this instructor to others

---

Course Content

7	How valuable was the course material for helping you perform your job more effectively?

Not at All Effective	Not Sure	Very Effective

8	How effective was the course material for helping your team, unit, department, or division increase its productivity?

Not at All Effective	Not Sure	Very Effective

Exhibit 10-1 (continued)

Facilities	
9	How well did the facilities match up to the requirements of the course, in your opinion? **Not at All** **Not Sure** **Very Effective** **Effective**
Other Remarks	
10	What did you find *least useful* about the course?
11	What did you find *most useful* about the course?
12	What other remarks do you have to make about the course?

Please Return this Training Evaluation to
(Name) at (Location) by (Date)

riences? In other words, how much did planned learning experiences help participants improve their job performance?

This form of evaluation is carried out with performance checklists, performance appraisals, critical incidents, self-appraisals, upward appraisals, after-course surveys of participants' immediate organizational superiors or subordinates, and other methods. One way to devise an evaluation of participant performance is to: (1) Draft questions to assess on-the-job change, (2) Administer the survey to participants' immediate organizational superiors and/or subordinates, (3) Compile the evaluation results, and (4) Feed back the evaluation results to participants, their immediate organizational superiors, and their immediate subordinates in order to stimulate future development and improve the planned L & MD program. The greatest single barrier to carrying out this form of evaluation is lack of motivation. L & MD specialists must *want* to collect information about on-the-job change resulting from planned learning experiences. They should also be willing to follow up after long time spans. (A sample after-course survey appears in Exhibit 10-2.)

Organization Results

Most decision makers who invest in L & MD programs would like to know the answer to one simple question: *How much was organizational performance*

Exhibit 10-2
Evaluation of On-the-Job Change

Participant's Name	
Participated in (*Course Title*)	On (*Date*)

Directions: We need *your* help, as an immediate organizational superior or subordinate, of the participant listed above. He/she participated in the learning experience, and we would like to have your opinion--in confidence--about how much, if at all, the course has influenced the participant's on-the-job behavior. For each question below, provide your frank answers *in complete confidence of anonymity*. Your responses will *not* be communicated to the participant listed above; rather, they will be helpful to the Management Development program for future reference in designing planned learning experiences.

1	Have you noticed any *change* in the participant's on-the-job behavior since he/she returned from the course? (*Circle one response below*) YES NO
	If you circle "no," then skip to question 5 below. If you circle "yes," then continue on to question 2.
2	What change did you notice? (*Describe the situation[s] and your perception of how the participant behaved.*)
3	How often has the participant behaved this way?
4	How do you feel about the change in behavior noted in response to question 2 above?
5	What comments do you wish to make?

Please Return this Training Evaluation to
(Name) at (Location) by (Date)

affected or improved by L & MD experiences? Yet that is a singularly difficult question to answer.

Common ways of measuring organization results include: employee or management suggestions, manufacturing indices, attitude survey results, union grievances, absenteeism rates, customer complaints, and other ultimate measures of organizational results. Unfortunately, it is rarely possible to control for so-called *intervening variables* so as to ensure that organizational changes stem from L & MD efforts *only*.

To devise an evaluation of participant performance, you should:

1. Identify important measures, based on organizational needs/plans, to be changed as a result of L & MD experiences

2. Clarify the degree of change desired

3. Control for intervening variables to the extent possible

4. Compare organizational results *after* planned L & MD experiences to those existing *before* the experiences

To measure organization results, L & MD specialists require much knowledge about the organization and about evaluation methods.

Distinguishing Between Formative and Summative Evaluation

Kirkpatrick's hierarchical model of evaluation focuses on the *results* of learning experiences, chiefly as they affect learners. But another model is needed to evaluate and improve learning materials or methods in L & MD programs. To that end, L & MD specialists must turn to *formative* and *summative evaluation*. Formative evaluation tests out materials and methods for leadership or management training, education, or development before widespread use; summative evaluation assesses changes resulting from leadership or management training, education, or development after widespread use.

Many L & MD specialists associate formative and summative evaluation with internal group training, since classroom methods were first used as the focus of evaluation. Moreover, classroom methods easily lend themselves to formative and summative evaluation. But other L & MD methods also lend themselves, though less obviously, to formative and summative evaluation.

THE IMPORTANCE OF EVALUATION

Evaluation is critically important because it affects the willingness of an organization's decision makers to support a planned L & MD program. Without evaluation, L & MD specialists cannot demonstrate that L & MD has contributed to performance improvement for organizations, work groups, or individuals. That makes L & MD a ripe target for cost-cutting, as dramatically illustrated by the introductory case study. After all, decision makers are reluctant to invest precious resources in programs for which payoffs are uncertain or problematic.

OBSTACLES TO EVALUATION

Despite the importance of evaluation, few organizations progress beyond participant evaluation or devote substantial resources to assessing the payoffs of L & MD. Unfortunately, participant reaction measures by themselves are inadequate to demonstrate *what changes* in performance occurred, *how much change* occurred, *what value* resulted from the changes, or *how much value* resulted from the changes.

If L & MD methods and programs are not evaluated as they should be, then that raises several questions: Why aren't they? What obstacles block the path of evaluation? How can the obstacles be overcome?

COMMON OBSTACLES

Five key obstacles block effective evaluation of L & MD methods and programs.

The first obstacle is *reluctance to evaluate*. Some L & MD specialists see no real or immediate payoff from evaluation—even at a time when dramatic cost-cutting and employee-slashing in organizations is more the norm than the exception. While top managers pay lip service to evaluation, they reward only highly visible efforts—such as internal group training or flashy new L & MD programs on trendy topics. Evaluation is seldom visible enough to command real resources or interest.

Moreover, some L & MD specialists are not sure that L & MD experiences produce real payoffs because they know few learners are held accountable on their jobs for applying what they learned. This is the *transfer of learning problem*.[4] Examples of this problem are easy to describe:

- Management employees—or those with leadership potential that are not in management—are sent to internal group training. When they return to their jobs, they are asked what they learned. When told, their immediate organizational superiors remark that "we don't do things like that around here." That one remark destroys the incentive for participants to apply what they learned—and creates enormous frustration for the learners, leading them to believe that the training was a waste.

- Management employees are sent to an expensive external seminar at a prestigious Ivy League University. But they are not told, before they leave, why they are being sent, what they are expected to learn, or why they should care about what they learn. Nor are they later evaluated in any measurable way on how well they applied on their jobs what they learned. (The sponsors of the event claim that transfer of learning is "not important" and, indeed, that transfer of learning is not even appropriate for a "true developmental experience.") Some participants conclude that the seminar is merely a vacation in disguise.

The transfer of learning problem leads to wasted time and resources. One expert estimated that less than 10 percent of what employees learn off-the-job is actually applied on-the-job.[5] Since L & MD specialists cannot control the job environment, they express the results to be achieved by measurable end-of-course performance objectives rather than by more appropriate—but difficult to measure—on-the-job results.

Lack of resources is another common obstacle, and a frequent excuse for not evaluating L & MD. For evaluation to be carried out successfully, adequate time, money, and staff must be budgeted, approved, and used. Not all employers are willing to approve expenditures on evaluation, preferring instead to invest funds where payoffs are more visible, flashy, or trendy. While good evaluation results can help defend L & MD from the budget cutter's ax, finding the time, money, and people to carry out a worthwhile evaluation effort is not easy when L & MD specialists struggle to meet the demand for high-priority services with diminishing resources.

Nor does evaluation enjoy a large, interested constituency that is breathlessly awaiting results.

Lack of know-how also stymies evaluation efforts. Many L & MD specialists do not have adequate knowledge of research or statistical methods. Both are critically important for carrying out evaluation.[6] Since funding may not be available to hire outside experts possessing the know-how, in-house evaluation efforts may suffer as a result. Even when appropriate expertise is available, top managers and other stakeholders may not be knowledgeable enough about statistics and research methods to make sense of sophisticated evaluation results that are expressed in social science jargon.

Low credibility is also an obstacle to successful evaluation. Few organizations have the luxury—as the world-class benchmark organizations do—to segregate evaluation from service delivery. When responsibilities are not segregated, L & MD specialists must deliver services *and* evaluate them. The credibility of that effort is not high. Indeed, it is about as credible as a bank president who heads up a financial audit of her own bank. While the results may be unbiased, skeptical users may worry that they are being fed self-serving or misleading results. That undercuts the credibility of the evaluation effort.

Finally, evaluation is plagued by *difficulties in using traditional research methodologies*. The same difficulties plague OD evaluation efforts.[7] These include problems with using control groups, lack of long-term (longitudinal) follow-up, and poor research designs.

OVERCOMING OBSTACLES

To overcome the obstacles identified in the previous section, L & MD specialists should adopt four major strategies:

- Overcome reluctance to evaluate by making a commitment. Take this step first. Go on the record to announce that this commitment has been made. Publicize how evaluation is being carried out, why it is important, and what results from L & MD activities have been realized by the organization and by individuals. If possible, tie L & MD results to the organization's strategic plan and/or individual career plans.

- Overcome lack of resources by a twofold strategy: publicize results and adapt evaluation methods to available resources. Aim to satisfy the information needs of stakeholders. Find out what the stakeholders need to know to make decisions and then provide it as cost-effectively as possible.

- Overcome lack of know-how by stepping up efforts to increase knowledge about evaluation. Educate stakeholders and L & MD specialists alike by sending L & MD staff members and line managers on field trips so they can see how competitors—or organizations renowned for the L & MD programs—conduct evaluation.

- Overcome low credibility by involving stakeholders in the evaluation process. Use that involvement to increase stakeholder participation in the program. Above all, avoid jealously controlling evaluation efforts. Remember that quality guru W. Edwards Deming made a significant impact on quality by training frontline employees in how to measure what they do and involving them in improvement efforts.

Exhibit 10-3
Collecting Information about the Results of L & MD from the Users: The Success Case Approach

Directions: Use this approach to collect information from participants in L & MD experiences, such as internal group training or on-the-job training. Visit with randomly selected learners. Pose the questions appearing below. Record the responses on this Worksheet. Later, compile results from several such interviews.	
Note: Begin the interview by explaining to the respondent that you are collecting information about the results of L & MD activities in your organization and that you need his or her help. Then pose the following questions:	
1	Since participating in (*name the course or other L & MD experience in which the individual participated*: _____), describe the worst situation you have encountered that was directly related to it. *Description of the situation*:
2	What did you *do* in this situation? *Description of actions taken*:
3	What were the *consequences or results* of what you did in this situation? *Description of consequences*:
4	How do you think you would have handled this situation if you had *not* participated in L & MD? Be truthful and explain what you think you would have done. *Description of probable actions*:
5	What would have been the negative consequences of your actions in question 2, in your opinion? In other words, what bad results would you or the organization have faced? *Description of negative consequences*:
6	How could we place a price tag or value on the difference between what you actually did, having participated in the L & MD experience, and what you would have done if you had not participated in L & MD? Is there any way you could estimate the cost? *Description of ideas about measuring the cost*:
7	If you were an investor, how much would you have been willing to pay to avoid making a mistake in this situation? *Estimate of willingness to pay*:

Take the same approach to evaluating L & MD by training learners—and their immediate organizational superiors—in how to measure results. Publicize the results they provide (see Exhibit 10-3). This approach increases stakeholder involvement in evaluation.

Overcome difficulties in using traditional research methodologies by matching methods to stakeholder needs. Do *not* pursue evaluation with the rigor needed to satisfy academic purists when that is unnecessary; rather, aim to produce credible results for stakeholders. If possible, work with skeptical stakeholders to identify approaches and results *they* find convincing. Then work to achieve those results.

CARRYING OUT EVALUATION

When evaluating L & MD, choose an appropriate blueprint for formative evaluation, summative evaluation, or program evaluation.

Carrying Out Formative Evaluation of L & MD

Formative evaluation is conducted to improve planned learning experiences *before* learners participate in them on a widespread basis. It masquerades under other names—pilot tests, structured walkthroughs, and previews.

Carrying out a formative evaluation is usually a multi-step process of repeated tests and revisions. First, assess materials under controlled conditions with one or two randomly selected learners from the targeted population or with several subject matter experts (SMEs). Second, assess materials with a group of randomly selected learners under controlled conditions. Third, assess materials with randomly selected learners under field conditions resembling those in which the planned learning experience will actually be carried out. Fourth, preview materials with a group of immediate organizational superiors of the targeted learners. Variations of these steps may be used. Step-by-step procedures for applying formative evaluation to internal group training are summarized in Exhibit 10-4. The same procedures may be modified for evaluating such other L & MD methods as external group training or on-the-job training.

Carrying Out Summative Evaluation of L & MD

Summative evaluation measures the results of L & MD methods. A secondary aim is to reinforce the impetus for change by focusing attention on the results of successful application. This form of evaluation usually occurs after L & MD methods have been used.

There are various procedures for carrying out summative evaluation. They were first perfected with internal group training. But they may be modified and applied to after-the-fact evaluation of other L & MD methods (see Exhibits 10-5 and 10-6). For instance, internal group training may be evaluated at the end of a classroom session by asking learners for their opinions about it. Learners may also be tested for mastery of the subject matter. Their on-the-job behaviors or performance may be evaluated through surveys or interviews—directed at them, their immediate organizational superiors, or their immediate subordinates. Or-

Exhibit 10-4

Step-by-Step Procedures for Conducting Formative Evaluation of Classroom Management Training

Before the test begins, prepare all instructional materials in draft form. Have everything ready to use for Phase 1.	
Phase 1: Under controlled conditions, assess the instructional materials with one or two subject matter experts.	
Step 1	Pick a controlled environment, such as a quiet room.
Step 2	Identify subject matter experts from inside or outside the organization and ask them to set aside a few hours to go over the instructional materials with you.
Step 3	Explain that the purpose of the test is to obtain expert help in assessing the quality of the instructional materials.
Step 4	Deliver the instructional materials to the expert(s) as you intended them to be delivered.
Step 5	Ask a colleague to attend the session to take notes on what the experts say about revisions needed in the instructional materials.
Step 6	When you finish, make revisions to the materials in line with the experts' recommendations for revision. If major modifications were recommended by the experts, then ask them to review the instructional materials again once you have finished the revisions and before you proceed to Phase 2.
Phase 2: Assess the instructional materials with a handful of people from the population of targeted learners.	
Step 1	Pick a controlled environment, such as a quiet room.
Step 2	Identify one or more people from the population of targeted learners.
Step 3	Ask participants to set aside a few hours to go over the course material with you.
Step 4	At the outset, explain the purpose of the test: to determine how well participants are able to understand the instructional materials, how participants feel about the methods used to deliver the instruction, and to identify areas in which the instructional materials may be improved for clarity or delivery.
Step 5	Deliver the instructional materials exactly as you intended them to be delivered.
Step 6	Ask a colleague to attend the session to take notes on what the learners say.
Step 7	Ask learners for their feelings and impressions about the training material as well as about the quality of the content.
Step 8	When you have finished the test with participants, make revisions to the instructional materials in line with what they recommended. If major revisions were made, ask the participants to review the instructional materials with you before proceeding to Phase 3.
Phase 3: Under field conditions, assess the instructional materials with a small, randomly selected group chosen from the population of targeted learners.	
Step 1	Repeat all activities in Phase 2 with a group of people—more than one or two—from the population of targeted learners.

Exhibit 10-4 (continued)

Step 2	When you finish, make revisions to the instructional materials in line with what the learners have recommended. If major modifications must be made, ask the learners to review the instructional materials again before proceeding to Phase 4.
Phase 4: Preview the instructional materials with a randomly selected group of the targeted learners' immediate organizational superiors.	
Step 1	Schedule the briefing/walkthrough in a location resembling that in which the instructional materials are intended to be used.
Step 2	Identify the participants.
Step 3	Invite the participants to a one-hour overview of the instructional materials and methods.
Step 4	Explain that the test is intended to determine what the participants think of the instructional materials and methods and brainstorm with them about ways to hold learners accountable on the job for what they learn from the instructional materials.
Step 5	Highlight the instructional materials, describing what you plan to do rather than doing it.
Step 6	Ask a colleague to take notes on what recommendations for improvement are made by the participants.
Step 7	Ask the participants for their impressions of the instructional materials and methods.
Step 8	Ask participants how they can hold the learners accountable for applying on the job what they learn from the instructional materials.
Step 9	When you finish the test, revise the instructional materials and methods in line with the participants' recommendations. If major revisions must be made, ask the participants if they would be willing to review the materials again once the revisions have been made.

ganizational results may be evaluated by measuring changes in production, quality, or other factors.

CARRYING OUT A PROGRAM EVALUATION OF L & MD

A program evaluation assesses the contribution of a planned L & MD program to the organization it serves. It thus resembles a *program performance audit*, a comprehensive review of an entire governmental program or business function. Such comprehensive reviews are rarely undertaken because they are expensive and time-consuming. Moreover, their payoffs are difficult to assess.

But, much like a comprehensive review of any other organizational system—such as data processing, human resources, financial management, or inventory methods—a program evaluation of L & MD can provide useful guidance for charting the long-term direction of a planned L & MD program and tying the program to the organization's strategic plan. In this respect it is akin to a broad-

Exhibit 10-5
Step-by-Step Procedures for Conducting Summative Evaluation of Internal Group Management Training

Do not wait until the end of a planned learning experience to prepare for summative evaluation; rather, lay the foundation as you design instructional materials and choose instructional methods. While there are many ways by which to apply summative evaluation to internal group training, here are some suggested steps:	
Step One	Prepare competency tests based on performance objectives. Use the performance criteria appearing in performance objectives as a starting point for writing test items, developing on-the-job performance tests, or contriving other methods of measuring learning mastery.
Step Two	Prepare a simple questionnaire to measure how well participants liked an internal group training session. Pose open questions like these: • What were the chief strengths of this session? • What could be improved most in this session? • Or pose scaled questions like these: How much do you feel you learned in this session? *(Mark an X above the space on the line below that best indicates your response)* Nothing Very Little Little Much Very Much Everything Needed
Step Three	Administer written or oral tests—or ask participants in an internal group training session to demonstrate what they learned—at the end of the session.
Step Four	Follow up several weeks or months after the session by sending a questionnaire to participants, their immediate organizational superiors, and/or their immediate subordinates to inquire about any noticeable on-the-job changes. Use open questions or scaled questions.
Step Five	Before delivering the instructional experience, establish control and experimental groups to assess the effects of internal group training on the organization's performance. (Experimental groups consist of those who participated in internal group training; control groups consist of those who did not participate.) Then compare individuals in both groups, promotions occurring to members of both groups, and (if possible) the financial performance of areas led by those who did and did not participate in the internal group training. Note differences. (Do not automatically assume that training leads to improvement, even if significant differences are apparent between control and experimental groups. After all, so-called *intervening variables*—such as individual motivation—may account for differences more than the training does.) If all else fails, measure organization performance using the "success case" approach described in Exhibit 10-3.

scope assessment of functional operations conducted by professional consulting organizations.

Before undertaking a program evaluation of L & MD, decision makers should come to grips with several key questions:

• *What is the reason for conducting the program evaluation?* Is the aim to assess how much the planned L & MD program contributes to achieving strategic objectives, personal growth, or some other purpose? Since a program evaluation is expensive to conduct, considerable thought should be devoted to reason(s) for carrying it out.

• *How clear are the desired outcomes of the program evaluation?* Appropriate outcomes

Exhibit 10-6
Step-by-Step Procedures for Conducting Summative Evaluation of Formal,
Informal, and Special L & MD Methods (Excluding Internal Group Training)

It may seem that there would be no way to apply summative evaluation to L & MD methods other than internal group training. But that is not true. It is possible to evaluate participant reactions, participant learning, participant performance, and organization performance for on-the-job training, job rotations, self-study, and other L & MD methods.	
Here are some suggestions:	
Step One	Plan to measure participant reactions by preparing an attitude survey for use at the end of such L & MD experiences as on-the-job training, job rotations, or self-study. Administer the survey just as you would at the end of an internal group training session. (In fact, one approach is to modify the participant evaluation questionnaire you use in internal group training so it can be used with other L & MD methods. That way, results can be expressed in similar ways.)
Step Two	Plan to measure participant learning by testing what the participants learned. To minimize participant anxiety, call these something other than "tests"—such as the more neutral term "learner activity." Although paper-and-pencil tests can be used with some on-the-job training, facets of job rotations, and with external training, you may find it preferable to ask learners to demonstrate what they learned.
Step Three	Plan to measure participant performance by including items on employee performance appraisals to inquire how much L & MD methods—such as on-the-job training, job rotations, self-study, or external education—contributed to the individual's performance.
Step Four	Collect information about organizational performance by asking participants to provide information about "success cases" resulting from what they learned (see Exhibit 10-3).

may include information on which to base a new L & MD strategy, improve the linkage between L & MD and the organization's strategic plan, or re-focus a planned L & MD program after a change of leadership.

• *Who should conduct the program evaluation?* Should expertise from inside or outside the organization be used? Each choice has unique advantages and disadvantages. By using internal staff members, the organization can avoid sizable out-of-pocket expenditures because staff salaries and benefits are relatively fixed. Moreover, internal staff members are—or should be—familiar with the organization's culture and traditions in a way external vendors rarely are, so they should require less time to understand the environment in which the planned L & MD program is functioning. But there are disadvantages to using internal staff members: they may lack credibility and may be perceived as having a stake in the evaluation results. On the other hand, external vendors may enjoy more credibility, may be perceived as unbiased about outcomes, and may be more familiar with state-of-the-art evaluation techniques than internal staff members. But vendors are expensive to employ and are rarely aware of the organization's culture. While the use of both internal staff members and external vendors is expensive, it often strikes an ideal balance by capitalizing on the advantages of both groups while minimizing their separate disadvantages.

Take eight basic steps when conducting a program evaluation of L & MD.

First, secure a strong signal of support for the evaluation effort from top management. Top managers signify their support by providing a mandate for it, such as a memo to employees authorizing the program evaluation and setting forth the reason(s) it is being carried out. This mandate should at least: (1) Establish the evaluation's scope (how much of the L & MD program is being examined?), (2) Set a deadline for completion (*when should the program evaluation be completed?*), and (3) Request cooperation from others in seeing the evaluation through to a successful conclusion (*who* needs to help, and what help should they provide?).

Second, select or appoint an evaluation administrator to bear project management responsibility. Place someone in charge to ensure the project is carried to completion.

If external consulting help is to be used, the evaluation administrator becomes the organization's chief liaison with the consultant(s). He or she prepares a Request for Proposal (RFP) setting forth the mandate, purpose, scope, deadline, and other key issues for the program evaluation; identifies consulting firms qualified to carry out the evaluation project; encourages them to submit proposals; and oversees the proposal review process.

But if internal staff is to be used, the evaluation administrator becomes the project manager. He or she conducts background research on the program evaluation and the planned L & MD program, finding out as much as possible about what led up to the perceived need for the program evaluation, results desired from it, and the scope of the planned L & MD program. He or she then forms initial judgments about how the program evaluation should be conducted, determines what information should be collected, decides what analytical methods will be performed, lists project steps, establishes a project time line, and selects a project team whose collective skills are adequate to complete the project successfully.

Third, set up an entrance meeting with those who authorized the program evaluation. The meeting's purpose is fourfold: (1) To introduce members of the evaluation team, (2) To collect additional background information about the need for evaluation and the results desired from it, (3) To explain the flow of project events, and (4) To clarify the desired ''deliverable'' (product) stemming from the program evaluation, such as a written or oral report. After this meeting, the evaluation administrator and team members jointly finalize a detailed program evaluation plan to guide the project.

Fourth, collect and analyze data. At this point, the program evaluation team collects information from surveys, interviews, document reviews, or observations. They may also compile results of previous program evaluations. This step is the core of the program evaluation.

Fifth, draft the evaluation report. Having completed data collection and analysis, team members review the fruits of their labors. Team members prepare a written report to describe the background of the program evaluation, the scope of existing L & MD activities in the organization, the questions addressed during the program evaluation, how the questions were answered, and how the answers were analyzed. They also identify "strengths" and "areas for improvement" in the planned L & MD program and make recommendations for improvements.

Sixth, seek response and reaction. Team members submit a draft report to top managers, the L & MD director, the L & MD coordinator, or L & MD specialists of the organization's planned L & MD program. At this time, the representative of the planned L & MD program is given an opportunity to respond to conclusions reached in the program evaluation. These responses are included in the evaluation report.

Seventh, present the results to key stakeholders and decision makers. They should receive copies of the final report detailing the program evaluation results. They may also attend an oral briefing over the report and its recommendations (see Exhibit 10-7). Representatives of the planned L & MD program are invited to attend this briefing.

Eighth and finally, implement the recommendations. Of course, the aim is to improve the planned L & MD program and establish or maintain a long-term direction for it. The program evaluation should help preserve and strengthen the linkage between the planned L & MD program and the organization's strategic plan. On the whole, a program evaluation provides a chance to assess the L & MD program as it contributes to the organization's mission, goals, activities, and results.

While the basic steps of a program evaluation are outlined above, other features may be added. For instance, members of a program evaluation team may:

- Conduct a competitive benchmarking study as part of the program evaluation to determine how much and how well the organization's planned L & MD program is funded and staffed in comparison to other organizations of the same size or in the same industry.
- Compare the organization's planned L & MD program to criteria set forth in the Malcolm Baldrige National Quality Award—or to the organization's ability to meet those criteria.
- Collect additional information from *external sources*—such as suppliers, distributing wholesalers, retailers, customers, franchise holders, or others—about L & MD needs.
- Collect information about learning needs from such *internal sources* as exempt and nonexempt employees and assess how well the organization's planned L & MD program contributes to satisfying those needs.

SUMMARY

This chapter showed how evaluation can provide valuable information for continuously improving a planned L & MD program. We also defined evalua-

Exhibit 10-7

Recommended Solution to a Case Study on Evaluation in L & MD

John will not fend off a budget cut if he has not already established a continuing evaluation process for the L & MD program and the L & MD methods of his organization. But he could have headed off the problem if he had taken the following steps before he received the call from Budgeting:

Step	Activity	Remarks
1	Establish an L & MD Committee in the organization composed of representatives from more than one organizational level.	This approach builds employee involvement and creates management "buy-in."
2	Ask committee members for their help to calculate the dollar value return on investments in L & MD, explaining why that is important to do.	
3	Ask committee members to pick *one* problem that they believe has been addressed effectively by the L & MD program. (Examples might include reduced turnover in the management ranks, reduced orientation time for supervisors, or some measure of organizational effectiveness such as improved quality or reduced scrap rates.)	There should be at least one "success story."
4	Ask committee members to help identify two or three individuals who can attest that • *their* orientation period was reduced due to the L & MD program. • *they* chose not to quit due to the L & MD program. • *actual cost savings* or *returns on investments* were realized in their organizational units as a direct result of the L & MD effort.	By using one or two real people, John develops persuasive circumstantial evidence supporting the L & MD program.
5	Estimate the value of the savings or return on investment for the actual cases in Step 4 above.	While this approach will not convince serious skeptics, it will be emotionally appealing and persuasive.
6	Multiply the value of Step 5 by the total number of people who participated in the L & MD experience or course.	Estimate the value added.
7	Estimate the total cost to operate the L & MD experience (fees, staff salaries, etc.) and subtract that from the product of Step 6.	Estimate the program cost and subtract from estimated value added.
8	Use the total estimated savings or return on investment (ROI) realized by the one L & MD experience/course and multiply it by the number of other courses/experiences administered by the L & MD program in the organization.	Develop a rough estimate of total value added.
9	Ask committee members to reduce the estimate as they wish.	This step gives skeptics a chance to have their say and give their input.
10	Ask committee members to sign off that the cost savings or return on investment accurately reflects the added value provided to the organization by the L & MD program, in their opinion.	This sign-off indicates management "ownership" and provides independent verification of value added.
11	Publicize the results of steps 1–10 periodically in organizational periodicals (such as company newsletters).	This step publicizes the value of the L & MD program.
12	Keep track of any criticism received when using this approach, challenging critics to participate on the committee to come up with more effective approaches to evaluate the dollar value return on investments of the L & MD program.	This step heads off critics before their skepticism about the value of the L & MD program becomes infectious and undermines its continuation.

While not foolproof, these steps would have helped John (1) estimate the dollar value return on investments of L & MD efforts, (2) build management support for the L & MD effort, and (3) head off the budget cutter's ax—or at least make cost-cutting of the L & MD program difficult to justify! Try the approach yourself.

tion, described different types, summarized key obstacles to evaluation, described methods to overcome those obstacles, and provided step-by-step guidance for conducting a program evaluation.

NOTES

1. D. Kirkpatrick, "Techniques for Evaluating Training Programs," *Journal of the American Society for Training and Development* [now called *Training & Development*], Vol. 14, No. 1, pp. 13–18.

2. M. Smith and D. Brandenburg, "Summative Evaluation," *Performance Improvement Quarterly*, Vol. 4, No. 2, pp. 35–58.

3. D. Kirkpatrick, *Evaluating Training Programs: The Four Levels* (San Francisco: Berrett-Koehler, 1994).

4. D. Laker, "Dual Dimensionality of Training Transfer," *Human Resource Development Quarterly*, Vol. 1, No. 3, pp. 209–224.

5. D. Georgenson, "The Problem of Transfer Calls for Partnership," *Training & Development*, Vol. 36, No. 10, pp. 75–78.

6. W. Rothwell, E. Sanders, and J. Soper, *ASTD Models for Workplace Learning and Performance: Roles, Competencies, Outputs* (Alexandria, VA: American Society for Training and Development, 1999).

7. C. Argyris, "Some Unintended Consequences of Rigorous Research," *Psychological Bulletin*, Vol. 70, pp. 185–197.

Chapter 11

Epilogue: Special Issues in Leadership and Management Development

L & MD is influenced by the same issues affecting management practice and leadership theory. For this reason, we feel that three important topical issues deserve special attention as we conclude the book: (1) globalism; (2) downsizing; and (3) team-based management. The three issues are related.

Managers and thought leaders in the United States are being forced to think globally. As they do, they find that foreign competitors enjoy a significant comparative advantage over U.S.-based corporations due to lower labor costs, supportive governmental policies, permissive regulations, and increasing labor productivity. That has prompted U.S. corporations to reduce operating expenses so as to become more internationally competitive. Downsizing is one way to slash operating expenses dramatically. And downsizing, in turn, has led to a groundswell of interest in team-based management, which makes more efficient use of employees than traditional top-down and centralized approaches to management decision making or job and organization design. By encouraging nonexempt employees to develop themselves, work cooperatively, and assume additional responsibility, team-based management reduces the need for control-minded supervisors, middle managers, and executives and cultivates future leadership talent. And, as nonexempt employees are cross-trained to perform other jobs, fewer are needed to cover for absent co-workers.

In this chapter, we shall define globalism, downsizing, and team-based management and leadership and offer suggestions for modifying a planned L & MD program to take these issues into account.

GLOBALISM

Immediately following World War II, the U.S. market was the largest in the world. U.S. businesses reigned supreme as the world-class leaders in their industries. But times have changed: "The global economic arena is no longer exclusively driven by, or designed to favor, the United States."[1] At present, "of the 500 largest industrial corporations in the United States, at least 25 earn more than half of their profits overseas. Today, 68 of the 156 largest multinational organizations are U.S. firms."[2]

If we could reduce the world to a village of just 1,000 people, the relationship of North Americans to their fellow villagers would be starkly clear: "of our 1,000 'neighbors,' 564 would be Asians, 210 would be Europeans, 86 would be Africans, 80 would be South Americans, and only 60 of that 1,000—a mere 6 percent of the world's population—would be North Americans."[3] The economies of the nations in this global village are interconnected in a transnational economy in which money flows are of key importance. The effects of a transnational economy have prompted increasing interest in *globalism*, "perhaps the hottest business buzzword around."[4] The term connotes a full appreciation of the need to plan, market, and serve customers internationally as well as domestically.

Effects on Businesses

Globalism has affected U.S. businesses in at least two major ways. First, U.S. business executives can learn valuable lessons from successful foreign competitors so that domestic management practices benefit from an organization's international experience. Second, U.S. business executives increasingly value international markets as much as, if not more than, domestic ones. Strategic thinkers realize that the U.S. market is no longer necessarily the largest nor the most lucrative. But, to take full advantage of foreign markets, managers and other leaders must possess special knowledge and skills—including appreciation of different cultures, legal systems, tariff structures, and exchange rates. The lack of requisite management knowledge and skills poses a significant barrier to U.S. international competitiveness: "An estimated 80 percent of U.S. businesses that could export do not, partly because their managers lack the skills and experience to respond to international competition."[5]

Effects on Management Employees

Successful management employees of the future will possess the knowledge and skills to do business internationally. In fact, a "Korn/Ferry survey of 1,500 CEOs and senior managers [revealed that], by the year 2000, the shortage of U.S. managers equipped to run global businesses will be the major concern of human resource management."[6] Experienced managers will have to do more to exert leadership in the international arena than take a college course on international business, learn a foreign language, attend a university-sponsored seminar on international business, or make jaunts to foreign work sites. While those experiences can become important starting points on the road to globalism, they are no substitute for firsthand experience in doing business abroad. Often, that experience can be gained only by lengthy international assignments and international job rotations. Many large organizations have already made such experiences part of their career paths.[7]

To succeed on international assignments and job rotations, management employees must possess special competencies. The same competencies needed to succeed internationally are also required domestically so that businesses have appropriately equipped all their workers to function competitively on the international scene. Building these competencies may become a centerpiece of an L & MD curriculum, a long-term learning plan for an organization's employees.

Effects on L & MD

How can a planned L & MD program contribute to an organization's ability to "go global"? How can a planned L & MD program help equip employees at all levels with the skills they need to succeed internationally?

To answer those questions, L & MD directors and L & MD coordinators must be willing to facilitate a change in corporate culture. They should start by building top management support, as well as appropriate skills among top management ranks for conducting business internationally. That makes L & MD the driving force to help an organization "go global" from inside out. In consultation with key decision makers, the L & MD director or coordinator should:[8]

1. Formulate a clear and simple mission statement
2. Have the systems and structures in place to ensure an effective flow of information
3. Create "matrix minds" to facilitate conflict management
4. Develop global career paths
5. Use cultural differences among employees and markets as a resource
6. Implement worldwide management education and team development programs

A new mission statement will be needed to drive the organization—and provide a mandate for a new *global* L & MD program. The L & MD director or coordinator also needs to review pending or existing learning experiences abroad in order to increase communications between international and domestic operations. When assessing needs, establishing curricula, formulating performance objectives, preparing instructional materials, or selecting L & MD methods, the L & MD director or coordinator must take international business needs and other cultures into account. Career paths that include international assignments or job rotation programs must also be established. The organization must use available talent within the organization—or hire it from outside—so that culturally diverse perspectives are integrated into planned L & MD efforts. Finally, the L & MD program as a whole must be reviewed so that its quality is consistent on a worldwide basis even when activities and methods differ by cultural context.

Often, an L & MD program will have to be established on-site in other locations abroad. That decentralizes the effort, making it more responsive to local (national) cultures and business conditions. In large corporations, the corporate-level L & MD program can serve as troubleshooter, braintrust, and helper. But the knowledge of the culture resides locally.

DOWNSIZING

The term *downsizing* was coined in the 1980s. A more recent euphemism is *rightsizing*. Both terms connote layoffs, voluntary retirement programs, or other reductions in force (RIFs) among full-time employees working for an organization.

In recent years, U.S. corporations have continued to downsize on a massive scale. Large-scale workforce cuts at General Motors and IBM generated national and even international publicity, but similar reductions have been occurring in other *Fortune* 500 firms for some time.

Causes of Downsizing

Downsizing stems from myriad causes. To cite a few:

- *Tough international competitive conditions* in which foreign firms enjoy a comparative advantage due to lower labor costs
- *Deregulation and industry competition* in which employee reduction efforts in one organization stimulate similar cuts across the industry
- *High employee benefit expenses* that now approach 50 percent on top of employee salary expense, due primarily to skyrocketing employer health insurance premiums and workers' compensation
- *A simple desire by top managers to realize increased profits by reducing staff* to mollify sophisticated consumer advocates
- *A belief that reducing staff, particularly at middle and higher levels, will increase efficiency* by pushing decisions down and reducing unnecessary paperwork
- *A desire to increase employee involvement and decision making by enriching jobs* and reducing unnecessary supervisory, middle management, and even top management positions so as to encourage and leverage leadership at all levels
- *Structural changes in the U.S. economy* in which high-paying manufacturing jobs are being replaced by lower-paying service jobs
- *Automation*, the substitution of technological devices and/or methods of work processing for human workers
- *Plant shutdowns and business relocations*, prompted by lower labor costs abroad

Some industries may also be affected by unique conditions that stimulate downsizing. One example: government agencies are caught between inflationary employment costs on one side and proportionally declining tax revenues on the other side.

Approaches to Downsizing

Downsizing too frequently conjures up an unpleasant scenario in which recently hired employees are herded into a room on a Friday and are unceremoniously handed the dreaded "pink slips." That is a *scorched Earth approach* to downsizing. While it is fast and efficient, its effects can be devastating to organizational productivity and employee morale. Its aftereffects haunt an organization for years to come, by

- Increasing turnover, an echo of the job insecurity felt by the survivors of a downsizing experience
- Complicating an organization's ability to find replacements for key positions as they become available, a result of eliminating an entire generation from an organization's workforce, and
- Increasing problems in meeting affirmative action goals, since (in many organizations) downsizing particularly affects women, minorities, and the young whose job seniority is less than that of other employees

However, there are alternatives to the ignominious scorched Earth approach.

One is a reduction through attrition. As employees resign, retire, or otherwise leave an organization, they are not replaced. This avoids a bloodbath. But a major problem is that not all positions are equally important to production or service delivery. Some are critical. The organization may thus be unable to sustain a naively established but well-intentioned policy of across-the-board staff reduction through attrition. Management may be forced to replace some positions to preserve production or service levels. Moreover, turnover in different functions or job classes may occur in a lopsided way, leading to harsher penalties on some areas than on others. A more advisable approach is a *selective* reduction through attrition, with staffing goals and parameters for each function and job class clearly established in advance.

A second alternative to the scorched Earth approach to downsizing is a reduction through voluntary retirement or termination programs. Employees are given special incentives to retire early or quit voluntarily. To qualify, employees may be required to meet objective criteria, such as a specified length of service. This approach, like downsizing through attrition, avoids a bloodbath. But a major problem is that management may have trouble selectively applying the incentives: key job incumbents may choose to take advantage of the incentives before the organization has time to prepare replacements. Spot talent shortages result. Many will have to be handled through external recruitment. A succession planning program, put in place some time before a voluntary retirement or termination effort, can mitigate the loss of key job incumbents.

A third alternative to the scorched Earth approach is *layer reduction* or *delayering*. It has been practiced by such well-known organizations as General Electric, 3M, Firestone Tire & Rubber, Ford, Westinghouse Electric, Hewlett-Packard, Apple Computer, and many more.[9] Advocates tout its value in reducing the "information filters" separating hourly employees and higher-level management, purportedly leading to faster and clearer information flow up and down the organization. As layers are reduced, higher-level managers find they have more—and different kinds—of people to supervise. This broad span of control will be successful so long as the jobs are not highly specialized. But if the jobs are highly specialized, the incumbents require sophisticated attention. That is difficult when managers have too many people assigned to them. When the span of control grows too large, employees suffer from too little individualized attention, coaching, and feedback. What could create leverage to build leadership is not encouraged. A fourth alternative to the scorched Earth approach is a reduction of full-time employees through various methods: (1) Substituting part-time (temps) for full-time employees, (2) Substituting permanent part-time employees for full-time employees, or (3) Increasing overtime for full-time employees rather than hiring additional staff. These options turn out to be suitable only as short-term measures.

Substituting part-time for full-time employees does hold down labor costs. But it can become expensive, especially when an organization must pay a temporary agency an hourly fee that is much higher than the hourly wage of a full-time employee. The trend points toward employing professional or managerial temps as well as clerical temps.[10]

Permanent part-time employees are another option. They can be substituted for full-time employees so as to hold down employee benefit expenses—since part-time workers are rarely eligible for benefits. While part-time employees can help organizations meet short-term staffing needs, they can be difficult to recruit and retain—especially for daytime employment. Often they are seeking full-time employment and will become turnover statistics as soon as they find it.

Overtime is yet another alternative. While it can be used to hold down the employee benefit expenses of full-time workers, it usually works as a short-term solution only. Employees who work overtime for prolonged periods suffer the effects of stress and burnout. Turnover will increase. The available evidence already suggests that U.S. employers are using overtime as a strategy for holding down staffing needs—and stress is building among the workforce as a result.[11]

A fifth alternative to the scorched Earth approach to downsizing is reduction by alternative cost-saving measures. Employers may establish ad hoc cost-saving teams to generate ideas to cut expenses and avoid unpleasant staffing reductions. Such teams may be cross-functional, composed of individuals from many areas of the organization. They operate much like Quality Circles, a popular fad several years ago. But the primary benefits of such teams will usually be realized in the first year. If they continue in operation beyond that, their results will rarely equal first-year cost savings.

A sixth alternative to the scorched Earth approach to downsizing is *work process re-engineering*. It is a popular concept, sometimes linked to a TQM effort. The essence of work process re-engineering is "out-of-box" (creative) thinking. Exempt and nonexempt employees alike are asked to approach what they do and how they do it with a fresh perspective. Work process re-engineering does share similarities with zero-based budgeting—except that a work process rather than a budget is the focus of attention. Key questions posed by work process re-engineering include:

1. What are the most costly—and most important—work processes performed by the organization?

2. If the organization were *starting* these functions for the first time, how would they be set up?

3. What other organizations are especially well-known for these processes?

4. How do those "world-class" organizations perform the processes?

5. What changes can be made to streamline an organization's work processes so as to bring them in line with "world-class" organizations, cut needless costs, and reduce superfluous staff?

The answers to these questions can provide valuable guidance for introducing innovation. Useless paperwork is often the first thing eliminated. Employees displaced by changes to work processes are retrained for more organizationally beneficial processes.

A seventh alternative to the scorched Earth approach to downsizing is team-based management (see the next part of this chapter). Employees are cross-trained to perform the work of others in the same or other work units. That can reduce the need for backup employees to fill in for those who are ill, vacationing, or absent for other reasons. They are also expected to exercise increasing self-management, thereby leading to reductions in the ranks of higher-paid management employees.

Downsizing's Effects on Management Employees

Downsizing's effects on workers depend, to a considerable extent, on the approach used. If a scorched Earth approach is used, downsizing's effects can be profoundly unpleasant. Quality vanishes. Turnover increases. Morale suffers dramatically. Stressed-out people go on overload. These negative feelings affect exempt as well as nonexempt employees, posing a major challenge to management—especially since management also keenly feels downsizing's effects.

The available evidence suggests that wholesale staff reductions of the scorched Earth variety are rarely effective.[12] Some firms end up downsizing more than once. They are like undisciplined dieters who gain weight after going off their diets and must later diet again to keep the weight off.

Managing the Effects of Downsizing

At least ten strategies may be used to rethink the way work is performed in the wake of downsizing:[13]

1. *Focus on purpose*: The organization and each work group should clarify its mission and focus solely on it.

2. *Focus on inputs*: Each work group, and the organization as a whole, should re-examine how the work is received to see if the work can be streamlined so as to reduce staffing needs.

3. *Focus on time and scheduling*: Managers must be acutely aware of the importance of mobilizing resources quickly, to cover spot needs when they occur.

4. *Focus on existing work first*: Avoid time-consuming new initiatives that distract management and staff from getting the work out.

5. *Restructure jobs*: Enrich and enlarge jobs.

6. *Restructure work groups*: Re-examine the way work groups are organized and seek more effective organizational structure.

7. *Contract out*: Shift work outside the work group or organization.

8. *Use part-time assistance*: Rely, as much as is practical and cost-effective, on part-time assistance.

9. *Use overtime*: Ask full-time employees to work overtime in brief spurts to hold down benefit expenses and meet short-term needs for additional staffing.

10. *Combine the methods*: Do not rely on a single method to cope with the aftereffects of downsizing.

Each approach above suggests that management employees must cultivate special skills to handle the aftereffects of downsizing. Those skills are a rightful focus of the planned L & MD program.

Downsizing and L & MD

Downsizing affects management employees by

- Changing the responsibilities associated with exempt and nonexempt jobs
- Creating increasing attitudinal problems resulting from stress, pressure, job insecurity, and more work for the same compensation
- Altering career paths and reducing opportunities for upward mobility
- Creating increasing pressures on management employees to see that the work gets out despite adverse conditions created by too few people to do the work

• Creating increasing pressures from higher-level management to maintain product or service quality and work output with fewer people

In addition, a downsized organization generally creates an environment in which L & MD programs of all kinds become more difficult to sponsor. For instance, employees in a downsized organization feel they have less time to participate in *any* planned learning experience. Even when they hunger for these opportunities, they may be unable to get away from the work site during the work day and too exhausted to take materials home at night. Downsizing is often accompanied by cost reduction efforts, and L & MD efforts are usually hit the hardest.

To cope with these efforts, L & MD directors and coordinators must be creative. They must come up with ways to ensure that the planned L & MD program continues despite the tough conditions created by downsizing and cost reduction. To that end, they may:

• Appeal to top management for special support

• Focus learning activities on "survival skills"—ways to do more with less, cope with stress, handle overtime, and similar issues of topical value

• Ask for suggestions from steering or advisory committees with which they work

• Engineer special incentives for employees who participate in, or sponsor, L & MD efforts

• Build accountability for L & MD results into management job descriptions, performance appraisals, and other employment decisions

Use the Activity appearing in Exhibit 11-1 to structure your thinking about ways to encourage L & MD efforts in an organization following downsizing.

TEAM-BASED MANAGEMENT

Team-based management is an exciting new philosophy about managing people and organizing work. When defining a team, we find it helpful to distinguish variations of it on a continuum from the traditional work group (see Exhibit 11-2). Teams may be project-oriented, semi-autonomous, or autonomous. Autonomous teams are usually called *self-directed teams*. Some key differences between a traditional work group and teams are described in Exhibit 11-3.

A *traditional work group* consists of a supervisor and nonexempt employees. The supervisor controls others to ensure that work output and quality are sustained. A traditional work group is responsible for *only one part* of a work process. Employees have tightly structured jobs that are akin to "boxes" of tasks governed by job descriptions. As a result of the way the work is organized and divided up, cooperation among group members is not necessarily encouraged. Indeed, each employee competes with others for individual merit pay

Exhibit 11-1
An Activity on Encouraging Leadership and Management Efforts in the Wake of Downsizing

	Directions: Use this Activity to help structure your thinking—and that of others in your organization—about L & MD in the wake of downsizing. Answer the following questions individually or in small groups. Then compare answers.
1	How was downsizing handled in the organization? (*Describe how many employees were affected, over what time period, and what organizational needs led to the downsizing effort.*)
2	What have been the effects of downsizing on nonexempt and exempt employees? (*Describe how the downsizing has affected work processes, turnover, product or service quality, and other key strategic organizational issues.*)
3	What special learning needs have been created by the downsizing? (*Describe them below.*)
4	How can the special needs, created by downsizing, be met through the planned L & MD program? (*Describe what can be done.*)
5	What should be done by the organization to encourage L & MD in the wake of downsizing? (*Provide an action plan.*)

raises, work group resources, and the supervisor's attention. If employees are asked to help co-workers, they may object by noting "that's not in my job description."

A *project or cross-functional* team is an effort to bridge the chasm separating activities of work groups, hierarchical levels, geographic locations, and organizational functions. Exempt and/or nonexempt employees work together on special tasks—such as troubleshooting a problem, preparing for a new product line, or discussing ways to streamline production. The project leader is elected by the project team itself or appointed by a top manager whose authority spans the groups represented. The project leader's authority is limited solely to the project. The project or cross-functional task may endure for some time, and members may rotate on or off the project or cross-functional team. On the other hand, the task may have a limited time horizon and disband when the mission is completed.

A *semi-autonomous team* is preparing for expanded responsibilities. The supervisor is called a *team leader*. The team leader's role is to serve as encourager, coach, on-the-job helper, and group facilitator. Team leaders do not order others around; rather, they help group members interact among themselves better. Members of a semi-autonomous team, like a traditional work group, focus their attention on *only one part* of a work process. However, they may be in training to absorb all the parts of a process. Work responsibilities are not divided up into the "boxes" of individual jobs; rather, the sides of "boxes" are being broken out so *all* work responsibilities are shared by team members. There may

Exhibit 11-2

A Continuum from Traditional Work Group to Autonomous Team

Traditional Work Group	Project or Cross-Functional Team	Semi-Autonomous Team	Autonomous or Self-Directed Team
• Supervisor "controls"	• Leader is elected or appointed	• Team leader "facilitates"	• There is no supervisor or team leader
• The work performed is only part of a larger process	• Co-exists with traditional work groups	• The work performed is part of a larger process, but workers are cross-trained	• Workers perform the whole task or process
• Jobs are specialized	• Spans the gap separating traditional work groups	• Jobs are increasingly "generalist" in their orientation	• Jobs are generalized (a team-based job description may exist, for instance)
• Decision making is top-down	• Some decisions are bottom-up but most are top-down	• Some decisions are top-down but most are bottom-up	• Decision making is bottom-up
• Supervisors select workers	• Workers have say in the selection of team members but supervisors make the final decisions	• Team leaders have a say in selection of team members but team members make the final decision	• Supervisors do not exist; team members make all decisions about team selection
• Roles of team members are determined by management and by work group mission	• Roles of team members are primarily determined by management and by work group mission	• Roles of team members are influenced by management but are primarily decided upon by the team	• Roles are entirely decided by team members

be one or two job descriptions for an entire team, because so many duties are jointly shared. Cross-training is heavily emphasized, and each team member is expected to master all tasks performed on the team.

Employees often react to the introduction of semi-autonomous teams with enthusiasm, since teams promote job enrichment and job enlargement. A few, however, may complain that they are being asked to do more while pay increases are not matching the heavier work load. That may create pressure to review, and change, a traditional compensation program to one that "pays for knowledge."

Exhibit 11-3
Differences Between a Traditional Work Group and a Team

Characteristics of a Traditional Work Group	Characteristics of a Team
• Large—18 to 20 people	• Smaller—10 to 12 people
• Not cohesive	• Team-spirited
• More individual incentives and more credit given to individual contributors than to the work group	• More group-oriented and incentives and credit are accorded to group/team accomplishments
• People tend to think of their own "box" of tasks	• People think in terms of the team's tasks
• People occasionally remark that a task is "not my job"	• Everyone shares responsibility for all the work
• Great emphasis is placed on individual accountability	• Great emphasis is placed on team accountability

An *autonomous* or *self-directed work team* "is an intact group of employees responsible for a 'whole' work process or segment that delivers a product or service to an internal or external customer."[14] There is no supervisor or team leader; those duties are dispersed across team members. Employees must therefore exercise self-management and self-control, and cooperation is highly valued. There is a *team job description* that encompasses all team responsibilities. Gone is the bureaucratic view of jobs as "boxes." Team members are expected to gradually master all activities or responsibilities listed on the team job description and are cross-trained to that end. Cooperation, because it is synonymous with teamwork, is very important and highly valued.

Benefits of Team-Based Management

Team-based management has three major benefits. First, it decreases the need for staff by reducing dependence on supervisors, managers, and executives in decision making and by reducing the need for backup workers to cover for sick, vacationing, or otherwise absent employees. Workers are trained to do all the tasks of a work group and are encouraged to make independent decisions.

Second, team-based management increases the speed and quality of decisions. It has the potential to build leadership skills at all levels, giving everyone a chance to exert influence and creativity. Employees do more than participate in decision making. Indeed, they are empowered to act on their own without receiving advance approval from higher-level management. Because decisions rest in the hands of those who do the work and/or interact directly with customers, team-based management is frequently tied to TQM programs.

Third, team-based management promotes work group cohesiveness. It helps people meet deep-felt human belongingness needs at precisely the time in the United States when social conditions outside the work place are undermining the satisfaction of those needs. Teams can, on some occasions, become a substitute for family.

Effects of Team-Based Management

To introduce team-based management successfully in an organization, workers must often accept and live by values different from those that they have historically embodied. Evidence suggests that management values are indeed changing, with interest in workers increasing faster than self-interest.[15] Against that backdrop, management roles must change, and management employees must master new skills to enact those roles.

Of course, the values, roles, and skills they need depend on the type of team-based management adopted by the organization. As Exhibit 11-3 illustrates, employees in an organization with cross-functional teams must be comfortable working amid the ambiguity often present in a project-oriented environment. They must be willing to accept matrixed responsibilities in which more than one person is accountable for getting results. Above all, they must prize creativity, since it is creativity that leads to breakthrough thinking and cost savings.

Management employees in an organization with semi-autonomous teams must function as group facilitators. They must exude enthusiasm and excitement, serving as work place cheerleaders for team efforts. More often than not, they must be very knowledgeable about group dynamics, possess strong interpersonal skills, and be capable of handling conflict resolution with expert skill. Management employees in an organization with self-directed teams are usually limited to middle managers and executives only—since nonexempt employees assume most responsibilities traditionally accorded to supervisors. In that setting, management employees function as coaches, group facilitators, and trainers. Their aim is to build leadership skills and infuse management knowledge, skills, and abilities throughout the organization—spreading self-management to the lowest level possible. That requires a fundamental culture change in most organizational settings, made all the harder because it goes against the grain of the top-down approach to decision making that has been prevalent in the United States since the days of Frederick Taylor and a changing, more leisure-driven, work ethic among many U.S. workers.

Team-Based Management and L & MD

The introduction of team-based management requires a radical culture change in most organizations. The L & MD director or coordinator is usually the spearhead or spiritual leader of this change. Frequently, it means that exempt and nonexempt employees alike must discard notions they have acquired over years of experience about the best or most appropriate approaches to management practice. Some can't or won't make the change. They may prefer alternatives—such as early retirement, transfer, or even departure from the organization. Such moves, when motivated by what is best for the organization and the individual, should be permitted or even encouraged.

The introduction of team-based management should be handled in a way that reflects the high value placed on employee involvement in decision making. Involvement is one important goal of such an effort. To that end, many organizations will begin with one or more retreats. Facilitated by the L & MD director or coordinator—perhaps with the valuable assistance of an outside vendor who has experience in introducing such changes in other organizations—the retreat(s) will first review the competitive and business needs driving the change. From there, the participants will formulate their own definitions of teams, clarify desired roles of nonexempt employees in a team setting, clarify desired roles of employees *at each level* after the change, pinpoint key issues affecting implementation, and devise a unified action plan. High-level retreats should be followed up by retreats at lower levels in the organizational hierarchy. Once participants understand the reasons to make changes and have been involved through *action learning* in the changes that are to be made, they should receive detailed training to build the skills they need to make the culture change successful.

Typically, the introduction of team-based management will necessitate a review of the responsibilities expected at *each* level in the organization. One way to do that is to form task forces to revise executive, management, supervisory, and nonexempt job descriptions as they "should appear" after the successful introduction of teams. These job descriptions will then provide a useful starting point for subsequent changes in the planned L & MD program, leading to new efforts to assess needs, formulate performance objectives, identify or prepare instructional materials, select and deliver appropriate L & MD methods to meet identified learning needs, and evaluate results. Another, related way is to conduct DACUM sessions at each level to formulate desired job responsibilities.

Team-based management has now established a solid track record in many organizations. It has offered a valuable alternative to traditional management approaches and has the capability to cultivate leadership talent. But the jury remains undecided whether team-based management lives up to its promises to increase productivity.

SUMMARY

In concluding this book, we have devoted attention to three important topical issues that are influencing planned L & MD programs in the U.S.: (1) globalism; (2) downsizing; and (3) team-based management. The three issues are related. In this chapter we defined what they are, how organizations can approach them, how they affect employees, and how a planned L & MD program can take them into account.

NOTES

1. C. Howard, "Profile of the 21st-Century Expatriate Manager," *HRMagazine*, Vol. 37, No. 6, p. 94.

2. D. Ricks and V. Mahajan, "Blunders in International Marketing: Fact or Fiction," *Long-Range Planning*, February 1984, p. 78.

3. P. Howard, "Worldshrink," *HRMagazine*, Vol. 36, No. 1, pp. 42–43.

4. B. Geber, "The Care and Breeding of Global Managers," *Training*, Vol. 29, No. 7, p. 32.

5. Howard, "Worldshrink," p. 43.

6. Ibid.

7. Geber, "The Care and Breeding of Global Managers," p. 32.

8. S. Rhinesmith, "Going Global from the Inside Out," *Training & Development*, Vol. 45, No. 11, p. 46.

9. R. Nelson, "Common Sense Staff Reduction," *Personnel Journal*, Vol. 67, No. 8, p. 50.

10. M. Messmer, "Right-Sizing Reshapes Staffing Strategies," *HRMagazine*, Vol. 36, No. 10, p. 60.

11. "Moonlighting Madness," *Personnel Journal*, Vol. 71, No. 6, p. 18.

12. C. Lee, "After the Cuts," *Training*, Vol. 29, No. 7, p. 19.

13. W. Rothwell, "Ten Strategies for Rethinking How Work Is Performed After Downsizing," in W. Rothwell, ed., *The Emerging Issues in HRD Sourcebook* (Amherst, MA: Human Resource Development Press, 1995).

14. R. Wellins, W. Byham, and J. Wilson, *Empowered Teams: Creating Self-Directed Work Groups That Improve Quality, Productivity, and Participation* (San Francisco: Jossey-Bass, 1991), p. 3.

15. B. Geber, "Managers Are A Changin'," *Training*, Vol. 29, No. 7, p. 73.

Bibliography

Abdalla, I. "A Survey of Management Training and Development Practices in the State of Kuwait." *Journal of Management Development*, Vol. 14, No. 3, pp. 14–25.

Ackers, P. "Born Again? The Ethics and Efficacy of the Conversion Experience in Contemporary Management Development." *Journal of Management Studies*, Vol. 34, No. 5, pp. 677–701.

Adler, G. "When a New Manager Stumbles, Who's at Fault?" *Harvard Business Review*, Vol. 74, No. 2, pp. 22–28.

Allerton, H. "News You Can Use." *Training & Development*, Vol. 51, No. 10, pp. 12–13.

Alpert, M. "The Care & Feeding of Engineers." *Fortune*, Vol. 126, pp. 86–95.

Analoui, F. "Training and Development: The Role of Trainers." *Journal of Management Development*, Vol. 13, No. 9, pp. 61–72.

Argyris, C. "Some Unintended Consequences of Rigorous Research." *Psychological Bulletin*, Vol. 70, pp. 185–197.

Arkin, A. "Breathing Fresh Air into Training." *People Management*, Vol. 1, No. 15, pp. 34–35.

Arkin, A. "An Education in Training." *Personnel Management*, Vol. 25, No. 12, pp. 42–45.

Arkin, A. "From Supervision to Team Leadership." *Personnel Management*, Vol. 26, No. 2, pp. 48–49.

"The Art (And Maybe Science) of Multicultural Management." *Institutional Investor*, Vol. 31, No. 3, pp. 98–99.

Badaway, M. *Management as a New Technology*. New York: McGraw-Hill, 1993.

Baird, L. "World Class Executive Development." *Human Resource Planning*, Vol. 17, No. 1, pp. 1–15.

Ballin, M. "Who Taught You to Do What You Do?" *People Management*, November 30, 1995, pp. 32–33.

Barclay, I. "A Survey of the Activities, Problems and Training Needs of Technical Managers." *Engineering Management International*, Vol. 3, No. 4, pp. 253–259.

Barrier, M. "The Changing Face of Leadership."*Nation's Business*, Vol. 83, No. 1, pp. 41–42.

Bartlett, T. "Put Down That Keats, Maggot!" *Business Week*, No. 3533, p. 42.

Batley, T. "Management Education for Professional Engineers." *Journal of European Industrial Training*, Vol. 14, No. 7, pp. 9–16.

Bazemore, G. "Institutional and Management Building in Sub-Saharan Africa: The Role of Training." *International Journal of Public Administration*, Vol. 18, No. 9, pp. 1447–1483.

Beddowes, P. "Re-Inventing Management Development." *Journal of Management Development*, Vol. 13, No. 7, pp. 40–46.

Belasen, A. "Downsizing and the Hyper-Effective Manager: The Shifting Importance of Managerial Roles During Organizational Transformation." *Human Resource Management*, Vol. 35, No. 1, pp. 87–117.

"Benefits of Competence-Based Management Development." *IRS Employment Review*, No. 616, p. SSS16.

Bennis, W., and B. Nanus. *Leaders: The Strategies for Taking Charge*. New York: Harper and Row, 1985.

Betters-Reed, B. "Shifting the Management Development Paradigm for Women." *Journal of Management Development*, Vol. 14, No. 2, pp. 24–38.

Bittel, L., and J. Newstrom. *What Every Supervisor Should Know* (6th ed.). New York: McGraw-Hill, 1990.

Blakely, G. "Management Development Programs: The Effects of Management Level and Corporate Strategy; Invited Reaction: Level and Strategy Should and Do Make a Difference!" *Human Resource Development Quarterly*, Vol. 5, No. 1, pp. 5–25.

Blau, B. "How IBM Technical Professionals See Their Work Environment." *Research Technology Management*, Vol. 32, No. 1, pp. 27–30.

Bolt, J. "Achieving the CEO's Agenda: Education for Executives." *Management Review*, Vol. 82, No. 5, pp. 44–48.

Bolt, J. "Ten Years of Change in Executive Education." *Training & Development*, Vol. 47, No. 8, pp. 43–44.

Bredin, J. "Broadening Horizons." *Industry Week*, Vol. 246, No. 18, p. 68.

Broadwell, M. "The Case for Pre-Supervisory Training." *Training*, Vol. 33, No. 10, pp. 102–108.

Broadwell, M. "How to Train Experienced Supervisors." *Training*, Vol. 30, No. 5, pp. 61–66.

Brown, T. "Are You 'Growing' into an Executive?" *Industry Week*, Vol. 243, No. 6, p. 25.

Brubaker, S. "Promoting from Within: The Best Way to Build Management." *Telemarketing Magazine*, Vol. 13, No. 2, pp. 64–67.

Buchanan, B. "Building Your Management Team." *Healthcare Executive*, Vol. 12, No. 6, pp. 52–53.

Buhler, P. "Managing in the 90s." *Supervision*, Vol. 55, No. 1, pp. 17–19.

Buhler, P. "Managing in the 90s: Becoming More Effective—Lessons from Covey." *Supervision*, Vol. 57, No. 7, pp. 24–26.

Buller, P., J. Cragun, and G. McEvoy. "Getting the Most Out of Outdoor Training." *Training and Development Journal*, Vol. 45, No. 3, p. 58.

Bunning, R. "Action Learning: Developing Managers with a Bottom-Line Pay-Back." *Executive Development*, Vol. 7, No. 4, pp. 3–6.

Burack, E. "The New Management Development Paradigm." *Human Resource Planning*, Vol. 20, No. 1, pp. 14–21.

Burgoyne, J. "Management Development for the Individual and the Organization." *Personnel Management*, June 1988, p. 41.

Butler, R. "Key Indicators Can Help Improve the Performance of Your Business." *Industrial Management*, Vol. 37, No. 3, pp. 2–3.

Byham, W. "Interaction Modeling: A Supervisory Training Concept." *Training & Development*, Vol. 50, No. 7, pp. 30–33.

Camp, R. *Benchmarking: The Search for Industry Best Practices That Lead to Superior Performance*. Milwaukee, WI: Quality Press; White Plains, NY: Quality Resources, 1989.

Campanelli, M. "James Champy on Reengineering Managers." *Sales & Marketing Management*, Vol. 147, No. 4, p. 36.

Cannon, F. "Business-Driven Management Development: Developing Competences Which Drive Business Performance." *Journal of European Industrial Training*, Vol. 19, No. 2, pp. 26–31.

Cannon, T. "Learning Linkages." *People Management*, Vol. 2, No. 25, p. 19.

Capowski, G. "Anatomy of a Leader: Where Are the Leaders of Tomorrow?" *Management Review*, Vol. 83, No. 3, pp. 10–17.

Carnevale, A., and L. Gainer. *The Learning Enterprise*. Alexandria, VA: The American Society for Training and Development and the U.S. Department of Labor, Employment and Training Administration, 1989.

Cash, J. "The Age of Execution." *Informationweek*, No. 637, p. 122.

Champ, H. "Between a Rock and a Damp Place." *Accountancy*, Vol. 119, No. 1244, p. 45.

Cianni, M. "CEO Beliefs, Management Development, and Corporate Strategy: An Exploratory Study." *Group & Organization Management*, Vol. 19, No. 1, pp. 51–66.

Cocheu, T. "Building a Leadership Foundation for Quality." *Training & Development*, Vol. 47, No. 9, pp. 51–58.

Cole, K. "Management Development to the Millennium." *Management Development Review*, Vol. 8, No. 3, pp. 20–23.

"Coming of Age." *Business China*, Vol. 22, No. 16, pp. 1–2.

Conant, J. "The Manager's View of Management Education and Training." *Review of Public Personnel Administration*, Vol. 16, No. 3, pp. 23–37.

Cone, J. "Creating a Good Manager Is All in the Training." *Nation's Restaurant News*, April 22, 1996, p. 34.

"Confidence Boost." *Business Asia*, Vol. 29, No. 11, pp. 5–7.

Cooper, R. "Applying Emotional Intelligence in the Workplace." *Training & Development*, Vol. 51, No. 12, pp. 31–38.

Cope, N. "Well Trained and Up to Speed." *Accountancy*, Vol. 112, No. 1200, p. 35.

Cordero, R., and G. Farris. "Administrative Activity and the Managerial Development of Technical Professionals." *IEEE Transactions on Engineering Management (IEE)*, Vol. 39, pp. 270–276.

Cosier, R. "Management Training and Development in a Nonprofit Organization." *Public Personnel Management*, Vol. 22, No. 1, pp. 37–42.

"Course Tips." *Business China*, Vol. 20, No. 18, p. 12.

Covington, W. "Motivating Engineers." *Broadcast Engineering*, Vol. 39, No. 10, p. 18.

Csoka, L. "The Rush to Leadership Training." *Across the Board*, Vol. 33, No. 8, pp. 28–32.

Currie, G. "Competence-Based Management Development: Rhetoric and Reality." *Journal of European Industrial Training*, Vol. 19, No. 5, pp. 11–18.

Currie, G. "Evaluation of Management Development: A Case Study." *Journal of Management Development*, Vol. 13, No. 3, pp. 22–26.

Curry, L. "Exterior Motives." *People Management*, Vol. 3, No. 11, pp. 32–33.

Dalton, M. "Are Competency Models a Waste?" *Training & Development*, Vol. 51, No. 10, pp. 46–49.

Dalton, M. "Conflicts Between Staff and Line Managerial Officers." *American Sociological Review*, Vol. 15, pp. 342–351.

Daudelin, M. "Learning from Experience Through Reflection." *Organizational Dynamics*, Vol. 24, No. 3, pp. 36–48.

Davis, R. "New Principles for Management Development." *Management Development Review*, Vol. 8, No. 6, pp. 5–8.

Davis, T. "Whose Job Is Management Development? Comparing the Choices." *Journal of Management Development*, Vol. 9, No. 1, pp. 58–70.

de Groot, H. "Multirater Feedback: A Primer for Public Sector Managers." *Optimum*, Vol. 26, No. 4, pp. 5–13.

DelMar, D. "Making the Transition from Engineer to Manager." *Industrial Management*, Vol. 32, No. 1, pp. 26–28.

"Developing Managers a Priority." *Personnel Management*, Vol. 26, No. 1, p. 53.

"Developing People Through Role-Plays." *People Management*, Vol. 1, No. 11, p. 50.

Dhebar, A. "Rethinking Executive Education." *Training & Development*, Vol. 49, No. 7, pp. 55–57.

DiPietro, R. "TQM: Evolution, Scope and Strategic Significance for Management Development." *Journal of Management Development*, Vol. 12, No. 7, pp. 11–18.

Dixon, J. "Human Resource Development and Management Education in Commercialising Public Sectors: Some Australian Trends." *International Journal of Public Administration*, Vol. 19, No. 11, pp. 2059–2093.

Drew, S. "Executive Development Observations: Prague 1993." *Journal of Management Development*, Vol. 13, No. 3, pp. 4–14.

Drew, S. "Simulation-Based Leadership Development and Team Learning." *Journal of Management Development*, Vol. 12, No. 8, pp. 39–52.

Dutton, G. "Executive Coaches Call the Plays." *Management Review*, Vol. 86, No. 2, pp. 39–43.

Edelstein, B. "A Model for Executive Development." *Human Resource Planning*, Vol. 16, No. 4, pp. 51–68.

Egan, K. "What Is Curriculum?" *Curriculum Inquiry*, Vol. 8, No. 1, pp. 65–72.

Ekerson, W. "Techies Need Training for Management Roles." *Network World*, Vol. 6, No. 14, pp. 27–28.

Eller, D. "Motorola Trains VPs to Become Growth Leaders." *HRMagazine*, Vol. 40, No. 6, pp. 82–87.

Ellington, H. *Producing Teaching Materials: A Handbook for Teachers and Trainers.* London: Kogan Page, 1985.

"Embracing the Witch Doctors." *Training*, Vol. 34, No. 7, pp. 41–45.

Engelbrecht, A. "The Managerial Performance Implications of a Developmental Assessment Center Process." *Human Relations*, Vol. 48, No. 4, pp. 387–404.

Ensman, R. "Management Blunders: Ten Common Mistakes Any Manager Can Make." *Manage*, Vol. 48, No. 1, pp. 4–5.

Ettorre, B. "How Are Companies Keeping the Employees They Want?" *Management Review*, Vol. 86, No. 5, pp. 49–53.

Evans, J. "A Targeted Approach to Management Development." *Personnel Management*, Vol. 26, No. 3, p. 52.

"The Executive as Coach." *Harvard Business Review*, Vol. 74, No. 6, pp. 111–117.

Feuer, D. "Paying for Knowledge." *Training*, Vol. 24, No. 5, pp. 57–58, 60, 61–66.

"Filling a Critical Gap: Sutter Health's Leadership Lab." *Health Systems Review*, Vol. 30, No. 5, p. 35.

"Firms Face Leadership Skills Gap." *People Management*, Vol. 3, No. 6, pp. 15–16.

Fitzgerald, W. "Personal Empowerment Key to Managers' Development." *HRMagazine*, Vol. 38, No. 11, pp. 84–89.

Folk, L. "Management Style as an Element of Management Development Programmes: Is It Worth the Trouble?" *Journal of Management Development*, Vol. 13, No. 9, pp. 25–33.

Fowler, A. "How to Use Games to Choose Winners." *People Management*, June 13, 1996, pp. 42–43.

French, W. "Organization Development: Objectives, Assumptions, and Strategies." *California Management Review*, Vol. 12, No. 2, p. 26.

Frost, P. "Bridging Academia and Business: A Conversation with Steve Kerr." *Organization Science*, Vol. 8, No. 3, pp. 333–347.

Fulmer, W. "Anticipatory Learning: The Seventh Strategic Imperative for the Twenty-First Century." *Journal of Management Development*, Vol. 12, No. 6, pp. 61–66.

Fulmer, R. "Building Organizations That Learn: The MIT Center for Organizational Learning." *Journal of Management Development*, Vol. 14, No. 5, pp. 9–14.

Fulmer, R. "Corporate Management Development and Education: The State of the Art." *Journal of Management Development*, Vol. 7, No. 2, p. 65.

Fulmer, R. "The Evolving Paradigm of Leadership Development." *Organizational Dynamics*, Vol. 25, No. 4, pp. 59–72.

Fulmer, R. "The Merlin Exercise: Future by Forecast or Future by Invention?" *Journal of Management Development*, Vol. 12, No. 6, pp. 44–52.

Fulmer, R. "A New Era of Management Education." *Journal of Management Development*, Vol. 12, No. 3, pp. 30–38.

Gagné, R., and L. Briggs. *Principles of Instructional Design* (2nd ed.). New York: Holt, Rinehart and Winston, 1979.

Galosy, J. "Curriculum Design for Management Training." *Training and Development Journal*, Vol. 37, No. 1, p. 48.

Garavan, T. "Supervisory Training and Development: The Use of Learning Contracts." *Journal of European Industrial Training*, Vol. 18, No. 2, pp. 17–26.

Geber, B. "The Care and Breeding of Global Managers." *Training*, Vol. 29, No. 7, p. 32.

Geber, B. "Managers Are A Changin'." *Training*, Vol. 29, No. 7, p. 73.

Geiger-DuMond, A. "Mentoring: A Practitioner's Guide." *Training & Development*, Vol. 49, No. 3, pp. 51–54.

Georgenson, D. "The Problem of Transfer Calls for Partnership." *Training & Development*, Vol. 36, No. 10, pp. 75–78.

Goodwin, J. "The Beer Distribution Game: Using Simulation to Teach Systems Thinking." *Journal of Management Development*, Vol. 13, No. 8, pp. 7–15.

Greco, J. "Corporate Home Schooling." *Journal of Business Strategy*, Vol. 18, No. 3, pp. 48–52.

Greco, J. "Long-Distance Learning." *Journal of Business Strategy*, Vol. 18, No. 3, pp. 53–54.

Greenberg, E. "Knowledge: It's There for the Asking." *HR Focus*, Vol. 75, No. 2, p. 2.

Guarriello, M. "The Management of Leadership." *Hospital Materiel Management Quarterly*, Vol. 17, No. 3, pp. 17–20.

Gunter, H. "Jurassic Management: Chaos and Management Development in Educational Institutions." *Journal of Educational Administration*, Vol. 33, No. 4, pp. 5–20.

Gutman, J. "Developing Cases and Scenarios for Anticipatory Learning." *Journal of Management Development*, Vol. 12, No. 6, pp. 53–60.

Hall, D. "Executive Careers and Learning: Aligning Selection, Strategy, and Development." *Human Resource Planning*, Vol. 18, No. 2, pp. 14–23.

Hargie, O. "Communication Skills Training: Management Manipulation or Personal Development?" *Human Relations*, Vol. 47, No. 11, pp. 1377–1389.

Harrison, R. "Challenge Should Be Linked to Performance." *HR Focus*, Vol. 70, No. 10, p. 9.

Hatlevig, T. "Departing Managers a Sign of More Basic Problems." *Personnel Journal*, Vol. 74, No. 3, p. 88.

Haydock, W. "Management Development: A Personal Competency Approach." *Training & Management Development Methods*, Vol. 9, No. 4, pp. 7.13–7.27.

Heifetz, R. "The Work of Leadership." *Harvard Business Review*, Vol. 75, No. 1, pp. 124–134.

Hemphill, J., and A. Coons. "Development of the Leader Behavior Description Questionnaire." In R. Stogdill and A. Coons, eds., *Leader Behavior: Its Description and Measurement*. Columbus, OH: Bureau of Business Research, The Ohio State University, 1957.

Hilgert, A. "Developmental Outcomes of an Executive MBA Programme." *Journal of Management Development*, Vol. 14, No. 10, pp. 64–76.

Hills, F. *Compensation Decision Making*. Chicago: The Dryden Press, 1987.

Hilton, P. "An Accelerated Route to the Top for Graduates." *Personnel Management*, Vol. 25, No. 7, pp. 36–39.

Hite, L. "Gender Issues in Management Development: Implications and Research Agenda." *Journal of Management Development*, Vol. 11, No. 4, pp. 5–15.

Hitt, M. "Human Capital and Strategic Competitiveness in the 1990s." *Journal of Management Development*, Vol. 13, No. 1.

"A Holistic View." *Training & Development*, Vol. 50, No. 5, p. 61.

Hopfl, H. "A Whole Can of Worms! The Contested Frontiers of Management Development and Learning." *Personnel Review*, Vol. 24, No. 6, pp. 19–28.

"Horses for Courses." *Business Asia*, Vol. 29, No. 11, p. 6.

Houle, C. *The Inquiring Mind*. Madison, WI: University of Wisconsin Press, 1961.

"How Do Professionals Define Their Productivity?" *Harvard Business Review*, Vol. 71, No. 4, p. 130.

Howard, C. "Profile of the 21st-Century Expatriate Manager." *HRMagazine*, Vol. 37, No. 6, p. 94.

Howard, P. "Worldshrink." *HRMagazine*, Vol. 36, No. 1, pp. 42–43.

Hubbard, A. "Supervisory Development." *Mortgage Banking*, Vol. 57, No. 1, pp. 166, 170.

Huczynski, A. *Encyclopedia of Management Development Methods.* London: Gower, 1983.

Hussey, D. "Effective Management Training and Development." *International Review of Strategic Management*, Vol. 4, pp. 277–299.

James, S. "Recent Advances in Management Development: Self-Directed, Continuous Development Through 'Smart Software.' " *Journal of Management Development*, Vol. 13, No. 7, pp. 35–39.

Judge, W. "The Brave New World of Executive Coaching." *Business Horizons*, Vol. 40, No. 4, pp. 71–77.

Katz, S. "Management Training for a Technical Population." *Training and Development Journal*, Vol. 41, No. 10, pp. 71–73.

Kelley, R. "How Bell Labs Creates Star Performers." *Harvard Business Review*, Vol. 71, No. 4, pp. 128–139.

Kets de Vries, M. "The Fast-Track Factor: Developing Tomorrow's Directors." *Director*, Vol. 49, No. 5, pp. 44–47.

Keys, J. "Microworlds and Simuworlds: Practice Fields for the Learning Organization." *Organizational Dynamics*, Vol. 24, No. 4, pp. 36–49.

Keys, J. "The Multinational Management Game: A Simuworld." *Journal of Management Development*, Vol. 13, No. 8, pp. 26–37.

Keys, L. "Action Learning: Executive Development of Choice for the 1990s." *Journal of Management Development*, Vol. 13, No. 8, pp. 50–56.

Kharbanda, O., and E. Stallworthy. "Management for Engineers." *International Journal of Operations & Production Management*, Vol. 10, No. 6, pp. 2–91.

Kilcourse, T. "Developing Competent Managers." *Journal of European Industrial Training*, Vol. 18, No. 2, pp. 12–16.

Kirkpatrick, D. *Evaluating Training Programs: The Four Levels.* San Francisco: Berrett-Koehler, 1994.

Kirkpatrick, D. "Techniques for Evaluating Training Programs." *Journal of the American Society for Training and Development* [now called *Training & Development*], Vol. 14, No. 1, pp. 13–18.

Knowles, M. *Using Learning Contracts: Practical Approaches to Individualizing and Structuring Learning.* San Francisco: Jossey-Bass, 1986.

Kolb, D. *Experiential Learning: Experience as a Source of Learning and Development.* Englewood Cliffs, NJ: Prentice-Hall, 1984.

Koper, C. "Executive Continuity: Building Leadership for the Future." *Optimum*, Vol. 26, No. 4, pp. 24–31.

Kouzes, J., and B. Posner. *The Leadership Challenge: How to Get Extraordinary Things Done in Organizations.* San Francisco: Jossey-Bass, 1987, p. 285.

Kovner, A. "Management Development for Mid-Level Managers: Results of a Demonstration Project." *Hospital & Health Services Administration*, Vol. 41, No. 4, pp. 485–502.

Kraut, A., P. Pedigo, D. McKenna, and M. Dunnette. "The Role of the Manager: What's Really Important in Different Management Jobs." *Academy of Management Executive*, Vol. 3, No. 4, p. 287.

Kubr, M., and J. Prokopenko. *Diagnosing Management Training and Development Needs: Concepts and Techniques*. Geneva: International Labour Office, 1989.

Laabs, J. "Community Service Helps UPS Develop Managers." *Personnel Journal*, Vol. 72, No. 10, pp. 90–94.

Laabs, J. "How Gillette Grooms Global Talent." *Personnel Journal*, Vol. 72, No. 8, pp. 64–76.

Laird, D. *Approaches to Training and Development* (2nd ed.). Reading, MA: Addison-Wesley, 1985, pp. 49–50.

Laker, D. "Dual Dimensionality of Training Transfer." *Human Resource Development Quarterly*, Vol. 1, No. 3, pp. 209–224.

Landry, J. "Arrive on the Ground Running." *Harvard Business Review*, Vol. 75, No. 2, p. 13.

Lapp, H. "Is It Time to Go Back and Reevaluate Engineer and Scientist Training and Development for the 90's and Beyond?" *Performance and Instruction*, Vol. 31, No. 7, pp. 8–15.

Larwood, L. "Training Women for Management: Changing Priorities." *Journal of Management Development*, Vol. 14, No. 2, pp. 54–64.

Lary, B. "Now, Coach?" *Across the Board*, Vol. 34, No. 6, pp. 28–32.

Lawrie, J. "Differentiate Between Training, Education and Development." *Personnel Journal*, Vol. 69, No. 10, p. 44.

Lee, C. "After the Cuts." *Training*, Vol. 29, No. 7, p. 19.

Leibowitz, Z., C. Farren, and B. Kaye. *Designing Career Development Systems*. San Francisco: Jossey-Bass, 1986.

Leigh, A. "Coaching Managers in the Art of Teamwork." *People Management*, Vol. 2, No. 24, p. 41.

Lewey, L., and B. Davis. "When Techies Manage." *Training and Development Journal*, Vol. 41, No. 10, pp. 66–69.

Lichtenstein, B. "Leadership and Ethical Development: Balancing Light and Shadow." *Business Ethics Quarterly*, Vol. 5, No. 1, pp. 97–116.

Lipton, M. "New Age Organizational Training: Tapping Employee Potential or Creating New Problems?" *Human Resources Professional*, Vol. 3, No. 2, pp. 72–76.

Loeb, M. "Where Leaders Come From." *Fortune*, Vol. 130, No. 6, pp. 241–242.

Lombardo, M., and R. Eichinger. *Eighty-Eight Assignments for Development in Place: Enhancing the Developmental Challenge of Existing Jobs*. Greensboro, NC: The Center for Creative Leadership, 1989.

McCall, M., M. Lombardo, and A. Morrison. *The Lessons of Experience: How Successful Executives Develop on the Job*. Lexington, MA: Lexington Books, 1985.

McCauley, C. "Assessing the Developmental Components of Managerial Jobs." *Journal of Applied Psychology*, Vol. 79, No. 4, pp. 544–560.

McCauley, C. "Linking Management Selection and Development Through Stretch Assignments." *Human Resource Management*, Vol. 34, No. 1, pp. 93–115.

McClelland, S. "Gaining Competitive Advantage Through Strategic Management Development (SMD)." *Journal of Management Development*, Vol. 13, No. 5, pp. 4–13.

McCune, J. "The Game of Business." *Management Review*, Vol. 87, No. 2, pp. 56–58.

McDermott, L. "Reengineering Middle Management." *Training & Development*, Vol. 49, No. 9, pp. 36–40.

McDonald, J. "Developing the Influential Manager: Experiences with Deans of Business Schools." *Journal of Management Development*, Vol. 12, no. 1, pp. 13–19.

McGee, M. "People Skills Can Pay Off." *Informationweek*, January 8, 1996, p. 62.

McGehee, W., and P. Thayer. *Training in Business and Industry*. New York: John Wiley, 1961.

Mani, B. "Progress on the Journey to Total Quality Management: Using the Myers-Briggs Type Indicator and the Adjective Check List in Management Development." *Public Personnel Management*, Vol. 24, No. 3, pp. 365–398.

Messmer, M. "Right-Sizing Reshapes Staffing Strategies." *HRMagazine*, Vol. 36, No. 10, p. 60.

Meyer, P. "Why Make Managers?" *Business Horizons*, Vol. 39, No. 1, pp. 1–2.

"Moonlighting Madness." *Personnel Journal*, Vol. 71, No. 6, p. 18.

Moore, T. "The Corporate University: Transforming Management Education." *Accounting Horizons*, Vol. 11, No. 1, pp. 77–85.

Moravec, M. "A 21st Century Communication Tool." *HRMagazine*, Vol. 38, No. 7, pp. 77–81.

Morrisey, G. *Management by Objectives and Results in the Public Sector*. Reading, MA: Addison-Wesley, 1976, p. 25.

Mullen, T. "Toward Improving Management Development's Contribution to Organizational Learning." *Human Resource Planning*, Vol. 16, No. 2, pp. 35–49.

Mumford, A. "Learning in Action." *Industrial & Commercial Training*, Vol. 27, No. 8, pp. 36–40.

Mumford, A. "Managers Developing Others Through Action Learning." *Industrial & Commercial Training*, Vol. 27, No. 2, pp. 19–27.

Mumford, A. "Myth and Realities in Developing Directors." *Personnel Management*, Vol. 19, No. 2, p. 29.

Murphy, J. "Results First, Change Second." *Training*, Vol. 34, No. 5, pp. 58–67.

Nadler, L., and Z. Nadler. *Developing Human Resources* (3rd ed.). San Francisco: Jossey-Bass, 1989.

Naisbitt, J., and P. Auburdene. *Reinventing the Corporation: Transforming Your Job and Your Company for the New Information Society*. New York: Warner Books, 1985.

Nelson, R. "Common Sense Staff Reduction." *Personnel Journal*, Vol. 67, No. 8, p. 50.

"A New Role for HR People." *Training & Development*, Vol. 50, No. 5, pp. 62–63.

Nowack, K. "Coaching for Human Performance." *Training & Development*, Vol. 51, No. 10, pp. 28–32.

Nowack, K. "The Secrets of Succession." *Training & Development*, Vol. 48, No. 11, pp. 49–54.

O'Brien, M. "Executive Coaching." *Supervision*, Vol. 58, No. 4, pp. 6–8.

Ohlott, P. "Gender Differences in Managers' Developmental Job Experiences." *Academy of Management Journal*, Vol. 37, No. 1, pp. 46–67.

Olivero, G. "Executive Coaching as a Transfer of Training Tool: Effects on Productivity in a Public Agency." *Public Personnel Management*, Vol. 26, No. 4, pp. 461–469.

Orr, J. "Re-Engineering the Engineer." *Computer-aided Engineering*, Vol. 15, No. 12, p. 68.

Oshagbemi, T. "Management Development and Managers' Use of Their Time." *Journal of Management Development*, Vol. 14, No. 8, pp. 19–34.

Paddock, S. "Benchmarks in Management Training." *Public Personnel Management*, Vol. 26, No. 4, pp. 441–460.

Payne, T. "Go Forth and Manage Wisely." *Supervision*, Vol. 55, No. 8, pp. 10–12.

Pearn, M. "Learning from the Good, the Bad, and the Ugly Mistakes." *People Management*, November 30, 1995, p. 43.

Pearse, R. "Career Success in Different Corporate Cultures." *Compensation & Benefits Management*, Vol. 14, No. 1, pp. 26–35.

Pearson, A. "Management Development for Scientists and Engineers." *Research-Technology Management*, Vol. 36, No. 1, pp. 45–48.

Penrice, D. "The Changing Organization: Why Do Managers Derail?" *Harvard Business Review*, Vol. 73, No. 3, pp. 10–11.

Phillips, A. "Effective Communications Skills Are Career Essentials." *Healthcare Financial Management*, Vol. 52, No. 2, p. 90.

Pineda, R. "The Effects of Ethnic Group Culture on Managerial Task Activities." *Group & Organization Management*, Vol. 22, No. 1, pp. 31–52.

Preston, D. "APL: Current State of Play Within Management Education in the UK." *Journal of Management Development*, Vol. 12, No. 8, pp. 27–38.

Quick, T. *Training Managers So They Can Really Manage: Confessions of a Frustrated Trainer*. San Francisco: Jossey-Bass, 1991.

Raelin, J. "Action Learning and Action Science: Are They Different?" *Organizational Dynamics*, Vol. 26, No. 1, pp. 21–34.

Ragins, B. "Barriers to Mentoring: The Female Manager's Dilemma." *Human Relations*, Vol. 42, No. 1, pp. 1–22.

Rancourt, K. "Real-Time Coaching Boosts Performance." *Training & Development*, Vol. 49, No. 4, pp. 53–56.

Rauch, C., and O. Behling. "Functionalism: Basis for an Alternate Approach to the Study of Leadership." In J. Hunt, D. Hosking, C. Schriesheim, and R. Stewart, eds., *Leaders and Managers: International Perspectives on Managerial Behavior and Leadership*. Elmsford, NY: Pergamon Press, 1984.

Read, R. "The Engineer in Transition to Management." *IIE Solutions*, Vol. 28, No. 9, pp. 18–23.

Redman, T. "Management Development Under Adversity? Case Studies from Poland." *Journal of Management Development*, Vol. 14, No. 10, pp. 4–13.

Reingold, J. "Corporate America Goes to School." *Business Week*, No. 3549, pp. 66–72.

Reyna, M. "A Framework for Individual Management Development in the Public Sector." *Public Personnel Management*, Vol. 24, No. 1, pp. 53–65.

Rhinesmith, S. "Going Global from the Inside Out." *Training & Development*, Vol. 45, No. 11, p. 46.

Ricks, D., and V. Mahajan. "Blunders in International Marketing: Fact or Fiction." *Long-Range Planning*, February 1984, p. 78.

Rimler, G. "The Transition from Engineer to Engineer/Manager." *Industrial Management*, Vol. 33, No. 6, pp. 17–18.

Roberts, K., and J. Biddle. "The Transition into Management by Scientists and Engineers: A Misallocation or Efficient Use of Human Resources? *Human Resource Management*, Vol. 33, No. 4, pp. 561–579.

Rodrigues, C. "Developing Three-Dimensional Leaders." *Journal of Management Development*, Vol. 12, No. 3, pp. 4–11.

Rosenbaum, B. "How Successful Technical Professionals Achieve Results." *Research Technology Management*, Vol. 33, No. 1, pp. 24–26.

Rosenbaum, B. "Leading Today's Technical Professional." *Training & Development*, Vol. 45, No. 10, pp. 55–66.

Rothwell, W. *Effective Succession Planning: Ensuring Leadership Continuity and Building Talent from Within*. New York: AMACOM, 1994.

Rothwell, W. "HRD and The Americans With Disabilities Act." In W. Rothwell, ed., *The Emerging Issues in HRD Sourcebook*. Amherst, MA: Human Resource Development Press, 1995.

Rothwell, W. "Strategic Curriculum Design for Management Training." *Journal of Management Development*, Vol. 3, No. 3, pp. 39–52.

Rothwell, W. *A Survey about Management and Leadership Development*. Unpublished survey results. University Park, PA: The Pennsylvania State University, 1998.

Rothwell, W. "Ten Strategies for Rethinking How Work Is Performed After Downsizing." In W. Rothwell, ed., *The Emerging Issues in HRD Sourcebook*. Amherst, MA: Human Resource Development Press, 1995.

Rothwell, W., and H. Kazanas. "Curriculum Planning for Training: The State of the Art." *Performance Improvement Quarterly*, Vol. 1, No. 3, pp. 2–16.

Rothwell, W., and H. Kazanas. *Human Resource Development: A Strategic Approach* (rev. ed.). Amherst, MA: Human Resource Development Press, 1994.

Rothwell, W., and H. Kazanas. "Issues and Practices in Management Job Rotation Programs as Perceived by HRD Professionals." *Performance Improvement Quarterly*, Vol. 5, No. 1, pp. 49–69.

Rothwell, W., and H. Kazanas. *Mastering the Instructional Design Process: A Systematic Approach* (2nd ed.). San Francisco: Jossey-Bass, 1998.

Rothwell, W., and H. Kazanas. "Structured on-the-Job Training (SOJT) as Perceived by HRD Professionals." In W. Rothwell, ed., *Emerging Issues in HRD Sourcebook*. Amherst, MA: Human Resource Development Press, 1995.

Rothwell, W., E. Sanders, and J. Soper. *ASTD Models for Workplace Learning and Performance: Roles, Competencies, Outputs*. Alexandria, VA: American Society for Training and Development, 1999.

Rothwell, W., and H. Sredl. *The ASTD Reference Guide to Professional HRD Roles and Competencies* (2nd ed.). 2 vols. Amherst, MA: Human Resource Development Press, 1992.

Rothwell, W., R. Sullivan, and G. McLean, eds. *Organization Development: A Guide for Consultants*. San Francisco: Jossey-Bass/Pfeiffer, 1995.

Russ, F. "Leadership, Decision Making and Performance of Sales Managers: A Multi-Level Approach." *Journal of Personal Selling & Sales Management*, Vol. 16, No. 3, pp. 1–15.

Saari, L., T. Johnson, S. McLaughlin, and D. Zimmerle. "A Survey of Management Training and Education Practices in U.S. Companies." *Personnel Psychology*, Vol. 41, pp. 739–740.

Sauser, W. "Encouraging Pluralism in Management Education Programs." *SAM Advanced Management Journal*, Vol. 58, No. 2, pp. 6–16.

Schein, E. *Organizational Culture and Leadership* (2nd ed.). San Francisco: Jossey-Bass, 1992.

Schlosberg, J. "Learning to Lead." *Computerworld*, Vol. 30, No. 37, pp. 81–82.

Seibert, K. "Strengthening the Weak Link in Strategic Executive Development: Integrating Individual Development and Global Business Strategy." *Human Resource Management*, Vol. 34, No. 4, pp. 549–567.

Shaw, M. "Management-Development Programs: A Canadian Perspective." *Cornell Hotel & Restaurant Administration Quarterly*, Vol. 36, No. 1, pp. 34–39.

"Shell's High-Test Program." *Training & Development*, Vol. 51, No. 5, pp. 72–73.

Shenhar, A. "A New Mixture of Management Skills : Meeting the High-Technology Managerial Challenges." *Human Systems Management*, Vol. 13, No. 1, pp. 27–40.

Sheperd, C. "The Training of Sales Managers: An Exploratory Study of Sales Management Training Practices." *Journal of Personal Selling & Sales Management*, Vol. 15, No. 1, pp. 69–74.

Shipton, H. "Tarmacademy 2."*People Management*, Vol. 4, No. 1, pp. 40–42.

Sifonis, J. "Changing Role of the CIO." *Informationweek*, No. 623, pp. 69–82.

Smith, A. "Management Development Evaluation and Effectiveness." *Journal of Management Development*, Vol. 12, No. 1, pp. 20–32.

Smith, B. "Building Managers from the Inside Out: Developing Managers Through Competency-Based Action Learning." *Journal of Management Development*, Vol. 12, No. 1, pp. 43–48.

Smith, M., and D. Brandenburg. "Summative Evaluation." *Performance Improvement Quarterly*, Vol. 4, No. 2, pp. 35–58.

Snyder, A. "Executive Coaching: The New Solution." *Management Review*, Vol. 84, No. 3, pp. 29–32.

Soderberg, K. "Leadership-Focused Management Development: Are Today's Practices Meeting Tomorrow's Needs?" *International Review of Strategic Management*, Vol. 4, pp. 141–154.

Sorohan, E. "Developing Leaders." *Training & Development*, Vol. 49, No. 8, p. 13.

Spector, A. *The Human Resource Development Policy Study: Identification and Analysis of Human Resource Development Policy in Selected U.S. Corporations.* Unpublished doctoral dissertation. Washington, DC: The George Washington University, 1985.

Spreitzer, G. "Empowering Middle Managers to Be Transformational Leaders." *Journal of Applied Behavioral Science*, Vol. 32, No. 3, pp. 237–261.

Springer, J., and J. Thomas. "An Experiment in Individual Leadership Development." *Performance and Instruction*, Vol. 31, No. 2, pp. 44–48.

Sternberg, R. "Managerial Intelligence: Why IQ Isn't Enough." *Journal of Management*, Vol. 23, No. 3, pp. 475–493.

Steven, L. "From Loner to Leader." *Training & Development*, Vol. 45, No. 10, pp. 56–60.

Stevens, T. "Follow the Leader." *Industry Week*, Vol. 245, No. 21, pp. 16–17.

Storey, J. "Management Development: A Literature Review and Implications for Future Research." *Personnel Review*, Vol. 18, No. 6, pp. 13–19.

Storey, J. "What a Difference a Decade Makes." *People Management*, Vol. 3, No. 12, pp. 28–30.

Strebler, M. "Developing a Competence-Based Management Training Programme." *Management Development Review*, Vol. 8, No. 3, pp. 32–35.

Stumpf, S. "Applying New Science Theories in Leadership Development Activities." *Journal of Management Development*, Vol. 14, No. 5, pp. 39–49.

Syrett, M. "The Best-Laid Plans." *Director*, Vol. 51, No. 4, pp. 107–108.

Syrett, M. "Changing the Face of Learning." *Director*, Vol. 50, No. 9, pp. 76–77.

"Tailored Plans for Managers Replace 'One Size Fits All'." *IRS Employment Review*, No. 612, p. SSS2.

Tapp, L. "Emerging Triumphant." *Business Quarterly*, Vol. 61, No. 3, pp. 27–28.

Taylor, B. "The Values of Leadership." *Optimum*, Vol. 24, No. 1, pp. 82–87.

Teal, T. "The Human Side of Management." *Harvard Business Review*, Vol. 74, No. 6, pp. 35–44.

Thamhain, H. "Developing the Skills You Need." *Research Technology Management*, Vol. 35, No. 2, pp. 42–47.

Thamhain, H. "From Engineer to Manager." *Training & Development*, Vol. 45, No. 9, pp. 66–70.

Thamhain, H. "Managing Technology: The People Factor." *Technical & Skills Training*, Vol. 1, No. 2, pp. 24–31.

Thompson, J. "Engineers Don't Always Make the Best Team Players." *Electronic Engineering Times*, September 30, 1996, pp. 124, 152.

Tough, A. *The Adult's Learning Projects* (2nd ed.). Toronto, ON: Ontario Institute for Studies in Education, 1979, p. 6.

"A Tour Guide to Management Meccas." *Business Week*, No. 3442, September 18, 1995, pp. 124–125.

Turpin, T., and A. Deville. "Occupational Roles and Expectations of Research Scientists and Research Managers in Scientific Research Institutions." *R & D Management*, Vol. 25, No. 2, pp. 141–157.

Van Gundy, A. *Techniques of Structured Problem Solving*. New York: Van Nostrand Reinhold, 1981.

Vicere, A. "Executive Development in Major Corporations: A Ten-Year Study." *Journal of Management Development*, Vol. 13, No. 1, pp. 4–22.

Vicere, A. "Executive Education: The Leading Edge." *Organizational Dynamics*, Vol. 25, No. 2, pp. 67–81.

Vroom, V. *Work and Motivation*. New York: John Wiley, 1964.

Wade-Benzoni, K. "Evaluating Executive Development: A Case Study." *Executive Development*, Vol. 7, No. 2, pp. 7–9.

"Wanted: A Mentor to Advance Your Career." *Supervisory Management*, Vol. 41, No. 1, pp. 4–5.

Welch, J. "Death Renews Charge of 'SAS Style' Training." *People Management*, Vol. 3, No. 5, p. 7.

Wellins, R., W. Byham, and J. Wilson. *Empowered Teams: Creating Self-Directed Work Groups That Improve Quality, Productivity, and Participation*. San Francisco: Jossey-Bass, 1991, p. 3.

Werther, W. "Global Deployment of Executive Talent." *Human Resource Planning*, Vol. 18, No. 1, pp. 20–29.

West, D. "Management Training: Why Bother?" *Accountancy*, Vol. 120, No. 1247, p. 37.

Westhead, P. "Management Training and Small Firm Performance: Why Is the Link So Weak?" *International Small Business Journal*, Vol. 14, No. 4, pp. 13–24.

Wightman, S. "Management Development: The Neglected Domain." *Journal of European Industrial Training*, Vol. 19, No. 5, pp. 3–10.

Wild, R. "The Management of Development." *Management Today*, October 1994, p. 5.

Willcocks, S. "A Local Authority Management Development Programme: Behavioural Versus Cognitive Development?" *Executive Development*, Vol. 8, No. 7, pp. 21–25.

Wilson, J. "360 Appraisals." *Training & Development*, Vol. 51, No. 6, pp. 44–45.

Winters, M. "Identifying and Supporting Potential Leaders." *HR Focus*, Vol. 74, No. 7, pp. 13–14.

Worts, C. "Building a Society with Special Skills." *People Management*, January 25, 1996, pp. 36–39.

Yelverton, J. "Adaptive Skills: Seven Keys to Developing Top Managers." *Vital Speeches of the Day*, Vol. 63, No. 23, pp. 725–727.

Yeung, A. "Developing Leadership Capabilities of Global Corporations: A Comparative Study in Eight Nations." *Human Resource Management*, Vol. 34, No. 4, pp. 529–547.

Zemke, R. "In Search of a Training Philosophy." *Training*, Vol. 22, No. 10, pp. 93–94, 96, 98.

Index

About the Authors

WILLIAM J. ROTHWELL is a Professor of Human Resource Development in the Department of Adult Education, Instructional Systems, and Workforce Education and Development in the College of Education at Pennsylvania State University. He also serves as Director of Penn State's Institute for Research in Training and Development. Previously, he was Assistant Vice President and Management Development Director for The Franklin Life Insurance Company and Training Director for the Illinois Office of Auditor General. He is also President of Rothwell & Associates, a private consulting firm. He is the author of numerous books.

H. C. KAZANAS is Professor Emeritus at the University of Illinois, Urbana-Champaign. He worked for 10 years in the manufacturing industry as a machinist and production supervisor and 35 years as an educator in human resource development (HRD). He has been an HRD consultant for the U.S. Departments of Labor and Education, the U.S. Agency for International Development, Motorola and Westinghouse Corporations, The World Bank, the UN Development Program, the International Labor Office, and UNESCO. He has written or co-authored 80 articles and numerous book chapters, monographs, and books.